# THOSE FEET

BY THE SAME AUTHOR

*Brilliant Orange: The Neurotic Genius of Dutch Football*

# THOSE FEET

An Intimate History of English Football

## DAVID WINNER

BLOOMSBURY

First published in Great Britain 2005
This paperback edition published 2006

Copyright © 2005 by David Winner

The moral right of the author has been asserted

Bloomsbury Publishing Plc, 36 Soho Square, London WID 3QY

A CIP catalogue record for this book is available from the British Library

ISBN 0 7475 7914 8
9780747579144

10 9 8 7 6 5 4 3 2

Grateful acknowledgement to the Estate of Philip Larkin
and Faber and Faber Ltd for permission to quote lines from
'Annus Mirabilis' from *Collected Poems* by Philip Larkin.

Typeset by Hewer Text Ltd, Edinburgh
Printed in Great Britain by Clays Ltd, St Ives plc

All papers used by Bloomsbury Publishing are natural,
recyclable products made from wood grown in well-managed
forests. The manufacturing processes conform to the environmental
regulations of the country of origin.

www.bloomsbury.com/davidwinner

For Valeria
And to the memory of Tamar Dromi and Suzan Harvey

# CONTENTS

# ACKNOWLEDGEMENTS

My heartfelt thanks to all the people quoted in the book who generously gave me their time, insights and knowledge. I'm equally grateful to all the others who helped in big and small ways, and without whom this book would be different and less. To my partner Valeria Vallucci, my parents Anthony and Monica, my agents Jane Judd and Jan Michael; at Bloomsbury my editor Mike Jones, Colin Midson, Will Webb, Mary Davis, Katherine Greenwood, Monica O'Connell and Larry Henry. Also to: Richard Adams, Shaul Adar, Iman Ahmed, Andrew Anthony, David Barber, Leon Berger, Neil Best, Colin Budd, Fiona Campbell, Peter Chapman, Ingrid Coltart, Paul Cooper, John Cowie, Bela Cunha, Andrew Dean, Maddalena Del Re, Sarah Duffield, Roland Dyong, Frances Edson, David Endt, Wayne Evans, Dave Godley, Alex Gordon, David Green, Mike Grenier, John Gustav-Wrathall, Lesley Hall, Neil Henry, Saskia Hantelmann, Uli Hesse-Lichtenberger, Colm Hickey, Anna Holtzman, Simon Inglis, Richard Jones, Dave Juson, Sean and Alexis Kelly, Su Kent, Chris Keulemans, Lucy Kimbell, Maike Korporaal, Momo Kovacevic, Simon Kuper, George Lewith, David Luxton, Chris Maume, Hugh Mcleod, Giovanni Maria Merola, Marcela Mora y Araujo, Sue Morgan, Jos Nagel, Tom O'Sullivan, David Owen, Gary Peatling, Tammy Perez, Mark Perryman, Jos de Putter, Graham Ramsay, Jennifer Rupp, Larry Shaw, Hugh Sleight, Barbara Smit, Henk Spaan, Joram ten Brink, the Thomsons (Ruth, Neil and Chloe), Hans van der Meer, Dalia Ventura, Ian Vosper, Edith Vroon, Andrew Waldon, Marie-Anne van Wijnen and Stéphane Zamparo.

Exercise No. 3.—For the arms, the legs, and the chest.

# INTRODUCTION

This project started out with something like a sneer. It ends, I hope, nearer to a kiss or a love letter. It was the summer of 2001. England had just lost badly to Holland in a friendly, and I was talking to a French friend about England's shortcomings: 'We're rubbish,' 'I don't know why, but we've always preferred running and fighting to being skilful,' and so on. Stéphane brought me up short by saying: 'You ought to write a book about it.' 'About England?' I said. 'I couldn't possibly. I'm much too close to it.' 'Close?' he said, incredulously. 'You're not close at all!' He was absolutely right. And completely wrong. But the conversation started the process which led to this book. On the face of it, it's a sequel to one I wrote a couple of years earlier called *Brilliant Orange: The Neurotic Genius of Dutch Football*. That was rooted in my straightforward fascination from afar with the Total Footballers and the culture which nurtured them. My feelings about my own country are much deeper and more complex.

Among other things, I think of football as a vehicle for love, especially between fathers and sons. I'm called David because of my great uncle Dave, who died two years before I was born. Uncle Dave used to take my dad to see Arsenal play when he was a boy during the war. By the early sixties, Dad had a Highbury season ticket of his own, high up in Block Z in the West Stand. Some time around 1962, he took me to my first match. It was a special day because the great Stanley Matthews was playing for Stoke. Naturally, I remember nothing at all about Stanley Matthews, or the game, or most subsequent games. But every other Saturday after that, Dad would ask me if I wanted to 'go to football' and I'd say: 'What colour are the other team wearing?' If the answer was 'bright blue' or 'black and white stripes' or 'old gold', I'd say yes. Tickets were never a problem: Dad simply assured the man on the turnstiles that I'd sit on his knee, and we were waved through. From high in the stand, the players on the field appeared no bigger than my little finger. Sometimes it rained, but we were dry. My favourite thing was the police band which marched at half-time. By the 1966 World Cup Final, I knew enough about football to realise that Germany's free-kick in the last minute of normal time was very frightening. I threw myself behind Dad's back on the old blue sofa in the living room, peeping out a few seconds later, just in time to be inconsolable when Weber scored Germany's equaliser. Within the hour, as every Englishman knows, Hurst had scored two more goals and restored my sense that every-thing was essentially right with the world. That blissful, sunny afternoon was one of the highlights in a long, uneventful and happy childhood.

I tell you these things, not because I'm about to launch into a Hornbyesque autobiography about my life as an Arsenal or England fan. The perfection of Nick Hornby's *Fever Pitch* makes all such books redundant. No, I tell you only to demonstrate that my English football roots predate and go deeper than my Dutch ones.

Some time between 1966 and 2001, my feelings about football and Englishness came to be coloured by more grown-up things such as teenage-dom, adulthood, Heysel and the writings of Brian Glanville. But my ambivalent attitude can be gauged by the joke I used in the early stages of this book. I'd explain 'I'm working on a sort of sequel to *Brilliant Orange*. That was about why the Dutch play beautiful football and lose all the time. But the English have a completely different problem: we play ugly football, and lose all the time.' For reasons explained in chapter 7, this joke was always very warmly received by English people. It was only a Dutch friend who took offence: 'Don't say that! English football is the *most* beautiful and exciting in the world.' His reaction got me thinking about the roots of my alienation.

Researching and writing this book has been a surprising emotional and intellectual journey which reversed many of my old assumptions. I discovered that things I thought I hated about England and its football – its spirit, its muddy, backward-looking battling – were things to which I felt deeply connected. If *Orange* was the result of a teenage infatuation, this has been more like the therapeutic unravelling of a relationship with a dysfunctional family, which, as any therapist will tell you, is much richer ground. I've discovered afresh how rich, weird, magnificent and exotic is the football of the country of my birth. And how much I love it.

It's certainly not intended as a conventional history – there are plenty of those already. Nor is it much concerned with hooligans, star players or sociology. Instead, I started with what I imagined to be the defining characteristics of the English style, and worked backwards to try to understand how they got that way. I came to see football as a potent and durable projection of a peculiarly late nineteenth-century kind of Englishness. That this culture, which has lasted more than 120 years, is finally showing signs of changing, makes me a little melancholy.

Rather than relying on videotape and interviews, as I had in Holland, I worked mainly in libraries. I started in Amsterdam, where I first discovered the strange, instantly recognisable world of Victorian boys' fiction (chapter 3), which led me to everything else. Later, I worked more at the British Library, where, on every visit, I was strangely delighted and uplifted by Paolozzi's huge bronze statue based on William Blake's painting of Isaac Newton. Exploring the world of Dutch football drew me to Dutch architecture, art and space. Reflecting on the essential Englishness of English football took me to deeper, more primal themes. Sex and memory. Grace and violence. Laughter and war. Manliness. History.

Along the way, strange things happened. Like with the title. In Holland the book is called *Zwaar Leer* (Heavy Leather), which evokes the material of old boots and balls and carries a pleasingly SM-ish double entendre. But it only has that name because Dutch readers wouldn't understand the correct title. 'Those Feet' are the third and fourth words of William Blake's sublime, exalting poem 'Jerusalem', that prayer and vision of a better England which ought to be our national anthem. The book's original working title had been *By God They Frighten Me*, from the Duke of Wellington's line about his army during the Peninsular War ('I don't know what they do to the enemy but, by God, they frighten me'). But a year or so into the research, it no longer seemed to fit. Influenced perhaps by the statue, I thought instead of borrowing from Blake. One day in May 2002 my editor, Mike Jones, and I met to thrash out the question, and it didn't take us long to agree that Blake's poetic vision had a lot more going for it than the acid wit of the Iron Duke.

The following day I was at the Angel in Islington, waiting to catch a bus towards the library when I saw a bus heading in the opposite direction. On a whim I decided to get on that instead. It was sunny, and the idea of exploring a part of London I didn't know at all was suddenly attractive. After a few stops, again on a whim, I got off the bus. I regretted this immediately because I was now in a dull street full of noisy traffic and boring buildings. The only interesting thing in sight was a small park behind a low wall, some distance on the other side of the road. I headed for it, crossed the road and realised that the park was some kind of old churchyard. I wandered in and found it pleasant; the rows of headstones behind the railings were peaceful. As I walked down the central path, the sound of traffic fell away. I became aware of birdsong and greenery and trees covered with blossom, but I paid little attention to anything else. After a couple of hundred yards and a turn to the right, the path opened out into a more open space, with a grassy field. I slowed. I stopped. I looked down, and found that I was standing beside the grave of William Blake.

David Winner, Rome, 2004

## SEXY FOOTBALL

The essence of the relationship between fancy foreigners and doughty Englishmen was captured by Sir Walter Scott in his novel *The Talisman*, written in 1825 and set during the Third Crusade. The key moment comes when the English king Richard the Lionheart meets the Muslim hero Saladin. The great men exchange pleasantries in an atmosphere of mutual respect. Then they show off their martial skills. First, Richard hefts his giant, glittering broadsword high overhead and smashes a big iron bar in half with a single mighty blow. Fantastic stuff! Saladin responds in a thoroughly un-English manner: he places a silk cushion on end, then deftly slices it in two with his razor-sharp scimitar. Both kings' weapons are perfect, but in completely different ways: power versus dexterity. Iron bars or fancy knick-knacks. Richard is impressed, but says he'll stick to what he knows best: 'Still, however, I put some faith in a downright English blow, and what we cannot do by sleight we eke out by strength.'

*What we cannot do by sleight we eke out by strength.* No more concise definition of English football exists. The game is and has always been 'a man's game'. English footballers are expected to display Lionheart qualities: strength, power, energy, fortitude, loyalty, courage. As for delicacy, cleverness, sleight-of-foot, imagination and cushion-slicing . . . Well, that's the sort of thing we prefer to leave to foreigners. This idea is rooted in what the Victorians called 'manliness', and it lies at the heart of all that's best and worst in English football. It accounts for the energy and power which make the English league exciting. It helps explain why English football rarely produces creative artists (and usually treats badly the ones who do emerge). And it provides an insight into the root cause of England's forty years of hurt in the World Cup.

England's failure against Brazil in Japan in 2002 was just one instalment in a long-running saga of decent, dull English footballers humiliated by technically superior foreigners. The first episode came at Wembley in 1953 when the 'Magical Magyars' humiliated the nation which invented the game. After that 3–6 defeat, the English admitted they had been taught a great lesson and vowed to improve their level of skill. But they won the World Cup at home in 1966 with mostly Lionheart football and never really concentrated on skill. So the same lesson has been handed down at regular intervals ever since. Brazilians, Argentinians, Dutchmen, Italians, Germans, Poles, Frenchmen, Portuguese, Spaniards, Romanians, Norwegians, Swedes, Greeks, Americans, Luxembourgeois, Sammarinese – just about everybody has on occasion shown England the limitations of their technically inferior ways. Every time it happens, English coaches, players and administrators solemnly affirm that they have been taught a great lesson and will do better in the future. But they never learn, never improve.

Against Brazil in Shizuoka (where some English fans actually dressed up as crusaders, in chain-mail and red-cross tunics), England started vigorously and drew first blood. But Brazil came back and scored two rather Saladin-like goals. The first was made by Ronaldinho's silky, flowing run through the heart of the English defence; the second was his precise (or lucky) long free-kick. Then Ronaldinho was sent off, but England were incapable of exploiting the advantage. When they had the ball (which wasn't often) they gave it away. When the Brazilians had it they used their superior skills to keep the ball between themselves. It became embarrassing as England failed to mount a single meaningful attempt on goal in the entire last thirty minutes. As the veteran Scottish journalist Hugh McIlvanney observed of England: 'There was not a trace of cunning or conviction or telling urgency in any of it. It was eunuch football, without the slightest promise of meaningful penetration.'

*Eunuch football.* How apt. In June 1996 Ruud Gullit, working as a pundit for the BBC, had introduced the pleasure principle to Britain's TV audience. Speaking during the warm-up before Portugal played Croatia in Euro '96, Gullit said he liked the Portuguese because they played 'Sexy Football'. Beside him presenter Des Lynam raised an eyebrow and asked what he meant. Gullit explained, it is best when it's 'sexy', when players perform with skill and style, when they express themselves playfully, reveal their fantasy, create rather than destroy. When it's a joy to play and a pleasure to watch. Lynam looked baffled. But sexy football won in Shizuoka. The Brazilians had extra dimensions of creativity and technique. England couldn't, in a purely footballing sense, get it up. So the question becomes: why don't the English play sexy football? And the answer, in part at least, is that the very idea of sexy football transgresses one of the English game's most sacred founding principles.

Perhaps the best way to understand the creation of English football (and therefore all football) is to see it as the diametric opposite of the creation of the universe. Creation of the universe, that is, according to the scriptures of ancient Egypt. Ancient Egypt had a highly sexualised culture, which was reflected in their creation myths. In one, all life begins when the god Atum appears on the Primordial Mound out of the Void of Nu. In a holy papyrus Atum explained in his own words what happened next: '. . . no sky existed, no earth existed . . . I created on my own every being . . . my first became my spouse . . . I copulated with my hand . . .' This act creates a god and goddess who copulate with each other to create everything else. In another story, the god Ptah, architect of the universe, maintains cosmic order through continual masturbation. The annual flooding of the Nile flowed from the secretions of the Nile god Hapy. Osiris, King of the Dead and Lord of Eternity, resurrected himself through an act of sacred masturbation . . . And so on. Now imagine something else. Instead of the Void of Nu, picture cold, wet playing fields in the English countryside in the middle of the nineteenth century. And in place of Atum, God of Creation, meet the brothers Thring.

The older of the two, the Revd Edward Thring, was headmaster of Uppingham School and one of the giants of Victorian education, equalled in importance only by Thomas Arnold of Rugby. In the mid-nineteenth century Thring was a key figure shaping Victorian ideas about manliness. He was also a pioneer of two of its key motors: organised sport and sexual repression. His younger brother, J. C. Thring, helped found one of the significant vehicles for this new manliness: the game of football. Edward was a muscular Christian who turned 'weaklings in to men'. He also preached a holistic, egalitarian educational doctrine which he called 'true life'. His aim was to produce well-rounded, spiritually alive, morally upright boys. A complex man, influenced by his German wife, Edward Thring built England's first public-school gymnasium and hired the first full-time music teacher. He was capable of subtlety, vision and tenderness. And he was obsessed with stamping out the heinous sin of masturbation, which (he was certain) led to 'early and dishonoured graves'.

Any boy at Uppingham who was found to have committed 'self-abuse' was instantly expelled. To maintain an atmosphere of 'purity', Thring encouraged boys to spy on each other. And, as we shall see, he used sport as a tool in the war against vice. He could be ferocious. 'When boys saw the lines of his upper lip stiffen like iron, and the sheet lightning begin to play in his steel grey eyes, they did not lightly provoke the discharge,' recalled his friend Edward Skrine. Thring saw himself as doing God's work. In one cheery (and unconsciously Freudian) sermon entitled 'Death, and Death, and Death', he thundered against the 'worm-life' of foul earthly desires: 'I say that, by and by, all of a sudden, you know not how, all that you have learnt to love through years of baseness will drop off.' *Drop off!*

Bizarre as all this may seem, it is crucial to understanding the culture and the era which created modern football. Thring's fears were widely shared. Victorian England was assailed by many sexual terrors. Prostitution, syphilis, the so-called 'white slave trade' and homosexuality were all seen as great moral and social evils. But masturbation was somehow thought to under-lie all of them. 'Self-pollution' was not only intrinsically vile; it also posed a danger to race and Empire because it was the crucial first step on the road to all other kinds of effeminate and dangerous sensuality. If only boys and young men could be taught not to masturbate, they would grow up chaste and pure and all other sexual evils would disappear. Masturbation was considered so appalling that moralists and teachers could barely bring themselves even to mention the word. The vast literature on the subject is full of euphemisms: 'that sin which I need hardly mention', 'this horrible thing done in secrecy', 'the pampered passion'. The campaign to stamp it out was one of the key cultural discourses of late-Victorian and Edwardian England.

Before we look more closely at the Thrings and the birth of football, we must take a detour into this world of anxiety.

The idea that masturbation could maim or kill had first surfaced around 1710 in an anonymously published French quack pamphlet called 'Onania; or the heinous sin of self-pollution, and its frightful consequences'. While the Bible has nothing to say on the subject except for an ambiguous reference to a character called Onan who sinned by 'spilling his seed on the ground' (which might be coitus interruptus), 'scientific' opinion now took a harsher line. The author of 'Onania', believed to have been a brothel-owner trying to drum up business by using scare tactics against a rival form of entertainment, claimed that masturbation wasted essential bodily fluids and 'destroys conjugal Affection, perverts natural Inclination, and tends to extinguish the hope of posterity'. The pamphlet was widely translated and for nearly 200 years underpinned a quietly burgeoning medical and quasi-medical literature on the subject (not to mention a gruesome trade in 'remedies' such as spiked metal rings). In most countries masturbation would remain mildly taboo, but nowhere else in Europe would it become the subject of national obsession. Only in Britain did a full-scale moral panic erupt, and then only in the late nineteenth century.

Doctors were partly to blame. Writing in the 1850s, the influential William Acton depicted sex as a source of danger. Acton believed in the 'spermatic economy', a theory in which sperm was viewed as an essential bodily fluid in short supply.

Masturbation, involving depletion of this fluid, therefore caused debility. At best, the symptoms were nasty: 'the pale complexion, the emaciated form, the slouching gait, the clammy palm, the glassy or leaden eye, and the averted gaze, indicate the lunatic, a victim to this vice'. At worst, it caused insanity and death. (A faint echo of this idea – and perhaps of the implicit violence in it – can be detected in Stanley Kubrick's movie *Dr Strangelove* when US Air Force General Jack D. Ripper launches nuclear war because he thinks the Russians are trying to pollute his essential bodily fluids.) Such was the ferocity of the taboo that even an enlightened, dissident doctor such as Sir John Paget, who was convinced that masturbation caused no physical harm, denounced it as 'an uncleanliness, a filthiness forbidden by God, an unmanliness despised by men'.

One key fear of the time was that British power was faltering. From the perspective of Britain's long post-Imperial decline, this seems odd. The late nineteenth century appears now as the zenith of British power, wealth and social stability, but that's not how it felt at the time. The Victorians were gripped by a sense of dread, seeing not stability but decay; they felt their world crumbling. Some of this anxiety reflected geo-strategic changes. Between the 1820s and the 1860s, Britain had enjoyed a period of assured, calm supremacy in the world. The Industrial Revolution had given her immense economic muscle; the Royal Navy ruled the waves. From the 1870s onwards other nations, notably America and Germany, started catching up – industrially, economically and as imperial rivals, but the British problem went deeper still.

In almost every cultural register of the time there is a sense of Britain under attack or threat. 'At base, it's economic, because of the massive problems with the British economy in the 1870s,' says one of Britain's leading gender historians, John

Tosh. 'And it's linked to anxiety about the Empire, which can be exaggerated but things like Gordon's death at Khartoum had a terrific resonance.' There were new anxieties about sexuality, too, with shifting boundaries between men and women and the emergence of the 'New Woman' phenomenon: women living alone, wearing bloomers, riding around on bicycles and reading 'suspect' novels. For this generation of English men, the world had changed sharply. 'It was an awful lot for the British to come to terms with psychologically,' says Tosh. 'And, since it's men who are supposed to defend the Empire and run the show, it was clearly all to their discredit. In some sense it was seen as their weakness.'

There were a number of markedly shrill responses to the perceived danger. One was the emergence of a harsh new ideology of Empire: 'imperialism'. The Empire had long existed, but had previously been seen more in terms of trade than military power, and few had thought to make an ideology of it. Yet now British attitudes to Empire changed. 'Imperialism' fuelled Britain's massive expansionist grab for territory in Africa and elsewhere. And, as Britain's relative industrial and economic power declined and its naval arms race with Germany escalated, British society became ever more militaristic, a trend accelerated by the sense of weakness revealed by the Boer War. Meanwhile, tremendous energy went into explicitly sexual neuroses. In an age when women were assumed to have no sexual energy at all, men's 'beastly' urges were terrifying. Victorian men were continually enouraged to 'master the beast' as if their bodies were like the wild animals of Africa. Even among the highest in the land, in this unprecedented atmosphere, strange things went on. The Prime Minister, William Ewart Gladstone, the most powerful man on earth, regularly scoured the streets of London at night, looking for prostitutes. When he found them, however, he did not have sex with them but gave them moral lectures, imploring them to turn from the ways of sin. When he returned home, Gladstone would whip himself until the blood flowed in an ecstasy of guilt over these encounters.

The literature of the era reflected sexual fear. Bram Stoker's *Dracula*, Robert Louis Stevenson's *Dr Jekyll and Mr Hyde* and Arthur Conan Doyle's Sherlock Holmes stories all share a theme. They depict the elemental battle between reason, order and control (epitomised by Van Helsing, Dr Jekyll and Holmes) and the evil, out-of-control forces of chaos, death and sex (Mr Hyde, Moriarty, Dracula). Intriguingly, Conan Doyle loved football. He helped to organise a Portsmouth Football Club where he played as goalkeeper or full-back. He also loved boxing, which he defended as 'an exhibition of hardihood without brutality, of good-humoured courage without savagery, of skill without trickery . . . Better that our sports should be a little too rough than that we should run a risk of effeminacy.' Similarly, the great journalistic stories of the day, such as Jack the Ripper, fed into the perception that sexual deviance was the heart of the moral problem of society. John Tosh: 'It's very, very sinister because that takes precedence over the problem of poverty, which, God knows, was *the* serious problem. You see a struggle between "Darkest England" by William Booth on the one hand, and all this sexual claptrap on the other. Should philanthropy go to helping prostitutes and helping young men "keep their vow" [of chastity]? Or to actually dishing out soup to those who are starving?'

Meanwhile, Britain's ruling elite, raised on the Greek and Roman classics, were haunted by imagined parallels between their own problems and the fall of the Roman Empire. According to Gibbon, Rome had fallen because its leaders lost sexual self-control and became decadent. The British were terrified that their Empire would go the same way. 'There is amply sufficient ground for alarm that the nation may be on the eve of an age of voluptuousness and reckless immorality,' warned the Revd J. M. Wilson, headmaster of Clifton School, in 1881. His fears were widely shared, as was his belief in savage remedies. Wilson's recommended 'treatment' for vulnerable boys, starting at the age of ten or eleven – before they went to school, before they even knew the meaning of words like 'immorality' or 'voluptuousness' – was to warn them against other boys' 'dirty and nasty ways' and to teach them to 'regard all dirty talk as being low and ungentlemanly'; they should also know that 'any offence will be followed by a whipping'.

John Tosh considers this late-nineteenth-century moral perspective to be a distortion of existing concerns rather than something completely new. 'Early-nineteenth-century ideas about manliness being put about by people such as Thomas Arnold were not lax by any means; Arnold was against any hint of sexual corruption, of homosexuality.' But the end of the century saw a pathological obsession with such issues. 'Obsessions are about kinds of transference or projections or displacement. They're faulty psychological mechanisms. Instead of doing something about what is happening with the Empire, you worry about what's happening with your willy. It sounds daft, but we know that's what people do – you displace the concern into something where you are fully responsible and, in theory, in control.'

Football was born in the English public schools of the nineteenth century, those weird and often brutal institutions where the sons of the English ruling class were educated. Much has been written about the influence on sport of Thomas Arnold at Rugby in the 1820s and 1830s, much of it based on the misleading image of Arnold presented in the novel *Tom*

*Brown's Schooldays* written by his former pupil Thomas Hughes. The novel influenced many, including Baron de Coubertin, the Frenchman who founded the modern Olympic movement. But in Arnold's day games were rather disorganised and played on a voluntary basis. Arnold wasn't particularly interested in games. Instead, as J. A. Mangan shows in his book *Athleticism in the Victorian and Edwardian School*, organised sport had a different genesis. Some twenty years after Arnold's death, several young headmasters, with Edward Thring prominent among them, began the process which turned games (principally cricket and various forms of football) into a fundamental element of education. Alongside the headmasters of Harrow, Marlborough, Lancing and Loretto, Thring played a key role in developing a radically new ideology – athleticism – which transformed the schools and the men educated in them. This new ideology (which, ironically, Thring later came to oppose for it was so at variance with his 'true life' concept) was a motor for the muscular new imperialism, for militarism and conformism. Suppression of sexuality, individuality – and even thought itself – were essential elements of this process, and were encoded in the games themselves.

Historian Katy Mullin, author of *James Joyce, Sexuality and Social Purity*, explains: 'The masturbation panic was so ubiquitous there was a strong emphasis against solitude, against privacy and against individualism. All sorts of team sports, football in particular, were brought in as an antidote. It was to stop solipsism.' As Mullin points out, it was considered 'sexually suspect' for boys to spend time on their own – so much so that by 1900 any boy expelled from a public school would have been suspected of masturbation. Even more weirdly, masturbation was seen as a communicable disease. 'The fear was not of homosexuality but of masturbation. That's really the important distinction. In the pamphlets, they say:

"It's really terrible. We found this older boy in bed with the younger boy, he might be teaching him to masturbate." Not that they might be having some kind of homosexual affair. That's not even considered.'

Back at Uppingham in 1853, Edward Thring had caused a sensation on his first day in charge. Headmasters were expected to remain aloof, but he joined in a boys' game of cricket. Over the next thirty years, he took Uppingham from obscurity to celebrity in part by turning it into a sports school. Playing cricket, football and fives became compulsory and highly organised, and Thring spent large amounts of money buying land for playing fields (a move soon emulated by other schools). Thring spoke 'with perfect plainness on lust, and its devil-worship, particularly noting its deadly effect on human life' and explicitly saw sport as an element of his purity crusade. His idea, which other educationalists later took to extremes, was that boys could be kept pure if they were kept busy and distracted by sport.

While he was thus fusing games with prudery, his younger brother was helping to shape modern football. In schools a wide range of muddy and often violent football games had been played for decades, descended mainly from various styles of rural and town-based 'folk football', which had existed in Britain for centuries. These were all variations on the general theme of kicking or throwing or running with a ball. Some games could be murderous semi-riots. Played in villages on feast days, they might involve hundreds of men on each side, 'pitches' up to three miles long and 'balls' which might be a sheep's head, an inflated bladder, or (as Durham legend has it) the severed head of a Viking warrior. By the 1840s – as football moved into its Primordial Mound phase – folk football traditions were in steep decline because of the Industrial Revolution and the displacement of rural populations to big new cities such as Manchester and Birmingham. But the public-school-based games were about to explode.

J. C. Thring, who lived in the shadow of his brother, had played football as a boy at Shrewsbury School. When he went to Cambridge University, he continued to play but found it difficult to arrange games with men from other schools, as they all followed different sets of rules. His first attempt, in 1846, to produce a standardised, universally accepted version of the game failed. But in 1862, by then working for his brother as a housemaster at Uppingham, he tried again. This was not quite the birth of modern football, but was perhaps the moment contractions began. J. C. called football 'The Simplest Game' and tried to lay it down, as God had done for Moses, in just ten rules. A year later, exploiting the momentum that Thring had helped create, a group of former Cambridge men met at a pub in London to settle the rules definitively and create the Football Association.

At this historic moment the sport split into two rival factions (rugby and association) over an argument about 'hacking' (kicking of the shins). Intriguingly, men on each side of this dispute made their case in terms of 'manliness'. Thring had stressed that football, by its 'very nature is rough enough, and cannot be made effeminate'. But 'to kick a player on the shins purposely is neither fair nor manly; nay I do not hesitate to call it thoroughly un-English and barbarous'. At the new FA's meetings the chief supporter of hacking, Mr Campbell of the Blackheath Club, insisted: 'Hacking is the true football game.' He claimed that anti-hackers were soft men who 'liked their pipes and grog or schnaps more than the manly game of football' and declared: 'If you do away with [hacking] you will do away with all the courage and pluck of the game, and I will be bound to bring over a lot of Frenchmen who would beat you with a week's practice.' Campbell lost the vote, and

Blackheath left the FA. Ironically, rugby soon outlawed hacking too. But the core idea – that football was, in essence, an arena for the display of manly Englishness, not to mention a vehicle for expressing contempt for effete foreigners – would last a lot longer.

In his humorous classic *How to be an Alien*, written in 1946, the Hungarian wit George Mikes poked fun at the English. His chapter on sex consisted of one line: 'Continental people have a sex life; the English have hot-water bottles.' In another chapter, he is at first delighted when a woman tells him, 'You foreigners are so clever.' Only later does he realise that this is an expression of 'contempt and slight disgust'. An Englishman, he explains, 'uses the word *clever* in the sense: shrewd, sly, furtive, surreptitious, treacherous, sneaking, crafty, un-English, un-Scottish, un-Welsh. In England it is bad manners to be clever'.

The attitude stemmed from the atmosphere in late-Victorian public schools. In contrast to what Thring taught, not only was 'effeminate' sensuality despised, but individuality, learning and orginality also came to be seen as dangerous.

That icon of the 1980s Gordon Gekko claimed that 'greed is good'. In the 1890s, in English schools, stupidity was super. In his book about public schools, *Boys Together*, John Chandos tells of a visit to Eton by a politician called Geoffrey Drage who admitted that, compared to foreign boys, the average Etonian 'could only be described as ignorant'. Drage meant this as a compliment. 'What is it that sets the ignorant above the learned and gives them repose and dignity, which all the knowledge contained in the *Encyclopaedia Britannica* fails to do?' he asked. The answer was 'respect for women' and performance of unpaid public service. He went on: 'I assure you that at this moment an Englishman who deserves the name stalks abroad through Europe like a Spartan through the fields of Greece in her degenerate days . . . and everyone says, "Great heavens,

why are not our boys like that?".' The purpose of this 'superiority' was 'the conscientious administration and defence under
the Queen and with God's help the greatest empire the world
has ever seen'.

Before the 1860s schools had been strange institutions, often
anarchic and savage, but at least they gave boys a high degree of
independence. Now, thanks to organised games, that changed
completely. Eton was the most important school of all, and its
dominant figure in the late nineteenth century, Dr Edmond
Warre, waged war on originality and sensuality. Chandos depicts
Warre, assistant master from 1850 and headmaster from 1884 to
1905, as champion of a new barbarism. Whereas in the old days
'the concept of human putty for manipulation' had been 'un-
worthy of free men, let alone Englishmen', by the 1860s it was
increasingly desirable. And Warre, 'far from rejecting the notion
of manipulable human putty, cherished the ambition that all the
pottery would be as nearly as possible identical'. Warre imposed
compulsory games and made a cult of them. 'He abhorred as
evils, with the zeal of moral righteousness, diversity and freedom
of choice, and he set himself the task . . . to weaken, and then
extinguish, the traditions of personal initiative and the independence of boys' personal lives. He went about this by ordaining
the official worship of a few chosen deities – rowing, cricket,
football, "the all devouring gods" – and officially exalting into a
privileged high priesthood the exponents of their rites.'

In the past, says Chandos, headmasters were indifferent or
hostile to games. Butler of Harrow said that football was 'only
fit for butcher boys'. To others, 'idle boys' meant boys who
played cricket. But when Warre used the expression, he meant
boys not playing games, or playing without sufficient zeal. He
even banned punting on the river, to stop 'drinking, idling and
vice of all kinds'.

Philistinism, games, 'manliness' and ever more bizarre levels of intolerant prudery all fused in 'a new educational doctrine of total control, according to which real leisure and liberty, that is to say, freedom of choice, were malign and undesirable'. The system aimed 'to make all the boys as far as possible alike . . . Independence of spirit and individuality of thought were discouraged as inimical to the object of the system.' Now even botany could be taboo. A boy at Wellington who was interested in gardening decorated his room with rare and beautiful flowers; the captain of the dormitory XI promptly swept them on to the floor and trampled them underfoot, saying, 'There is no room for this rotten effeminate stuff here.' At Harrow, in 1895, the headmaster, Montagu Butler, ordered all boys' pockets to be sewn up. At Clifton, boys' knees were considered 'immodest' and had to be covered. (In Afghanistan, the Taliban later took the same view and whipped members of a Pakistani football team for the crime of wearing shorts.) At Radley, headmaster William Sewell reminded boys that they were under perpetual scrutiny: 'constantly we shall be visiting the dormitory, coming upon you suddenly (until we feel you have strength enough to resist the temptation of being left alone) . . .'

J. A. Mangan shows how the new cult inculcated imperialist and militaristic values. Football, he notes, 'was a direct form of military education . . . Inexperienced youth learnt their lessons on the playing fields and innocently went off to fight.' He quotes another writer, Ronald Gurner, describing Marlborough boys at the beginning of the First World War as thinking of it as 'a glorified football match in which, if peace did not come, they might take their places in the England team'. He also pinpoints an absolutely central element, that 'manliness' excluded sex: 'To be manly was a condition that exuded the physical, but at the same time, it was an "asexual physicality" extended into early manhood, in which sexual knowledge and experience were taboo.' There was a sensuality, but one in which 'physical contact was channelled into football mauls, and emotional feelings into hero worship of athletic "bloods".' The games cult was awash with pain and sublimation. Edward Lyttelton, Warre's successor at Eton, complained that smooth cricket pitches, which lessened the chance of injury, made the game 'comparatively worthless'. Another teacher derided golf and lawn tennis as 'unsuitable' because they were insufficiently painful.

From the 1880s football became a mass movement, spreading quickly from its aristocratic roots to the wider population, via teacher-training colleges, churches, organisations such as the Boys' Brigade, and other routes. Most of the great clubs of England were created at this time, as was the Football League, based on clubs in industrial Lancashire and the Midlands. Historians have tended to focus on questions of class, identity and control in this era. But, despite conflicts between pro-fessionals and amateurs, between former miners and public-school-educated aristocrats, they all played the game in essentially the same 'manly' style. The sacred, fundamental values of the English game did not change. These were defined in 1901, by one E. A. C. Thomson in *The Boys' Champion Story Paper*, one of the many imperialist, militaristic, sports-obsessed magazines for boys:

> There is no more manly sport than football. It is so peculiarly and typically British, demanding pluck, coolness and endur-ance, while the spice of danger appeals at once to a British youth who is not of the namby-pamby persuasion. He loves the game for the sport's sake and thrives upon it. A sound mind in a sound body is produced by healthful exercise and effeminate habits are eschewed. He glories in the excitement of a hard-

fought match, disdains to take notice of a little bruise, and
delights to be in a vigorous charge, giving knock for knock.

Meanwhile, the new social-purity movement took public-
school values and attitudes to sex and sensuality to the middle
and working classes. Their message, delivered by speeches and
pamphlets, was clear: sport would save lives.

In 1884, for example, leading purity crusader Alfred Dyer
told an audience of 2,000 working men in the Plait Hall,
Luton, that 'this horrible thing done in secrecy' was killing
'thousands'. But his listeners could save themselves: 'Ride a
tricycle, play at cricket, skate, chop wood, go for a long walk,
take bodily exercise of some kind, and retire to bed physically
tired.' Pamphleteer Sylvanus Stall said that many men were in
prison because they masturbated or had syphilis. To avoid such
a fate, boys 'should devote at least two hours a day to physical
recreation'. Major Seton Churchill, in his pamphlet 'Forbidden
Fruits for Young Men', urged boys to 'crush' evil thoughts with
an 'iron will'. At night 'the habit of not thinking at all should be
cultivated. Thinking at night is a physical disease with some.'
He too thought that games were the solution, 'an excellent way
of working off that superfluous energy'.

James Wookey, whose pamphlet 'Human Wrecks' sold
150,000 copies, claimed to have knelt beside the death-beds
of numerous masturbators and witnessed their terminal agonies.
Typically, the wretched victim was stricken with remorse
before 'his worthless body tumbles into the grave, and his
guilty soul (guilty of self-murder!) is hurried into the awful
presence of its Judge!' The Social Purity Alliance urged mothers
to tell their sons (in a 'a tender loving' way) that boys who
'indulge in these wrong acts . . . often die young, or go mad, or
become idiotic'. Even during the First World War, when
young Englishmen were statistically more likely to be killed

by machine guns, howitzers or poison gas than by masturbation, the Alliance of Honour sent truckloads of purity pamphlets to soldiers on the Western Front. In one of them, the
eminent Baptist minister F. B. Meyer pleaded: 'Belong to a
gymnasium; ride a bicycle; get, once a week, a game of cricket,
football, lawn-tennis. Do this for the glory of GOD.'

In 1908, Sir Robert Baden Powell – once goalkeeper for
Charterhouse School, where he was known for 'the most
nerve-fluttering war-whoop imaginable when rushing the ball
forward' – founded the Boy Scout movement. His *Scouting for
Boys* and *Rovering to Success* were probably the most influential
children's books of the age, carrying his message of militarism,
the benefits of outdoor exercise, and terror of sex well into the
late twentieth century. In *Rovering to Success* he told boys to
control unhealthy urges during the 'rutting season' by bathing
the 'racial organ' in cold water.

Katy Mullin waded through mounds of such purity literature
and enjoyed its unintended humour. 'It was a pre-Freudian
age, so they always say things like: "Young man, take yourself
firmly in hand." When I'm reading this in a library I have to go
out of the room, laugh, and then come back in. It's funny to us,
but it must have been terrifying at the time.' Her favourite
metaphor was the popular one of the serpent that 'creeps into
many a school', an image which in the 1880s was taken a step
further by the Christian feminist campaigner Ellice Hopkins. In
a pamphlet addressed to young boys, she likens the desire to
masturbate to being bitten by a snake. Mullin: 'Hopkins says,
"Imitate an Australian sawyer who when he is stung in his little
finger by a rattlesnake takes an axe and chops it off", and you
think, "Oh! ouch!" The poor young boys reading this, thinking they should chop off their own penis!'

Ellice Hopkins founded and led the largest and most aggressive purity organisation to target the working class. Her

White Cross League produced a torrent of pamphlets and sent lecturers to gatherings of hundreds (sometimes thousands) of working-class men around the country, and its ubiquitous white-cross logo became synonymous with the demand for self-control.

One stronghold of the movement was Manchester where, in the early 1880s, White Cross activists worked through the city parish by parish, making converts, persuading men to take vows of chastity, setting up new branches. In the late 1870s the football club now known as Manchester City was founded in one of the poorest districts by the Revd Arthur Connell, vicar of St Mark's Church, West Gorton. The church records were destroyed some thirty years ago, so it's hard to know precisely why, but in 1884, as White Cross influence in the city surged, the team played in a new strip donated by the church warden, Mr William Beastow. The shirts were black and decorated with a large white cross.

Public-school-educated Christians sought to raise the moral condition of the working class through football, and their contribution to spreading the game was huge. Eight clubs now in the English Premiership – Aston Villa, Birmingham City, Bolton Wanderers, Everton, Fulham, Liverpool, Manchester City and Southampton – began as church teams. Barnsley FC was founded by the Revd Tiverton Preedy, a pugilist-turned-priest who later moved to London and built a boxing ring in the crypt of his new church. By 1885 twenty-five of the 112 football clubs in existence in Liverpool had religious connections.

But football and purity were not merely ideologically connected: they also shared personnel.

The national secretary of the White Cross was the Revd G. S. S. Vidal, who was goalkeeper for Oxford University for three years in the early 1880s. His older brother, R. W. S.

Vidal, who also became a vicar, was known as 'the prince of dribblers' and laid on the winning goal in the first FA Cup Final, in 1872. The younger brother's stance on moral issues can be judged from his comments at a meeting in Manchester in 1888, where he demanded a 'far less timid and hesitating method' of dealing with purveyors of so-called 'corrupt literature'. Instead of being fined or imprisoned, offenders should be flogged because those 'inoculating England with continental vices deserve neither quarter nor compassion'.

Edward Lyttelton, author of *The Causes and Prevention of Immorality in Schools* ('the gravest social question of the day'), played in the 1876 Cup Final for Old Etonians. One of his team-mates was J. E. C. Welldon, later headmaster of Harrow, where he had his staff take boys aside one by one to give them lessons in purity. Another was Quintin Hogg, who organised the first England–Scotland match and became an evangelist, founder of the London Polytechnic and a pioneer of Christian outreach to the working classes. Most striking of all was the team's captain, Arthur Kinnaird, perhaps the single most influential individual in the first sixty years of English football.

The son of an aristocratic banking and landowning family in Scotland, the Honourable Arthur, who became the Eleventh Lord Kinnaird, grew up with family connections to opposite ends of Britain's moral spectrum. His great-uncle (the Ninth Lord) was banker and friend to that most rebellious and sensuous of all English poets, the 'mad, bad and dangerous to know' Lord Byron. Arthur's mother, however, was a devout evangelistic Christian who founded the Young Women's Christian Association and supported missionary work and the social-purity and temperance movements. In moral matters, young Arthur followed in his mother's footsteps.

He learnt his football at Eton and became a legend in the game, first as a player for Wanderers and Old Etonians, and later as football's foremost politician, president of the Football Association for thirty-three years. Famous for his flowing red beard and boisterous exuberance, he played in nine of the first eleven FA Cup Finals, winning five times. Gibson and Pickford say that Kinnaird's vivacity, fervour and agility were remarkable; he was 'one of the most active men that the game ever produced'. He took part in a 'very hot' match played in 1866, in which one team 'were badly knocked about' but after which all the players 'dined happily together'. After winning the hard-fought 1882 Cup Final, Kinnaird celebrated by standing on his head in front of the main stand. At another final, as a mark of respect, the crowd pulled his carriage the last few hundred yards to the Oval stadium. The classic Kinnaird story has his mother worried that Arthur will get hurt. She tells a friend: 'I fear one day Arthur will come home with a broken leg.' 'Fear not, madam,' comes the reply. 'The leg will not be his own.'

Kinnaird was also one of the key leaders of the social-purity movement. In his book *Vice and Vigilance*, Edward Bristow describes him as 'an indispensable lifetime bankroller of purity causes'. He worked mainly behind the scenes. Uncontroversially, he was president of the Young Men's Christian Association, a director of Barclay's Bank and Lord High Commissioner of the Church of Scotland. One of the family's interests was the Pure Literature Society, which distributed morally uplifting books. Arthur was also treasurer of the Central Vigilance Society for the Repression of Immorality and, most intriguingly, vice-president of the National Vigilance Association (NVA), the most influential and aggressive of all purity groups.

The NVA was founded in the aftermath of the highpoint of Victorian sexual hysteria, the 'Maiden Tribute' scandal of 1885. The case involved the exposure by W. T. Stead (the founding father of tabloid journalism) of the so-called 'white slave trade'.

This monstrous trade involved the capture and sale of young English virgins for use in Belgian brothels, and did not in fact exist. Unable to find any real victims, or real slave traders, Stead and his fellow campaigners (whose objective was to force Parliament to raise the age of sexual consent) arranged the abduction of a thirteen-year-old girl who was later subjected to a forced gynaecological examination. Stead was jailed for six months for his part in this episode. The story, sensationally serialised in Stead's newspaper, *The Pall Mall Gazette*, created a hurricane of moral indignation and inspired one of the biggest political demonstrations in British history. More than 300,000 protestors crammed into Hyde Park to call for new laws and to 'express their shame and indignation at the prevalence of criminal vice in their midst'. Speakers at the rally included Quintin Hogg, the feminist pioneer Josephine Butler, Ellice Hopkins and James Wookey. The NVA was formed a week later; Kinnaird had helped to organise it all.

By now, says Bristow, 'one of the primary objectives of the social-purity movement was to sweep the streets of the erotic so that people would forget they had sex organs'. The NVA led the way with campaigns and prosecutions against 'indecency' and 'immorality' wherever they imagined it, which was almost everywhere. Their method was to set up 'vigilance committees' to press local and national authorities to take action. The NVA tried to close or bowdlerise the music halls, and persecuted the owners of theatres, exhibitions, newspapers, advertising hoard-ings, early film and 'mutascope' shows. They also attacked serious art and literature. In 1890 London police helped the NVA break up an exhibition of illustrations of the work of Rabelais. In Manchester they were behind the seizure and destruction of 25,000 copies of works by Balzac. One of the organisation's greatest triumphs was the prosecution of Henry Vizitelly, English publisher of the 'obscene and lewd' novels of

Emile Zola, Gustave Flaubert and Guy de Maupassant. After two trials, the NVA rejoiced when Vizitelly, seventy years old and in failing health, was jailed for three months.

None of this was enough for Kinnaird and his fellow campaigners, who demanded ever more laws, more police action, prosecutions and self-censorship. In June 1895, just one month after Oscar Wilde was jailed for homosexuality (he had an affair with the son of the very manly Marquess of Queensberry, who wrote the rules of boxing), the NVA met at the Duke of Westminster's home for their annual meeting. Lord Kinnaird chaired the event and was loudly cheered when he expressed 'the hope that from this meeting there will go forth a unanimous opinion that the time has come when public opinion will demand something further in the way of repression'.

About football Kinnaird once said: 'I believe that all right-minded people have good reason to thank God for the progress of this popular national game.' In a climate where, as Harry Enfield joked, the only part of an Englishman's body allowed to be stiff was his upper lip, it was hardly surprising that English football viewed creativity, delicacy and individuality with such extreme suspicion. In 1909 Arnold Bennett complained that 'the atmosphere of this island is enough to choke all artists dead'. In the same year the only significant artist in English football, Welshman Billy Meredith, the 'Wizard of the Wing', was banned from football for the second time. The first occasion, when playing for Manchester City three years earlier, had been for allegedly bribing an opponent. Now his offence was an attempt to found a players' union. Meredith, a showman who liked to play with a toothpick in his mouth, eventually won his battle to create a union but his career was dogged by official harassment.

Stylish, creative individualists like Meredith were rare as hen's teeth, and usually suffered for their skills. The press called them 'stormy petrels' and they were seen as trouble. 'Gatling Gun' George Hilsdon, a rare Edwardian sensualist – goalscorer, lover of women and addict of the bright lights of the West End – was often in trouble with his employers, West Ham and Chelsea, though his decline owed more to wartime exposure to mustard gas. In the 1920s Hughie Gallacher was said to have 'magic feet'. Small and stocky, he mesmerised opponents, scored unforgettable goals and was the star of the famous Scottish team that beat England 5–1 at Wembley in 1928. But he never felt he fitted in anywhere, moved restlessly from club to club, became an alcoholic and eventually threw himself under the wheels of the York to Edinburgh express train. The story stays the same over the years. Len Shackleton, the brilliant 'Clown Prince of Football' played just five times for England. He was ostracised by officialdom after he wrote a book in which the chapter entitled 'What the Average Director Knows About Football' consisted of a blank page. Jimmy Greaves, an instinctive goalscorer with gifts comparable to a Romario or Gerd Müller, was left out of the 1966 World Cup Final for workhorse Roger Hunt. Greaves never quite got over it, became an alcoholic and drifted out of the game early. Even the revered Stanley Matthews, another sensualist and artist who so hated the traditional heavy English football boots that he had his own lightweight versions, played only about half the number of games for England he should have done.

It didn't necessarily have to be this way. Everywhere in the world, football grew from English roots, and everywhere different styles and values developed. Argentina, which had the deepest English connection, is a particularly revealing case. In his book *Masculinities*, anthropologist Eduardo Archetti shows how football, along with tango and polo, was where a distinctive Argentinian masculinity emerged. For its first forty years, Argentinian football was an all-English affair, brought to Buenos Aires in 1867 by expats and dominated by Anglo-Argentines imbued with public-school values in teams such as the Alumni. Then, around 1910, Italian and Spanish immigrants and other non-Anglos, who resented English domination, overthrew the old ways and developed a new, explicitly anti-English *criollo* style. Force and discipline were out; sensual, elegant, creative football became mandatory. Archetti quotes the Anglo former Alumni star Jorge Brown lamenting in the early 1920s that the new football was 'weakened by an excess of passing close to the goal. It is a game that is more fine, perhaps more artistic, even apparently more intelligent, but it has lost its primitive enthusiasm . . . Football is not a delicate sport . . . It is a violent and strong game in which physical resistance and the muscles of the players are what is proved.' Argentina never produced Lionhearted centre-forwards like Tommy Lawton or Nat Lofthouse, or sturdy, reserved, gentlemanly defenders like Billy Wright or Bobby Moore. And England never produced a Di Stefano or a Maradona.

By 1914 most of English football's key tenets and institutions were set in stone. It was a game imbued with manly, martial virtues played with heavy leather balls in thick, ankle-high boots in seas of mud. Creative players, where they existed, tended to have been imported from Scotland. The carnage of the Great War put a stop to the more extreme doctrines of imperialism and militarism. And, by the 1920s, the influence of Freud and changed medical opinion saw the steam go out of the anti-masturbation hysteria (though as late as the 1960s embarrassed teachers were still warning baffled schoolboys not to 'damage themselves'). But England remained a hot-water-bottle culture, both on and off the pitch. In 1961 the historian

Percy Young wrote a famous paean to his home-town club, Bolton Wanderers, in which he celebrated 'the real virtues of the English game . . . its vigour, drama and sociability'. Skill was a potential threat to this fundamental Englishness, though 'from time to time standards of technical excellence are to be seen, and I believe that these can be built in without altering the local accent'.

The poet Philip Larkin mournfully observed: 'Sexual inter-course began/In nineteen sixty-three/(Which was rather late for me)/Between the end of the Chatterley ban/And the Beatles' first LP.' Football was in some ways the English institution least amenable to the cultural and sexual revolution of the sixties. Even so, a handful of a new breed of Byronic players briefly emerged. The journey of the greatest of them, George Best, from footballing sex god to alcohol-ravaged liver-transplant patient is well known. But what went wrong for the other extraordinary mavericks of the period – players such as Rodney Marsh, Peter Osgood, Charlie George, Alan Hudson, Tony Currie, Stan Bowles and Frank Worthington? Never before or since has England had so many gifted and creative forwards at one time. An England team built around just two or three of these players might have been a thing of joy and wonder. We'll never know, because the two main England coaches of the period, Alf Ramsey and Don Revie, tended to treat these players' genius as if it was a form of leprosy. And England failed to qualify for the 1974 and 1978 World Cups. My boyhood hero Charlie George, for example, who scored four goals in a European Cup tie against Real Madrid and could pass the ball like Dennis Bergkamp, played only once for England (and was substituted after only an hour). But his Arsenal colleague, the dull, brutal 'hard man' Peter Storey played nineteen times. In 1975 Alan Hudson led England to a demolition of world champions West Germany. He was never picked again.

Like their Dutch and German contemporaries, the mavericks were self-taught, and had learnt their football on the streets of austere, war-damaged cities. Their crime, when they reached maturity in the late sixties and early seventies, was sensuality. They caressed the ball, made it obey their whims and desires, performed outrageous tricks, scored dazzling goals. Disobedient, funny and colourful, they saw themselves as artists and entertainers, as queen bees rather than workers or soldiers. Off the field they were defiant hedonists. 'Yeah,' Stan Bowles later admitted, 'I spent all my money on booze, gambling and women – but at least I didn't waste any of it.'

Frank Worthington was a cheerful libertine and sensational goalscorer whose passion for football and sex is detailed in his autobiography, *One Hump or Two*. As a teenager, he was so entranced by Pelé that he decided he didn't want to be English any more and wandered around Yorkshire speaking a made-up language he thought sounded like Portuguese. He played for eleven different clubs ('twelve if you count Stringfellows') and turned up for the first of his handful of England appearances wearing a green velvet jacket, a flowered shirt, leather trousers and cowboy boots. He believes that his hero Elvis Presley once visited him in a dream; and after he retired as a player Worthington forged a second career as an after-dinner speaker and Elvis impersonator.

For Rodney Marsh the thrill of football was entirely sensual. Generally, he said, English football was 'a grey game played by grey people on grey days'. But he saw it differently: 'Nothing you do can get close to playing football at the highest level in front of a big crowd, and scoring a goal . . . when you score a goal and it's an important game, the high you get from that is ten times higher than sex. You can actually hear the blood going into your head . . . it's such a sensation. It's a rush of blood you'll never ever get from anything including probably cocaine.' Marsh grew up in a poor family in London's East End. His father spoke little and savagely beat him often. Rodney vowed never to be intimidated or take orders from anyone ever again. He played seven times for the national team but he and Sir Alf Ramsey, the old-school disciplinarian who won the '66 World Cup, inhabited different worlds. Marsh wanted to have fun; Ramsey told him: 'Run yourself into the ground.'

Their most revealing clash was their last. In 1973, in the dressing room before a game against Wales, the following conversation took place:

Alf Ramsey: 'Marsh, if you don't work hard, I'm going to pull you off at half time.'

Rodney Marsh: 'Blimey, boss! At Manchester City all we get is a cup of tea and an orange!'

Ramsey did not laugh, and Rodney Marsh never played for England again.

During their careers, the mavericks were hounded by tabloid newspapers, usually in dispute with their clubs or coaches, and punished on the pitch for their impertinence by hard men like Norman 'bites-yer-legs' Hunter and Ron 'Chopper' Harris. Against Don Revie's Leeds, Worthington once embarrassed Johnny Giles by delicately lobbing the ball over his head as he slid in for a tackle. Giles caught up with him later and informed him: 'Take the piss out of me or Leeds United again, I'll break your fucking leg for you.' Tommy Smith, captain of Bill Shankly's Liverpool, had the same approach. At Anfield, Worthington beat Smith neatly and was told: 'Do anything like that again and I'll snap your fucking back.' Later in that game, Worthington jumped for a high ball. 'As I made contact [Smith] hit me in the middle of the back. To this day I don't know what he did or how he did it. But, if you can, imagine being hit by a sledgehammer in the middle of your back. There was nothing you could do about it. I just lay there on the deck.'

Even more telling were the taunts of rival fans who saw flamboyant skill as a sign of effeminacy: 'Georgie Best superstar/Walks like a woman/And he wears a bra'; 'Where's your handbag, Charlie George?'; 'Oh, wanky, wanky/Wanky, wanky, wanky, wanky Worthington'. In the 1980s Glenn Hoddle was called 'Glenda' because his visionary passing and perfect technique marked him out as a 'poof' and a 'big girl's blouse'. Hoddle played fifty-three times for England – but only twice in his correct position. In 1987 he sought football asylum in Monaco. In the 1990s England under Graham Taylor became a parody of dullness as Taylor picked boring Carlton Palmer instead of brilliant Chris Waddle (who also fled for a while, to France). Stormy petrel Paul Gascoigne shone briefly before a long, slow, alcohol-assisted decline. Middlesbrough's hard man Paul ('the Guv'nor') Ince complained about being sent off for pushing an opponent in the face: 'This is a man's game – unless the FA wants us to walk out with handbags, wearing lipstick!' Meanwhile, England's only known gay footballer, Justin Fashanu (disowned by his brother John 'Fash the Bash' Fashanu, a member of the Wimbledon 'Crazy Gang'), stumbled out of the game, turned to born-again Christianity and ended up killing himself after sex-abuse allegations were made against him in the US, where he was coaching a boys' team.

Yet wider cultural changes were occurring. Some traditionalists came to believe that foreigners were ruining football. In 1998 Tommy Smith condemned the new rule against tackles from behind: 'Soccer has changed from a real man's game. People like to see a good, hard tackle going in, just like they like to see two boxers going hammer and tongs at each other. Taking tackling out of it is going to kill the game.' Smith regarded the elegant Argentine Ossie Ardiles as a 'fancy flicker' – and fouled him heavily when they first met on the pitch. Now, Smith claimed: 'The temperament of the foreign player is different from ours. Most of the worst incidents this season have involved foreigners, and they are bringing some bad habits into our game.'

Strangely enough, Smith was on to something. Foreigners, especially Frenchmen, had begun to spread their un-English ways through the kingdom, though not quite in the manner he or Edwardian moralists had feared. Thanks to satellite TV, globalisation, Europeanisation and the increasing cosmopolitanism of English society, foreigners came to dominate English football. The pivotal figure was Eric Cantona. From the moment he arrived at Leeds United in 1991, the English never ceased to marvel at a man able to combine arrogance, indiscipline, artistry (and a risible interest in poetry and philosophy) with aggression, power and achievement. At Leeds, his manager, Howard Wilkinson, took a traditional English view and decided that the wilful, skilful Frenchman was trouble. So, for a modest fee, Wilkinson sold Cantona to Manchester United, a club which hadn't won the championship in twenty-five years. It was the worst decision in English football history, maybe the worst anywhere in any sport since the Boston Red Sox offloaded Babe Ruth to the New York Yankees. Cantona promptly inspired Manchester United to an unprecedented decade of domination. Perhaps more importantly, he paved the way for the deepest challenge ever mounted to the ancient English code.

Cantona's impact on English football was rather like HMS *Dreadnought*'s effect on naval warfare before the First World War. In 1906 the new *Dreadnought* was so fast and well armed she rendered all existing battleships instantly obsolete. This triggered an arms race as other navies responded by building *Dreadnoughts* of their own in ever greater numbers. Likewise, Cantona was so manifestly superior to every English player of the time that rival clubs concluded that they had to get hold of brilliant foreigners too – and quick. At first, clubs acquired talent in ones and twos. Chelsea got Gullit; Spurs had Klinsmann; Bergkamp joined 'Boring Arsenal'; ambitious Newcastle splashed out on Ginola and Asprilla. Then the EU forced Uefa to scrap its rule allowing only three foreigners per team, and soon nearly all the best players at most of the top English clubs weren't English. In 1997 Zola (Gianfranco, not Emile) was voted Footballer of the Year, an honour which has been won by only one Englishman in the last eight years. Chelsea regularly fielded teams without any Englishmen at all. Arsenal kept some English defenders and goalkeepers, but won two Doubles without a single English forward and only a couple of (reserve) English midfielders. Even more tellingly, there was a shift away from English club coaches, with Arsène Wenger of Arsenal and Gérard Houllier of Liverpool leading a revolution in ideas about tactics, fitness and motivation.

The overall quality of the English Premiership has risen sharply in recent years as an army of clever foreigners helped club football throw off historical baggage. But it is still far too early to see where this process will lead or whether it will fundamentally affect the English themselves. The acid test is the England team. After the lumbering embarrassment of Euro 2000 and Kevin Keegan's admission that he wasn't up to the job, the FA did what was previously unthinkable. They appointed a Swede, Sven-Goran Eriksson, to take charge of the national team. When the jingoistic *Sun* newspaper organised a protest, the comedian Jeremy Hardy observed: 'I don't know why everyone's making such a fuss about a foreign manager when it's having all those English players in the team which is the problem.' Eriksson's calm intelligence and his refreshing lack of cliché-ridden Lionheart rhetoric slowly won over fans and the suspicious media. And, by leading England to two unexpected and popular victories (5–1 against Germany in

Munich, and 1–0 against Argentina in Japan), he at least guaranteed that the process by which English football opens itself to the wider world and to the possibility of further change will continue. Eriksson was aware from the start that most of his players had technical limitations. Before the 2002 World Cup, he admitted that 'Argentina, France and Holland are better at keeping the ball than us. It's their history to play that possession game. I am not here to do another style of football. In the World Cup, we must play to our strengths.'

Now, though, English football is at a crossroads. Will it cling to its old unsexy traditions? Or adopt the ways of foreign players and coaches? Or, as seems more likely, integrate both approaches to create some new kind of English player who is vigorous and tough like before but more skilful? The biggest stars in English football now are foreign players who have been changed as much by contact with old Englishness as Englishness itself is being changed by them. At Bolton, that bastion of old English football virtues, apparently washed-up old foreign stars such as Frenchman Youri Djorkaeff and Nigerian Jay-Jay Okocha found themselves astonishingly reinvigorated by Lion-hearted manager Sam Allardyce and the fans. The new synthesis was most noticeable at Arsenal. Under Arsène Wenger, yeoman defenders such as Tony Adams and Martin Keown became technically and tactically sophisticated, and foreign Fancy Dans such as Pires and Bergkamp learned to scrap. Before Robert Pires's first English game at Sunderland Wenger put him on the bench. At first Pires couldn't believe what he was witnessing: 'After thirty minutes I thought, "What am I doing here?" It was so tough. Attack, defend, attack, defend. Some of the tackles were like rugby.' A few months later, before his first North London derby at Tottenham, Adams warned him: 'You have to be ready for this, to fight for the team.' Pires recalled: 'It was wild, and you have to learn that the

English game is very different. People can tell you but it still takes time to change. You have to adapt, to show that you are not going to take anything or people will run over you.'

In the era of *Footballers' Wives* and 'roasting', it's clear that modern footballers don't share quite the same sexual codes as the game's founding fathers. Even so, other aspects of ancient English footballing manliness look pretty indestructible. It is striking, for example, that, even in the sexed-up modern game, heterosexuality remains the only kind allowed: there are still no openly gay professional players or coaches. The durability of old English manners was deliciously illustrated by a famous TV commercial for John Smith's Bitter. On a muddy recreation ground a group of trim new-style footballers in a circle silkily juggle with the ball. When the ball reaches the portly figure of comedian Peter Kay he wellies it triumphantly into a neighbouring garden, looks hugely pleased with himself and celebrates his blow for old-fashioned Englishness with a can of beer.

The contest between traditional manliness and a newer model can also be read through the shifting perceptions of David Beckham. Before the 1998 World Cup, Beckham was derided for wearing a sarong and because his wife had said he enjoyed wearing her underwear (though she later insisted this was a joke).

After his sending off against Argentina, the 'girlish', 'immature' Beckham was popular only as a scapegoat. The next season, he was 'Beckscum', booed at every ground by rival fans and hanged in effigy. (Naturally, almost no one criticised dour, manly David Batty for missing his penalty.) Beckham weathered the abuse, refused to change and quietly metamorphosed into a seemingly untouchable national icon. Unlike the frantic hedonism of seventies mavericks, Beckham seemed happily married and at ease with his feminine side. For the first time in history, the most creative footballer in England was its dominant figure on and off the pitch. For a few seasons he was England's most industrious and inspirational player. Then came Rebecca Loos and a poor Euro 2004. The anti-Beckham backlash that followed was huge, gleeful, venomous – and clearly tinged with relief. Beckham hadn't been the only national icon to play badly in Portugal. But no one in Spain, France or Italy questioned the manliness of Raul, Zidane or Totti. Here, though, Martin Amis sneered: 'How, by the way, did it ever get about that Beckham was good at penalties? He utterly lacks the steel for it.' In the week when Wayne Rooney suddenly became 'the new Pelé' and took over from Beckham as the nation's favourite sporting icon, Andrew Anthony observed that the shift had occurred in part because Rooney was seen as a more 'authentic' representative of the spirit of the nation and the game. Instead of the 'heterosexual gay poster boy who feminised football' we had a new hero whose primal appeal drew on peculiarly English tradition. 'Authenticity is back. After the product-selling moisturised man, we want a bit of rough. And there is no rougher than Rooney in football . . . His jutting jaw-line, that seems to have been drawn by a *Beano* cartoonist, harks back to another age – the Neolithic perhaps. He is Roy of the Rovers with the physique of Desperate Dan.'

The constable was just stooping down, with his back to the players, to pick up the errant dog, when the ball, miskicked by Banham, smote him a resounding smack on the back, bowling him over like a ninepin.

# ROYS, KEENS AND ROVERS

Does he reincarnate in the manner of the Dalai Lama? Or is he more like terrifying Jack Torrance who's 'always been the caretaker' in *The Shining*? Either way, it's clear that the fictional football character known in this lifetime as 'Roy Keane' has been here before. With his taut sinews, dark eyes and grim visage, Roy is a timeless archetype of the English game: the sporting warrior. Demon-driven but indomitable, Roy emerges victorious from almost every bone-crunching tackle. Even in the twilight of his career, he retains the power to inspire devotion in his followers and fear among his enemies. Quick-tempered but a born leader, he drives himself and his comrades to triumph in the eternal battle for victory. In this lifetime, we know Roy as the captain of Manchester United. We first heard of him as a troubled teenager in a Forest at Nottingham; earlier reports spoke of a troubled boyhood in Ireland. But what was 'Roy' doing before that?

The character is older than you might think. The first of
many recorded sightings comes in 1859 when he was the hero
of a racy Victorian novel called *Sword and Gown* by G. A.
Lawrence. For connoisseurs of what we should perhaps call
'Roy-ness' – that distillation of essential British footballing
manliness through the ages – the parallels between the hero of
the novel and the champion of United's midfield are striking.
These days Roy is a fighting sportsman with a quick temper; in
1859 he was a sportsman and fighting man with a quick
temper. The men under his command called him 'the Cool
Captain'. He had a big, thick, manly moustache, and he was
madly in love with a woman called Cecil. His name? Royston
Keene.

'There were passions in Royston Keene – difficult perhaps
to rouse, but yet more difficult to appease or subdue,' wrote
Lawrence, anticipating future storylines involving red cards,
raging furies and vendettas. 'It seemed as if some strange
doom was upon him.' Royston has a 'vast deep chest' and
'knotted muscles without an ounce of superfluous flesh'. But
his face is scary: 'The thin short lips could be very pitiless' and
his 'cold, steady, dark eyes seldom flashed or glittered; but,
when their pupils contracted, there came into them a sort of
sullen, suppressed, inward light, like that of jet or cannel coal'.
He has a taste for blood too. On a hunting expedition for
wild boar, Royston says casually: 'I should like to kill something before I turn homewards.' His approach to war is
similar. When he is ordered to lead a cavalry charge in India,
the red mist descends. 'I caught sight of Keene's face,' said a
comrade later.

It was so changed that I should hardly have known it: every
fibre was quivering with passion, and his eyes – I have not
forgotten them yet. We ought to have fallen back immedi-

ately on our old ground, but it was so evident he did not mean this, that I ventured to suggest to him what our orders had been . . . Royston faced round on me with a savage oath – 'How dare you interfere, sir! Are you in command of the squadron?' Then he turned to the troopers: 'Have you had half enough yet, men? *I haven't.*' I am very sure he had lost his head . . . It seemed as if the devil that possessed him had gone out into the others too, for they all shouted in reply – not a cheery honest hurrah! but a hoarse, hungry roar, such as you hear in wild beasts' dens before feeding time. An old troop sergeant, a rigid pious Presbyterian, spoke for the rest, grinding and gnashing his teeth: 'We'll follow the captain anywhere – follow him to hell.'

The novel, set before and during the Crimean War, is also a chaste love story in which Royston woos a Cornish beauty called Cecil Tresilyan. Page after page, they circle each other with growing desire ('Royston's eyes darkened strangely; and one glance flashed out of the gloom that made her shrink away from him then, and blush painfully when she thought of it afterwards alone'). Royston persuades Cecil to elope with him, but a jealous former suitor tells her this will ruin the family's honour, so she runs away from Royston. He is distraught, but buries his grief by signing up for the Crimean War and arrives in time to take part in that disastrous, defining moment of manly mid-Victorian English bravery, the Charge of the Light Brigade at Balaclava ('Theirs not to reason why/Theirs but to do and die', etc.). Keene – 'the best swordsman in the Light Brigade' – kills some Russians and survives the charge, but his horse is shot from under him on the way back to the British lines and, although run through by a bunch of 'bloody Muscovite spearmen', he doesn't die immediately. And who should be at the field station nursing the wounded? The gorgeous Cecil! (She has become a nun.) The star-crossed lovers are reconciled on Royston's deathbed. Royston tells Cecil: 'I loved you best of all. Darling, wish me good night . . .'

Being in love with a nun must take its toll on a soul for Keane/Keene disappears, returning in 1909 as a very bad man in a western. His name is now 'Royal Keene', women call him 'Roy', Indians know him as 'Death Shot', and he's the villain of a Buffalo Bill novel called *Wild Nell: the Amazon of the West*. Nell is 'wild' because Roy took away her honour by tricking her into a false marriage, but this is the least of his crimes. Royal Keene is the 'Prince of Evil': a smiling killer, highwayman, trickster and fugitive. He has long black hair and a droopy moustache, rides a black horse and wears high-top boots and a grey sombrero. His face is 'strangely handsome' but 'the eyes may be a little too black and piercing, and the look of recklessness and dissipation mars the almost perfect features'. Keene pursues a vendetta against Buffalo Bill and finally confronts him in a knife-fight. 'Royal Keene smiled grimly in anticipation of his deadly revenge over the man he so hated.' But Bill wins and knocks away Roy's knife. ' "Curse you – curse you!" broke from the lips of the infuriated and baffled Roy' who tries to flee but is shot through by an Indian arrow.

Wild Nell staggered forward and threw herself upon the dying form of the man who had so wronged her. 'Oh, Roy, Roy! Speak to me – speak! Even now I love you!' Her tone was piteous, and she bent over the dying man with moans that would touch the hardest heart as she wailed forth: 'Roy, only once look in my eyes – only once before you die.' The dark eyes opened, and the fire of his impetuous spirit yet burned within them as he turned upon the woman; then the expression changed to sadness as he murmured: 'I wronged you, Nellie, and you do not hate me!' Again his eyes closed, but all heard the word that trembled on his lips. It was simply: 'Farewell!'

He meant '*au revoir*', actually, for soon he was back again, this time as Barry Keene, wronged English sporting hero, cheated of the world heavyweight boxing championship by a 'swarthy' American called Bud Crane. During their title bout, Crane's evil trainer had shot a poisoned dart into Keene's leg with a blowpipe disguised as a cigar. Crippled for life, Keene vowed revenge. The story unfolded over thirteen exciting weekly episodes in the *Boys' Realm of Sport and Adventure* in 1920. Keene has a 'fragile, pretty' sister, Dolly Keene, who is outraged by the American's lack of sportsmanship. 'Dolly had risen to her feet, her eyes moist with tears. She clenched her little hands. "Oh, why am I not a man?" she said piteously. "Why am I not big and strong and firm, that I could give this – this creature the hiding he deserves?"'

Barry is motivated more by patriotism and he travels in search of a protégé to beat 'the most unsporting hound who ever entered a ring' and bring back to Britain the title 'which should rightly be hers'. One candidate is the hopeless 'One-Punch Smith' who 'goes down fighting, in the truly British fashion'. Eventually, Keene finds a miracle cure for his leg and beats Crane on his own. He softens up Crane with a barrage of punches before righteously smashing the American's jaw to 'pulp'. There is 'not a sign of pity or compassion upon Keene's face. He was strong, immobile and the stony eyes seemed to regard Bud as though he were a wild animal that had to be destroyed.'

We are obviously charting more than an unusually long and colourful footballing career here. To trace Keano's various manifestations and spellings through the vast literature of British boys' adventure stories is to get a sense of British fantasies over the last century and more. As we shall see, there were thousands more tales where these came from. In time, Roy would Rove. He and men like him would take a keen interest in football, and they would do it across the limitless arena of cheap novels, story papers and comics which provided pleasure to millions of British boys. It's easy to see why scholars have tended to ignore this material. Most of the stories are hack-written and without literary merit. Yet they are important, perhaps only because the stories we tell ourselves – as individuals, families or nations – are always important. Our stories define us. Stories are the way we make sense of the world and our place in it. More than other nations, the English love language and dwell in their imagination. Football is one of the stories the English tell themselves in order to know who they are.

One doesn't instinctively think of football as a narrative form, but that's a large part of the game's appeal: it's a vast, never-ending unscripted drama. As spectators, we yearn to know what happens next. Every free-kick, corner and penalty has dramatic tension. To fans, the progress of their team is more involving than any TV soap, and much less predictable. No novel or film ever held huge international audiences transfixed the way great footballing occasions do. These two kinds of story – the boys' yarns and the game itself – overlapped and reinforced each other. Real football blended seamlessly into the realm of imaginary football: the dream of one world shaped the imagination of the other. 'What happened then no scriptwriter could have penned because no editor would have accepted a story so far-fetched and outlandish,' wrote Stanley Matthews of his part in the last-minute winning goal in the 'legendary' 1953 Cup Final. One of the last jobs of Sir Alf Ramsey, England's greatest manager, was managing Melchester Rovers, England's greatest fictional team.

In her book *Manliness and the Boys' Story Paper in Britain: a Cultural History, 1855–1940*, historian Kelly Boyd, one of the few academics to mine this area, observes that the 'story papers served to entertain the average boy and provide him with a world view. They were cheap, easily purchased, traded, abandoned and lost. In their early days they were accused of corrupting the nation's youth in much the same way that television or music is today.' In the mid and late nineteenth century story papers for boys usually consisted of a few crudely printed sheets of text, enlivened by a few illustrations. Much later, after the Second World War, picture-based comic strips dominated. The stories themselves, though, always remained broadly similar, celebrating and promoting much the same vision of masculinity as that encoded into football in the late-Victorian period. The language changed slightly. After the Second World War, it was rare to find lines as sweetly arcane as ' "Dash my buttons!" ejaculated the boss as he watched. "It's the boy they've come to see" ' (from 'The Easter Monday Match – a Rousing Tale of the Football Field and Circus Ring', *Boys' Realm*, 15 April 1911).

Even so, post-war comics such as *Roy of the Rovers* faithfully continued the earlier traditions of stock characters who were remarkably alike down the decades. It didn't really matter too much if the heroes of these stories were footballers, spies, cowboys, schoolboys, spacemen, detectives or imperial warriors. Their core archetypal characteristics were interchangeable: the best kind of Englishmen were strong, decent and patriotic, brave and capable, men of action rather than words; honourable and chivalrous rather than cunning; daring fighters rather than sages, poets, lovers or priests. Lionhearts, not Saladins.

And from the 1880s onwards, as football became a mass-spectator sport, it figured ever more prominently in juvenile literature. Many publications were devoted entirely to sport, of which football was the most important, and anthology papers such as *Boys of England*, *Union Jack*, *Rover*, *Lion* or *Champion* usually had at least one football story in each issue. Aldine and Newnes published football stories, novels and fourpenny novelettes in the twenties and thirties. The Amalgamated Press owned *All Sports*, *Boys' Football Favourite*, *Football Favourite*, *Football & Sports Library*, *Football Weekly*, *Sports for Boys*, *Sport & Adventure*, *Sports Fun* and *Sports Budget*. Most school stories – that other uniquely English form which was turned into a global craze by the Harry Potter series – also included football matches. D. C. Thomson, the Dundee company famous after the war for comics such as *Beano* and *Dandy*, built its fortune in the twenties and thirties with titles like *Rover*, *Wizard* and *Hotspur*, all of which always included a football adventure.

The sweetest of all the Keane/Keen stories is probably 'Billy's Boots', a football yarn with echoes of King Arthur and Excalibur, which started in *Scorcher* in 1970 and ran for sixteen years. Billy Dane is an orphan who lives with his grandmother and is crazy about football but 'a duffer at the game'. Then he discovers a pair of magic old football boots which used to belong to an old England centre-forward called 'Dead-Shot' Keen. When Billy wears Keen's boots, he plays as Keen did. Billy's boots are forever falling apart the night before a big match or getting accidentally thrown away by his gran. But more interesting is the degree of reverence for and engagement with the past. The grandmother gives Billy a book called *'Dead-Shot' Keen – the Life of a Great Footballer* which he consults like the *I-Ching* for guidance at every turn of his career in the school team. When Billy goes a few games without scoring, he checks the book and finds 'Dead-Shot' had the same problem. When local bullies threaten Billy, he is inspired by reading how 'Dead-Shot' sorted it out. (As the series progressed, 'Dead-Shot', who appears in the form of flashbacks, changes. At first he looks like Billy Meredith: a slender figure from about 1910, wearing long shorts and an Edwardian moustache. Later, he is more of a Tom Finney lookalike from the 1950s. At other times he resembles Dixie Dean or Nat Lofthouse.)

Early on in the series Billy actually meets 'Dead-Shot'. The legend is silver-haired, wears a pullover and is mowing his lawn. The old man and boy bond, but not very interestingly. Keen gives Billy his first England cap and tells him: 'You can have it, Billy, and when you win your first cap you can give that to me.' Billy goes home and tells his gran: 'Fancy Mr Keen being such a nice bloke.' They don't meet again and the relationship works much better when Keen is a mythic, talismanic figure. On one occasion, Billy meets an old grounds-man who saw 'Dead-Shot' Keen in his prime: 'Best player I ever saw! Not much bigger than you . . . But as BRAVE AS A LION!'

Few Keens approached anything like this level of sophistica-tion. In 'A Perilous Mission for the Sheik' (*1959 Lion Annual*) we meet a 'tall, broad-shouldered man with an out-thrust granite-like jaw'. 'I live on danger,' smiles Tiger Keen 'grimly'. 'Tiger Keen lived for adventure. It was his profession. He would go anywhere anyhow, and at any time. Being unat-tached to the police or any other official body he received many strange commissions.' The story concerns shifty foreign-ers, false beards and diamonds. Gable Keen, an amateur detective on the trail of the gang which murdered his father, is the star of 'Get-His-Man Keen', an 'all-thrill yarn' in *Chums* in 1931. After a few episodes, Keen does indeed get his man:

'Keen's lips twisted into a peculiar, mirthless smile. "You've robbed me of my prey . . . but you've also saved me from a nasty, objectionable duty. And I fancy it is just as well that you'll have to hang for murdering him . . . It clears up the last of the gang."'

When a footballer gets kidnapped on his way to the big match in 'The Riddle of the Missing Star', a detective called Maxwell Keene is on hand. 'I scent a strange mystery here,' says Keene. He cracks the case by kicking a football through a window and finding a secret passageway under the evil groundsman's hut. 'Keene waited no longer. From his pocket he whipped out a gun and, moving it fanwise, stepped from the doorway. "Stick your hands up – all of you!" Tommy, the rescued player, doesn't know how to thank him, so Keene says: "You can thank me by playing a real blinder of a game in the match this afternoon"' (Tommy duly scores a brilliant goal). 'Maxwell Keene clasped the young centre-forward by the hand as he left the field. "Well done, Tommy!" he cried. "You played a great game. I'm pleased you won!"' In the *Super Thriller Annual* of 1957, we meet 'Edmund Keen Ace Detective', who foils a plot involving a pineapple-shaped bomb, a villain in a green suit wearing a false red beard, and an attempt to assassinate a visiting head of state. 'By Jove, Mr Keen, England has something to thank you for today!'

The most prolific and influential of all boys' story writers, Charles Hamilton, creator of Billy Bunter under the name 'Frank Richards', also dabbled briefly with Keane/Keene/Keen in a couple of stories which appeared in *The Vanguard* in 1909 under another pen-name, Robert Stanley. In 'Russell Keene for the Empire – a story of the Transvaal frontier' Keene was 'the iron Englishman' – a millionaire adventurer with a 'calm inscrutable face, seemingly moulded in iron, which told nothing of his thoughts and feelings' and had a faithful one-eyed Malay servant. 'I can promise you excitement and danger. I know you like both,' says Keene *en route* to a battle of wills with a 'swarthy' Portuguese enemy called Da Costa. Da Costa is treacherous, ruthless, and gnaws his moustache, but Keene beats him in a battle over diamond-rich mountains. Generously, the Englishman lets the foreigner live. Which was a mistake, because in the next issue Da Costa was back stirring up the natives supporting the Mullah's revolt against the British in Somaliland. Keene outwits Da Costa again and corners him. This time, Keene smiles 'grimly' and offers his opponent a choice between imprisonment or certain death if he fights on against superior British firepower. The Portuguese opts to fight. 'A shade of regret appeared for a moment on the face of Russell Keene. Only for a moment. "Fire!" . . . The British Maxim "growled out death".' After the killing, 'Russell Keene looked icily on the scene of destruction . . . The millionaire's face was tranquil . . . In the wilds of Somaliland the Mullah still, for a space, defies the British. But the victorious advance of the rebel ceased with the death of Da Costa, and the Mullah's design of driving the white man into the sea will never be carried out.'

Disdain for foreigners was a key component of this literature. 'One underlying assumption throughout all these stories is that the Englishman is really the greatest man on earth,' says Kelly Boyd.

In the earlier period, this means being English and middle or upper class. But after the First World War this is extended as the working class is included in the polity, and you see working-class heroes. Religion is usually elided over, though, of course, Catholics were never seen as a good thing. But British juvenile fiction is nearly always very negative about most foreigners. In India, for example, the Bengali middle class is despised for not being 'manly', because they want to be civil servants and are too much into book learning. But there is admiration for 'warrior races'. Gurkhas, Sikhs, Maoris and Zulus are 'noble', whereas Aborigines in Australia are seen as effeminate and soft.

Meanwhile, the English heroes are 'capable and clever, but this is the "school of the streets", not books. In the earlier period, the public schoolboys who are heroes are never bookish; just naturally bright, regular boys with common sense. That's very English. And they were not Welsh or Scottish either or even English with Norman influences.' The stories tried to inculcate moral attitudes:

> They're often about physical courage and facing up to danger. The idea is of standing up for your beliefs, and protecting people who are weaker than yourself, taking responsibility. You're not frightened of things, but if something is frightening, then you face up to it. It's always about putting yourself forwards, pushing yourself out in front. So in football you're always trying to take the lead. You're not playing a defensive game; you are always on the attack.

Steve Holland, who collects juvenile stories and runs a splendid website for other enthusiasts, observes:

> Most early boys' papers supported anything that was considered a healthy outdoor activity, and football was always that. It also promoted 'team spirit' and while many of the teams had good players, individuality and self-glorification was often something that lost a match. Football was not the only way of encouraging readers to develop 'fighting spirit', but anyone who didn't get involved in sport was deemed a slacker and it was usually the

bad types (smokers, drinkers and gamblers) who tried to avoid games practice.

In the 1920s, with so many sports papers around, writers injected large doses of adventure and mystery into matches: 'Dozens of mystery wingers wore masks, gangsters were always threatening to blow up the stadium, and teams were decimated by kidnappings every five minutes. This kind of behaviour continued all the way up to WW2 and beyond.'

In the best of the English boys' stories there's an irresistible mixture of imagination and bathos. This first paragraph of a story called 'Jack of All Trades' (*Football and Sports Favourite*, 1929) is typical: 'It was a dark, gloomy November morning and the big young man, who looked even gloomier than the weather, had switched on the electric light in the offices of Messrs. Crisp & Carter, the estate agents, of Marine Parade, Westpool in order to make some entries in a large ledger . . .' In a 1931 science fiction series in *Skipper*, a scientist from Surrey uses too much fertiliser in his garden and accidentally creates a colony of giant ants called 'Gi-Ants' ('as big as omnibuses!'). While the scientist rushes to the police station for paraffin, his friend Jim (an ex big-game hunter) and his black servant battle the insect monsters with a gun and a spear. Within a couple of episodes, the Gi-Ants are heading towards London, smashing bridges, demolishing houses . . . and using their giant mandibles to steal apples from a green-grocer's shop.

In *The Men Behind Boys' Fiction*, two enthusiastic chroniclers of this world, W. O. G. Lofts and D. J. Adley, recalled other unlikely heroes from the 1920s and 1930s. The Sapper 'caused a great upheaval in more ways than one – he travelled through the earth in a "burrowing" machine, shaped like a submarine, which sometimes cut right through the Underground, in

London!' 'The Truth about Wilson', a serial in *The Wizard*, concerned 'an incredible athlete who broke all the world records, and was dressed in a black Victorian bathing costume. He was reputed to be nearly 120 years old, and he attained this great age by a series of special breathing exercises and by eating wild roots, which he collected from the Yorkshire Moors.'

Scarcely less exotic were the Englishmen who penned this sort of stuff. Ernest W. Alais, who wrote for *Boys' Herald* and *Union Jack*, was:

> born with only one lung, yet was a continuous heavy smoker of the strongest tobacco, his favourite being the old Irish Twist. When he was writing there was a ceaseless volume of smoke from his pipe. A marvellous raconteur, he told all his yarns without a facial movement. He could literally smell a fog coming, when he would retire to his bed until it had cleared. He was the sixth of a family of seven and his tact in any emergency was unsurpassed.

Harry Egbert, creator of detective stories, wrote 'in the middle of an aviary in his garden with dozens of birds chirping and fluttering around'. Anthony Parsons, once a Royal Flying Corps pilot on the North-West Frontier, was 'shooting elephants for a living, but later came home and started to write for a living'. Edgar Joyce Murray 'was a countryman who used to write all his stories in microscopic handwriting, so small that an editor friend . . . had to get his wife to read them to him . . . another editor can recall him only by the large pair of squeaky boots he wore'.

Leslie Charteris, creator of 'The Saint', loved the stories.

> What fine lusty fare it was! In those simple bygone days, before the child psychologists were invented, there was meat in those

tales for a boy to get his teeth into – instead of getting them into his playmates. The pirates were unregenerate cut-throats, the international spies and criminals were prodigal with murder and torture; even the denizens of other planets were bloodthirsty monsters. There was no sparing of violence and gore. Before Our Side inevitably triumphed, the scuppers ran with blood, the sinister cellars rang with screams, the bug-eyed Martians devoured any available humans except our heroes. Hardly any of those stories would have survived today's namby-pamby criteria of what the young should be allowed to read. But they were a good introduction to the classics which we would move on to in adolescence, from Henty to Sabatini, from Rider Haggard to Sax Rohmer.

George Orwell, by contrast, was not a fan. In a famous essay in 1940, he attacked the boys' weeklies for being stultifying and reactionary:

You never walk far through any poor quarter in any big town without coming upon a small newsagent's shop. The general appearance of these shops is always very much the same: a few posters for the *Daily Mail* and the *News of the World* outside, a poky little window with sweet-bottles and packets of Players, and a dark interior smelling of liquorice allsorts and festooned from floor to ceiling with vilely printed twopenny papers, most of them with lurid cover-illustrations in three colours . . . Probably the contents of these shops is the best available indication of what the mass of the English people really feels and thinks.

He conceded that 'boys at certain ages find it necessary to read about Martians, death-rays, grizzly bears and gangsters' but worried that the stories came 'wrapped up in the illusions which their future employers think suitable for them'. The outlook of papers such as *The Gem* and *The Magnet* was 'that of a rather exceptionally stupid member of the Navy League in the year 1910', and he was appalled by the world-view in which 'foreigners are un-important comics' and the Empire 'a sort of charity-concern which will last for ever'. Nevertheless, Orwell insisted, boys' stories were hugely significant:

> . . . the worst books are often the most important, because they are usually the ones that are read earliest in life. It is probable that many people who would consider themselves extremely sophisticated and 'advanced' are actually carrying through life an imaginative background which they acquired in childhood from (for instance) Sapper and Ian Hay. If that is so, the boys' twopenny weeklies are of the deepest importance. Here is the stuff that is read somewhere between the ages of twelve and eighteen by a very large proportion, perhaps an actual majority, of English boys, including many who will never read anything else except newspapers.

(Charles Hamilton responded by insisting the stories were apolitical, harmless fun. In any case, he added, 'foreigners are funny'.)

One of Roy Keane's predecessors as warrior-like Manchester United captain was Bryan Robson, nicknamed 'Captain Marvel' after the American comic super-hero who flew faster than the speed of light, lifted 50-ton weights and shot blasts of pure energy. Bafflingly, Keane himself is known as 'Captain Fantastic', which is an Elton John song (Captain Fantastic wasn't a hero. He was 'just someone his mother might know'). It doesn't quite fit, whereas Keane could have had a genuinely fantastic monicker if only fans had tapped into the rich tradition of the boys' stories. He could have been 'Captain Hurricane', after the Royal Marine commando who flew into 'ragin' furies' and twisted gun-barrels with his bare hands in *The Valiant* in the 1960s. Or Captain Cactus . . . Captain Crimson . . . Captain Eagle . . . Captain Fury . . . Captain Future . . . Captain of Captains . . . Captain Quickwits . . . Captain Lightning . . . Captain Tubby Muffin . . .

Roy Keane's own contribution to literature was a ghost-written autobiography – *Keane* – which attracted much attention for its lurid revenge sub-plot. In 1997 Keane injured himself in fouling a foreigner from Norway called Alf Inge Haaland. Instead of being remorseful, Keane was righteously angry. Four years later the rivals met again and it was almost the end of the match before Keane got his man with a series of stabbing short sentences: 'I'd waited long enough. I fucking hit him hard. The ball was there (I think). Take that, you cunt. And don't ever stand over me sneering about fake injuries. I don't wait for Mr Elleray [the referee] to show the red card. I turned and walked to the dressing room.' This passage hardly gives a full picture of Keane as a player. Elsewhere, he talks revealingly about his grimly muscular approach to the game:

Neutrals said the 1996 Cup Final was a bore. Not if you were playing. It was grim all right, demanding every ounce of concentration, every gasp of breath. My job was to anchor midfield, to deny Liverpool time and space, to break up their rhythm, basically to destroy any notions they might have had about passing us to defeat. There's a lot of ground to cover at Wembley, but I covered it, getting my tackles in, and delivered the message: this is going to be hard work, boys, fucking hard work. Along with Nicky Butt, I won the midfield battle. Nicky is a tough lad, and an ideal partner for this kind of operation.

Footballers in other countries don't talk about football in this
rather martial way. But then they haven't the same background
of pleasure-fighting as the British. Football stories and war
stories were always close. Everyone knows the heart-warming
true tales of British and German soldiers playing football
together between the trenches at Christmas in 1914. On other
occasions, though, officers signalled an advance by kicking
footballs or rugby balls over the top. There were even instances
of Tommies dribbling footballs across no-man's land towards
German machine guns. And if war was a game, then the game
was both a training and metaphor for war. The righteously
English thrill of various kinds of combat is clearly present in
many football stories before and after the war. Take, for
example, this incident from a 1905 yarn called 'Playing to
Win', the prolific author A. S. Hardy's 'latest athletic master-
piece', published in the *Boys' Realm* ('a bright and up-to-date
paper for all British Boys and Young Men'). A football game is
interrupted by a fight:

> 'Look out Jack!' The young footballer instinctively ducked and
> wheeled round. He took the situation in at a glance, and,
> forgetting all about his attention to the game, he closed with his
> vile assailant like a flash, and with a heavy right-handed blow
> stretched the hulking brute at his feet.
>
> The man's friends, maddened by the non-success of their
> scheme to injure Jack, uttered a cry of rage and rushed at
> Andrews.
>
> Dick Talbot and Jack never gave them a chance. They saw
> the men meant mischief, and knew . . . more fighting
> follows . . .
>
> The man whom Jack had knocked down rose to his feet with
> a howl of rage. He was instantly laid low again by a smack that
> brought the tears to his eyes and the fight went out of him.

Boys' papers often featured columns by professional footballers giving advice. Typical in tone is this from 1920 by Celtic's Jimmy Quinn on the role of the centre-forward: 'The position bristles with difficulties . . . There are "enemies" before, behind and round about him.' The centre-forward who will make his mark must 'have a big heart, and be able to take a lot of punishment without losing his temper'. Martial notions of self-sacrifice and devotion to the cause are even present in the proto-feminist football stories which flourished in the 1920s. In 'Meg Foster – Footballer', mill girl Meg's team is involved in a 'Plucky Fight for Fame and Fortune'. When evil-doers burn the main stand and destroy the team's kit, the girls have to play in new boots. By half-time their feet are killing them, but when the coach suggests they stop, the girls 'pluckily refused to give in. "It's such a gradely game," said Bessie, "I wouldn't miss it if it crippled me for life!"'

Often the link between war and sport is more specific. Typical is 'The Guardsman Goalie' ('With a Tah-rah–rah—rah! this gripping yarn of Army life and footer gets right home') by C. Malcolm Hincks from the *Sports Budget* in October 1927. The hero is 'a big fair-haired young man' called Dick who is both a soldier and goalkeeper. This description of a match reads like a war story:

Then came an excited roar, the khaki-clad crowd on the ropes swayed inwards, a sea of faces were turned towards a big, red-haired man racing along with the ball at his foot.

Dick's opponents had broken through, the red-haired man had beaten the back. 'Shoot!'

Dick's blue eyes had narrowed, and were fixed upon the ball; he did not jump about but quietly stood his ground. Then the ball flashed towards him.

It was a fine, high shot; it looked all over a goal and the men of A Company were cheering loudly, when the goalie sprang upwards. Somehow, he caught and held the fast-travelling ball, and the next instant had dropped it to his feet and punted it well out of danger as the red-haired man rushed upon him.

A few pages later Dick's sporting instincts help foil an attempted assassination while he's on parade:

> Dick saw a man break through the police line behind him and spring into the roadway, levelling a revolver at the young foreign monarch who was the country's guest.
>
> A wild-eyed sallow-faced man, quick of movement. But quick as he was, Private Dick Weston was quicker. Football and boxing had taught him to think and act quickly. Even as the revolver was being raised, Dick's rifle came from the present and plunged at the man's arm with his bayonet. So good had he become at bayonet drill that his name had been taken for the big military tournament, and so quick and accurate was he now in this moment of dire peril, that his bayonet passed clean through the arm of the man who was about to press the trigger. With a howl of agony he stood writhing; the revolver clattered to the roadside.

In his book *Warrior Nation*, historian Michael Paris shows how boys' stories and other forms of popular culture developed a 'culture of pleasure in war' in the mid-nineteenth century – and kept it going ever after. In the Victorian era, 'the essentially aggressive nature of the British was reflected as a powerful theme within popular culture, a culture which legitimised war, romanticised battle and portrayed the warrior as a masculine ideal'. War was 'an exciting adventure, and through the experience of battle boys became men, made their mark in the world and gained honour and position'. In nineteenth-century literature, the novels of Walter Scott made mythic medieval chivalric values fashionable and paved the way for dozens of patriotic historical romances which underpinned the fantasy that British imperial soldiers were engaged in chivalrous warfare for moral purposes. Later, Charles Kingsley and Thomas Hughes fused imperialism with muscular Christianity, and the war stories of G. A. Henty 'taught his readers that war was inevitable if the empire, the greatest force for civilisation in the world, was to be preserved and extended'.

Surprisingly, the idea of war as fun survived the horrors of the trenches. 'The idea that the scale of devastation and suffering destroyed the appetite for glorification of war is a myth. Poets like Siegfried Sassoon and Robert Graves and Wilfred Owen and other writers were a minority,' Paris insists. The boys' stories archetypes after 1918 remained much as they had been before 1914. W. E. Johns, creator of the popular Biggles stories about a chivalrous fighter ace, said:

> I give boys what they want, not what their elders and betters think they ought to read. I teach at the same time, under camouflage. Juveniles are keen to learn, but the educational aspect must not be too obvious or they will become suspicious of its intention. I teach a boy to be a man, for without that essential qualification he will never be anything. I teach sportsmanship according to the British idea . . . I teach that decent behaviour wins in the end as the natural order of things. I teach the spirit of team-work, loyalty to the Crown, the Empire, and to rightful authority.

This culture also survived the Second World War. The post-war flood of comics, films and toys, portrayed the war as:

little different from earlier conflicts . . . The barbarity of the Eastern front, of Auschwitz, Dresden, Changi and the Burma railway, were simply ignored in favour of a representation of conflict that was sanitised, romanticised and reduced to exciting game in which Tommy and Fritz manfully slugged it out face to face. Perhaps because it was the nation's last great achievement on the world stage before relegation to the Second Division, 1939–45 has become, for the British people, a never-ending story told and retold to remind themselves of the glorious past, in a far less glorious and depressing present.

Meanwhile, boys' stories rapidly adapted old models to new realities. In a post-colonial world, the archetype of the imperial hero was repackaged as the Second World War hero. Imperial stories were made over too. Dan Dare, 'pilot of the future', star of *Eagle*, the most important comic of the fifties, travelled to the planet Venus and battled the evil Mekon, but the subtexts of his stories were of an earlier vintage. As the *Boy's Own Paper* was founded by the Religious Tract Society in 1879 to protect British boys from the evils of the 'bloods' and 'penny dreadfuls' of the day, so *Eagle* was inspired by the desire of its creator, Lancashire priest Marcus Morris, to counteract the influence of violent American comics. On the drawing board, Dan Dare was originally a charismatic East End parish priest called 'Lex Christian'. Later, he wore a dog collar as 'Chaplain Dan Dare'. Only in the final versions were the overtly Christian elements dropped. Meanwhile, Dare's actions and even his clothes made it clear he was a space version of the old colonial heroes. Second World War stories were hugely popular, not least in specialist war-story comics such as *Commando*. In the late 1990s, according to Michael Paris: 'German pilots were still made to exclaim: "*Himmel*! An Englander fighter" and dive away in panic as the Fleet Air Arm comes in to the attack. Second World War novels, films and comics put a new vocabulary into the public domain which reflected intense patriotism, is offensively racist and quite unknown among other nations which took part in the war.' Even now, 'the image of the warrior is still the most powerful heroic icon for boys and young men'.

One of the oddities of British juvenile fiction heroes is their frenzied alliteration. No one seems to know why it started, but it was already a tradition by the 1860s. Hence titles such as Bicycle Bob, Ned Nimble, Fighting Frank, Get-There Gunter, Hard-Luck Hamilton. Occasionally an editor would go crazy and splash out on a wild double-header such as 'The Risks that Roy Ran (A Topping Tale of the Turf)'. Long before Dan Dare there had been Dare of 'D' Division, Dick Daring, Dare-Devil Dick, Dare-Devil Don and Danny Donovan's Daring Deed. In 1954, a boy emerged in the pages of *Tiger* magazine who was to become the most famous alliterated hero of them all. Borrowing his first name from Mr Keane, and his surname from the eugenics movement (or was it athletics?) his name was Roy Race. He was destined to be Melchester Rovers' brave, battling, blond, boisterous, barnstorming, big-hearted battering-ram. We know him better as Roy of the Rovers.

Roy's immediate predecessor was Danny of the Dazzlers, a late 1940s serial in *The Champion* about an orphan who lived with his uncle. When *Champion* folded, Danny's creator John Marshall (real name of 'Frank S. Pepper') helped to come up with Roy for the new *Tiger*. But Mr Race is also descended from a more ancient line of Rovers and Roys. In the 1920s, for example, 'Film Fun' featured 'Roy of the Ranches', 'a tall, lean wiry figure, with a face deep tanned by years of open-air life in the West'. At first glance, this Roy seems just like most of the others we've met. 'Roy whipped out his six-gun with a speed that made Sam gasp. "Forget it!" said Roy grimly. "Throw your gun on the ground – look lively!" ' But he also had a rare tender side: 'It was a perfect moonlit night, warm and clear. The air was fragrant with the soft perfume of early summer flowers. Roy of the Ranches was sitting on the steps of Sheriff Jackson's white wood home, his arm encircling the waist of Dacia, the sheriff's daughter. He was feeling at peace with the world. And so was Dacia.' That soppy stuff couldn't last and Roy was soon replaced by the 'Rolling Stones' (a series about girlfriend-free Englishmen in 'the land of the cowboys and prairie').

There had been plenty of previous Rovers as well. In the early 1930s *The Wizard* had 'OK O'Keefe of the Rovers', a serial about a rich American who turns hopeless Rockvale Rovers FC into a winning team. In P. W. Batten's 1927 Aldine novel, *Dan of the Rovers*, we meet Rothsdale Rovers' centre-half Dan Burnby ('broad of shoulder and clean of limb'), who is drugged during a match by an evil odd-job man and falsely accused of accepting a bribe. Dan inherits £50,000 from the father he never knew but turns the money down to clear his name before rescuing a baby from a fire in which he gets horribly disfigured, which leads to a new identity, a new chance with another team . . . and you can probably guess the rest.

Eighty years before *Bend It Like Beckham*, a *Football and Sports Library* novelette of 1922 gave us a feminist 'Ray of the Rovers'. The heroine was spirited, red-haired Ray Lester, who takes a humble job at a Liverpool department store in order to play for the company football team. Her brilliance on the field persuades the dying boss to leave her his fortune, but a scheming lawyer keeps this hidden from her and gets Ray unfairly sacked. After what seems like thousands of pages, a man called Sir Frederick arrives in the nick of time to tell Ray she actually owns the place. Despite her new wealth and status, she insists on playing in the Cup Final and scores the winning goal:

> With the ball at her feet, Ray cleverly swerved and dodged the half-backs and was off like the wind towards . . . goal. The two backs, taken by surprise, hesitated for a moment, and then closed in on this daring centre-half.
>
> 'Shoot!' roared the crowd. But Ray was not to be bustled. Drawing away from her pursuers, she kept on. The backs were closing in, the goalie was alert. Ray waited until the two girls had almost closed in on her, and then suddenly she stopped and sent a swift, oblique shot that no goalkeeper on earth could have saved except by a fluke.
>
> Then, above the tumult came the phee-ep of the referee's whistle announcing the end of the game. And once again Ray of the Rovers had risen to a great occasion, and the Northern Drapers' Cup was going to Rinsford's, of Liverpool!
>
> Flushed and panting, the Rovers lifted her shoulder-high, and carried the sporting little boss of Rinsford's towards the stand to receive the cup she had done so much to win!

Roy of the Rovers, who later got his own magazine, came to be seen as the idealised embodiment of English football itself. 'Roy wasn't based on any one player,' says his former editor, Barrie Tomlinson. 'He was a real British Lionheart. He didn't dribble much, but when he was running on to a through-ball or meeting a cross with his head . . . *Vooomph!!* There was a long tradition of big English centre-forwards, wasn't there? Nat Lofthouse, Jackie Milburn, Ted Drake, Dixie Dean . . . Roy was obviously based on all of them. But then Bobby Charlton was Roy of the Rovers too. So was Bobby Moore. Malcolm Macdonald was identified with him in the seventies. Gary

Lineker in the eighties. Today it would be Alan Shearer. Look at the 1966 World Cup team: they were all Roy of the Rovers. Well, perhaps Jimmy Greaves wasn't, but everyone else was. Roy was just a true British hero who would never do anything wrong on or off the pitch, even when the character became much more realistic later on. On the pitch, there was no fancy stuff. Just basic, old-fashioned English football. It wasn't a matter of tactics but spirit.'

In 1973, Roy's Melchester Rovers won the European Cup, beating 'Corados' of Portugal ('one of the cleverest teams in Europe') in the final. The Portuguese are cunning continentals, inexplicably playing Italian-style *catenaccio*. ('They're concentrating on stopping us from scoring, while waiting for a sudden, unexpected break to snatch a goal of their own,' explains Roy.) The match turns on a duel between Rovers' English hard man Geoff Giles, and a swarthy Portuguese defender with a moustache who keeps winding Geoff up in Spanish ('lo siento, amigo', 'bravo, amigo!') and ruffling his hair. Geoff reacts with 'quick indignation':

'Keep your hands to yourself, mate!' says Geoff in a speech bubble.

The Portuguese claims: 'No spikka Inglees' but actually he understands English perfectly. So Geoff turns the tables, setting up the winning goal by shouting out the direction of a pass and sending the ball the other way.

It was the turn of Geoff's opponent to look bad-tempered!

'No spikka Inglees, eh?' Geoff taunts him.

Rovers hang on to secure a famous victory.

'Good old Roy!' shouts a voice in the crowd. 'Up the Rovers! They're the BEST in Europe!' yells another.

Roy holds the big cup aloft: 'What a climax to the season, eh, chaps?'

*       *       *

Patriotic fantasy was always crucial to boys' stories. This was never more evident than in 1978, after England had failed to qualify for the World Cup (again) and disgraced manager Don Revie had legged it to the United Arab Emirates: a special Roy story was written to show the way forward. In reality, England had been humiliatingly outplayed and beaten by the Dutch a year before, but now Roy returned as the national team's player-manager, inspiring a brilliant 5–1 demolition of 'silkily skilled' Holland. Barrie Tomlinson recalls: 'We wanted to do a story where England could be proud of the way it was playing. We were looking to get the old British characteristics into football: the fighting spirit. We picked Holland because they were the best at the time.'

With Roy up front, big defender Lofty Peak at the back, and cartoon versions of real-life stars Trevor Francis and Malcolm Macdonald on the field (both signed for their publicity value), how could England fail?

England score first. The Dutch equalise. England storm back into the lead. 'With their tails up, the England players really turned it on!' With Geoff Giles and his chum Johnny Dexter 'winning everything in midfield, England tore into the rattled Dutchmen'.

Trevor Francis makes an incredible goal-line clearance. 'Where are you, Trevor?' says Nipper. 'Right here, Nipper!'

Then England score again. GOAL!

And again. GOOAAL!

And again. GOAAAAAAAL!

'Malcolm Macdonald going at them like a juggernaut! England aren't wasting time with aimless crossfield balls. Everything about their football is positive,' says the TV commentator.

At the final whistle, 90,000 England fans go 'wild with delight': 'ENGLAAAAAND! ENGLAAAAAND!', 'YIP-PEEE! Good old Roy!' go the crowd's speech bubbles.

'We bow out to the better team, Roy,' says Johan, the Dutch captain.

'Just listen to that crowd!' says the TV commentator. 'With his untried team, Roy Race has combined courage, fitness and flair to give English football its greatest night in years!'

Barrie recalls it all fondly: 'You look at some of the foreign imports now. They're brilliant but they haven't quite got that British bulldog spirit. That Dutch story was a chance for us to say: we could have beaten the Dutch if only we had played the Roy of the Rovers way. It was the last big fling for Roy. After that you couldn't do it. The world changed, football changed. In a way, it was Roy's finest hour.'

Actually the story was a bit prophetic. Almost twenty years later, in Euro '96, England thrashed a real Dutch team 4–1. Everything England did that night was positive as they tore into the rattled Dutch midfield. Alan Shearer scored twice. The crowd went wild with delight. On the TV commentary, Brian Moore said: 'Listen to that crowd!' It was English football's greatest night in years. Moreover, had England won the competition, a set of 'Roy of the Rovers' postage stamps was ready to roll to commemorate the triumph. 'You can't show living people on stamps except for the Queen, so they came up with Roy instead,' explains Tomlinson. 'If only England had won the penalty shootout against Germany and beaten the Czechs in the final, the Royal Mail was going to produce a lot of stamps very quickly. But then Moller scored that penalty . . . Sob!'

'Sob!'? I ask Barrie why he's talking like a cartoon character. 'You cross the border between fantasy and reality all the time. I always said I was Roy's best friend, and I meant it. Roy was very much a real character, and to edit the comic successfully you have to believe in him. If the character is real in your mind, then hopefully, when you write strips they become real in the minds of your readers too.'

Fantasy and real life got mixed up all the time with Roy, especially under Barrie's stewardship in the late seventies and eighties when he persuaded celebrities to appear in the strip to raise the magazine's profile and boost circulation. The most intriguing was Sir Alf Ramsey. 'In 1982, when Roy of the Rovers was in a coma after being shot, we had to find a new manager, so we asked Alf Ramsey and he said yes. We sent him the script, and he loved it really. He was great fun, lovely to work with.' Alf Ramsey was fun? 'Yes, he knew the character and he'd read stories like that when he was a child. Once I asked him why he hadn't picked Roy in 1966, and he said: "Roy was too young at the time, too inexperienced." He really entered into the spirit of it, so we had a very good relationship, which surprised some people because Alf Ramsey hadn't appeared to be that sort of person. He wasn't a great one for talking about the past, not even 1966, but he really enjoyed getting involved with Roy of the Rovers.'

Football and boys' stories had together helped carry profoundly nineteenth-century ideas of Englishness and manliness deep into the twentieth century, but the culture was changing. Foreign players and coaches arrived in Britain. The low-tech traditional British children's comics were overwhelmed by television, video, computer games and technically superior American and Japanese comics. As English cuisine became a world cuisine, so English football was getting globalised. Roy of the Rovers was rapidly becoming obsolete, destined for a sad afterlife of being regarded not as a role model but as a kind of ironic postmodern joke.

In the 1950s and 1960s the comics which replaced the pre-war story papers were still a big part of British kids' lives, says Barrie. 'Going to the newsagent to buy a comic, or having one delivered to your home was the highlight of a kid's week.

Children swapped comics in the playground, kept them under their bed. Reading is very important for children. We used to get a lot of support from teachers. As long as their kids read something they were happy because it stimulated and developed their imaginations. Now, they'd just sit back and watch entertainment. Videos, TV and computer games are much more dramatic in one way, but there is less going on in the mind. When you look at a still picture in a comic, your imagination goes beyond that . . . But then television came along and a comic can't compete with a moving image on the screen. So from the early seventies comics start to gradually decline. We relaunched *The Eagle* with photo strips, but it didn't really work. And the final death knell was really computer games when they came along in the eighties. It didn't depress us at the time because we were working to reverse the circulation, but deep down I think we knew we were fighting a losing battle.'

*Roy of the Rovers* changed too, eventually out of all recognition. Even in the seventies, Roy's asexuality had become an anachronism. 'Children were watching television and seeing sexual content, so it became ridiculous. It was much more natural for them to see Roy as a father. I think we had to do it otherwise it wouldn't have lasted. But later on, after I stopped being involved, all sorts of strange things were introduced. They brought in the son of Roy. Then there was a coloured Roy. Then he started taking drugs, smoking and drinking. *Roy of the Rovers* had always basically been a football comic and they'd tried to make it something it wasn't. Right at the very end, it really disintegrated. For publicity, they thought up the idea of a helicopter accident. Then they killed off Roy's wife. Then they chopped off Roy's leg, which always seemed to me a rather strange thing to do for a football character.'

It's not quite all over for the British football comic. These days Barrie writes and edits the 'Scorer' strip for the *Daily Mirror*. The story concerns star striker Dave Storry who 'scores on and off the pitch'. 'Strip' is the right word, because lots of the action seems to be Dave's girlfriends taking showers. 'It's a *Roy of the Rovers* with sex,' says Barrie. 'It's read by people who like football and who like pretty girls.' Unlike Roy Race, Dave isn't big and powerful in the air, but technically accomplished and rather smaller. Where Roy played alongside Englishmen with names such as Jimmy Slade, Jumbo Trudgeon and Tubby Morton, Dave's team-mates include Alberto Spiratti, Santos Ralmar and Dieter Haller. The strip is in its fourteenth year and has spawned a computer-generated imitator at the *Sun*, 'Striker'. But next time England win a big tournament the Royal Mail won't be planning stamps of either of them.

Probably the last of the great British football comic strip characters is a different species altogether: goalkeeper Billy Thomson, who is half human, half halibut and only two foot long, the brightest star of that brilliant comic coda to the traditional British comics, *Viz*.

*Viz* magazine started out as a few photocopied sheets put together in their Newcastle bedroom by brothers Simon and Chris Donald, and went on to become a publishing phenomenon. Vastly popular with students, and an influence on comedians such as Vic Reeves and Bob Mortimer and *The Fast Show*, *Viz* represents a comedy version of what Freud called 'the return of the repressed'. All the references to sex, bottoms, farting, violence and drunkenness systematically banned from boys' reading matter for more than a century erupted into foul-mouthed hyper-sexualised, politically incorrect characters such as 'Sid the Sexist', 'Fru T Bun' and

'Roger Mellie, Our Man on the Telly'. At heart, the magazine is a long-delayed insurrection against Edwardian manliness. The essence was captured by a cartoon in one of its 'annuals', *The Big Pink Stiff One* (1988). The near-naked 'Fat Slags' are seen riding the cruel sea on a tiny pedalo in a blaze of pink and orange. Bearing down on them is a terrifying, slate-grey British battleship, red ensign flying in the storm, big guns blazing. The Slags cheerily hail the passing sailors: 'Anyone fancy a fuck?'

The ancient tradition of British football stories is lovingly mocked in 'Billy the Fish'. Billy is a phenomenon between the sticks for Fulchester United. He defies criminals, space aliens, bomb plots and kidnappers, and having no legs or arms or human body doesn't stop him being a wizard goal-keeper:

'What a save!'

'Amazing stop!'

'He just got his fin to it in the nick of time!'

'A breathtaking display of "aquabatics" by the man/fish maestro!'

Billy's team-mates include Johnny X, an invisible centre-forward; Brown Fox, a large-breasted Red Indian winger (who was orphaned in a plane crash and raised in the jungle by a tribe of football-playing Indians); and Professor Wolfgang Schnell, B.Sc., Ph.D. (the brains of the team). It simultaneously murders and breathes new life into the old clichés. Does Billy represent the Indian summer of the genre or its death rattle? The popularity of Japanese comics shows that the old hunger for comic strips still exists, and computer games now meet the need children always had for stories of adventure and excite-ment. But these new sources of children's fantasies mark a break. For good or ill, they simply don't carry the cultural baggage of Roy of the Rovers, or even Roy of Manchester

United. British children now play in new stories. They read, they watch, they dream. But their dreams will be different. Their imaginary world cannot be the same as that of previous generations.

*" Maybe you're feeling jumpy, Cassidy," said Dorgan quietly. " But remember, that I've never picked a failure yet ! " " Thanks," said Tom huskily. " I—I hope I won't be the first ! "*

# IN ANCIENT TIME

Common sense suggests that time in English football should flow in a reasonably orthodox manner. Last week's match: past. Today's game: present. Next Tuesday's cup replay: future. If only it were so simple. Einstein once said: 'The only reason for time is so that everything doesn't happen at once.' But in English football, perceptions are different. Certainly, other countries and football cultures view time slightly differently. In Holland, for example, when the country failed to qualify for the last World Cup, a leading journalist, Frits Barend, blamed the disaster on national coach Louis van Gaal's flawed sense of time. In early qualifying matches Holland dropped points because less effective young players played instead of tougher experienced older ones. This was because the coach was 'building for the future'. Barend complained: 'People talk a lot about the future in football. It's nonsense. Van Gaal said he was thinking of the future, but football only happens in the present. There is nothing else.'

This is exactly the opposite of what most Englishmen would say. Nick Hornby, author of *Fever Pitch*, once said that for a fan, football almost *never* exists in the present. The future has meaning because fans look to next season to erase the disappointment of the current one. And the past is an infinite trove of memory. By comparison, the present seems ephemeral and unimportant. In 1998 Hornby's feelings about time were thrown into confusion when he watched Dennis Bergkamp score three astoundingly good goals in one game at Leicester. For once, it occurred to Hornby that the present could be magnificent – but not because it was the present. What gave the moment resonance was his realisation that he was seeing Bergkamp laying down hallowed memories for the future – right now. Hornby understood that he was watching history.

'One can never ignore the deep worship of the past which exists within the British psyche. Britain is a very old country and, seemingly, a country which wants to remain old,' wrote the American historian Gerard de Groot. Literary historian Stephen Knight makes a similar point: 'In Australia, where I have spent quite some time, they are obsessed with the future. They want to forget the past whereas the English want to live in it.' One of the reasons the English love football is because it is seen as old. The game floats on an ocean of nostalgia, sentimentality, tradition and myth in which its historicity is constantly invoked and celebrated. Fans speak without irony of their club's 'heritage', 'heroes' and 'legends', and of their own part in the glory. Football performs a role not unlike that of the royal family, ruined castles and stately homes: it is a living symbol of stability and heritage.

Intriguingly, it always has been. Football's 'ancientness' was minted the moment the game was invented. It was what Eric

Hobsbawm called an 'invented tradition'. In this it shares
something with other 'timeless' symbols of national identity
such as royal ceremonial or the wearing of Scottish tartan, both
of which were invented in the nineteenth century. In 1986
Henry Kissinger remarked that English football was 'in nostalgic thrall to a bygone era'. But the same could have been said
a hundred years earlier.

In 1905 the game's first major historians, Alfred Gibson and
William Pickford, published their handsome four-volume
work *Association Football and the Men Who Made It*. They were
as keen to promote football's oldness as its bulldog masculinity
and imperial virtues. When they wrote, the 'venerable' FA Cup
was some thirty years old, the football league had been going
sixteen years. Yet the authors claimed ancient lineage. 'Many
reliable records' showed football had been part of 'the very
fibre' of Britain 'for centuries'. Gibson and Pickford's opening
chapter − 'Touching on the Antiquity of the Game' − is a
striking piece of racial myth-weaving:

> Great Britain may not have been the birthplace of football, but
> it was most surely its nursery and its home. Roman cohorts may
> have planted the seed; if so it was planted in good soil, for the
> temperament of these islanders was ever for rough and vigorous
> bodily exercise. It is true perhaps that the Saxon Thanes and the
> Norman Dukes may have considered the football of their day
> undignified and wanting in chivalry, but the yeoman and the
> burgher loved it deeply. It found no place in the annals of
> knight-errantry, but it found a warm corner in the breasts of the
> common people. Rough and ready it was as were the bow and
> pike men who won Agincourt and Crecy. It was beloved of the
> churl and ploughman, and at all times the 'lower orders'
> received it gladly. Interdicted by monarchs, it defied the
> law; fulminated against by prelates, it survived the onslaught;

attacked by the pens of the writers, it outlived them all. Outlawed it flourished; criticised it grew, it entered into the very life-blood of the most virile race on earth.

In English football the present defers to the past instinctively. When Rio Ferdinand emerged at West Ham he wasn't 'a talented young defender', he was 'the new Bobby Moore'. At Manchester United most promising young forwards of the last thirty years have been 'the new George Best'. No other footballing nation thinks quite like this. 'Perhaps it's because other countries either have polluted pasts, like Germany or Russia, or they don't have a particularly interesting past,' says the well-travelled football journalist Simon Kuper. 'I grew up in Holland in the 1980s but hardly anyone ever talked about the great Dutch team of 1974. It was simply absent. But in England, people never stop talking about England's 1966 World Cup win. It's as if it just happened. In England, the past always seems more real than the present.' In politics he sees the same process all the time. 'I remember when the Tories put up VAT, Michael Heseltine defended it by saying that twenty years earlier Labour's Prime Minister, Harold Wilson, had done something very similar. What struck me as odd was that this was seen as a perfectly valid argument. It was seen as a very normal and legitimate way to talk.'

Stephen Fry and Hugh Laurie mocked the English habit of looking back in their radio programme *A Bit of Fry and Laurie*, when they chatted mournfully about the passing of a lost 'golden age', a 'gentler time' when life seemed less hurried and more graceful. The young people of today might not understand, but 'back then' there really was 'a certain inno-cence'. The period in question turns out to have been last fortnight.

Comedy genius Johnny Speight also understood English

reverence for the past. His satirical creation, Alf Garnett, working–class racist and lover of West Ham United, who play at the Boleyn Ground in East London, tended to invoke history only in support of his bigoted rants. In Alf's snobbish mind, football, Empire and memories of the Second World War flowed together seamlessly. Bobby Moore, the royal family and Winston Churchill were interchangeable icons of English grace and superiority, and Alf's beloved Hammers were the most noble team in the land:

> We've got history, West Ham has, which none of yer other clubs have got. Anne Boleyn had a house right next door to West Ham's ground – Boleyn Castle – an' it was Henry the Eighth who founded West Ham so he'd have somewhere to go on Saturday afternoons when he was down at Boleyn with Anne. That is why West Ham United play in the colours of Henry the Eighth, even till this day: claret an' blue, claret which was his favourite drink and the blue of your Royal blood. The Directors' Box at West Ham is actually built on the spot where Henry used to sit while he watched the lads play. I think it was at West Ham where he might have met Anne, because she was a local girl.

English fans don't just live in the past, they commit its names and dates and scores to sacred memory. They remember players' shirt numbers, their own journeys to stadiums, their team's place in the league on a given day, the texture of the meat pie they ate at half-time, the temperature of the Bovril they spilled. And all of it is important. The more you know about your team's 'history' and 'heritage', the more authentic a fan you are. Near Arsenal's stadium there's a pub called the Drayton Arms that is barred after the match to everyone except real Arsenal supporters. The windows are shuttered and dark, but for those who know, there is a way to get inside and enjoy a pint and the warmth of the landlord's open fire. First you knock on a side door, which opens like at a Capone-era Chicago speakeasy. Then, if the landlord doesn't know your face, you'll have to prove you're a genuine Arsenal fan. How do you do that? By reciting the names of the entire Arsenal team that won the FA Cup in 1971.

'In Germany this would be an awfully empty pub,' says football writer Uli Hesse-Lichtenberger. German fans neither know nor really care about such stuff, not even the hardcore mullet-haired ones who go to all home and away games, wear the club shirt, bang the club drum and sport denim jackets plastered with club badges. Borussia Dortmund are reckoned to have the most passionate fans in Germany. 'But if you go on the Sudtribune and asked fans to name the most famous Dortmund team in history, the one which won the 1966 Cup Winners' Cup, they would really struggle. They would probably know Tilkowski was in goal. They might remember Emmerich and Held, and they would know Libuda scored. But then they would pause and say: "Who else was there?" I have a Scottish friend who has tons of Rangers games on videotape. But I don't have tons of Dortmund games. I have three or four maybe, and I'm considered a little odd. We just don't have these things in Germany. The club store at Dortmund doesn't even have tapes or DVDs of when we won the Champions League Final in 1997. A friend of mine works for the club and I told him they really should sell maybe four or five classic games. But they weren't interested. They said: "Who would buy such a thing? Who wants to buy a tape to watch a game where you already know the result?"'

'Living in the past' is usually a figure of speech, but for Rob Nichols it's a daily reality. The devout Middlesbrough fan bought a house on the holy ground of his club's old stadium,

Ayresome Park, which was demolished in the mid-1990s. Rob's back garden was once the edge of the pitch. The house itself, a neat, cream-coloured Wimpey-style starter home, is on the site of the old boys' enclosure where Rob stood on match days. And indoors, the décor is themed. Because Middlesbrough play in red the walls are painted red, and they're decorated with old team photos. The carpets are green to evoke the old turf. And the bookcase, with a circular gable, was chosen because it looks like the vanished main stand. I ask why he didn't paint little advertising hoardings along the skirting boards.

'What a good idea!'

'You could have those revolving ones.'

'No! That's tacky. And the mice wouldn't know where to go.' Rob laughs. 'It's like a joke and everyone always laughs about it. I've always thought I'd stay living here until I get sick of the joke. But I haven't got sick of it yet, and I've been here a few years. It's a good place to live. You feel the spirit of the place.' As editor of *Fly Me to the Moon*, the Boro fanzine, Rob is a bit of a celebrity around town; strangers stop him in the street to discuss the last match or indulge in transfer speculation. And when he moved to Ayresome Park, he persuaded former player Bernie Slaven to join him in an elegantly simple home-con-secration ritual. Slaven was famous in his prime for celebrating goals by jumping on to the stadium's perimeter fence and screaming at the fans. Now he and Rob ran together through Rob's back garden, jumped on to the garden fence and yelled at some photographers, neighbours and a TV crew.

In cinema, one of the most haunting explorations of the power of the passage of time comes in Orson Welles's *The Magnificent Ambersons*, which tracks the tragic decline of a once-powerful family. The key line is spoken early on by Eugene, the blithely confident and optimistic young inventor. When an older woman in the famous ballroom scene happily says of the dancing: 'It's just like old times', Eugene cuts her down: 'Old times? Not a bit! There aren't any old times. When times are gone they're not old, they're dead! There aren't any times but new times!' Something makes me think that Rob, who also works as a part-time archaeologist, might not share this philosophy. 'I say we can only explore the future through knowledge of the past.' He chuckles. 'Well, that's my excuse anyway.'

At core, though, Rob is serious. The town of Middlesbrough was founded in 1830 during the Industrial Revolution, but local coal and iron industries disappeared long ago. The steel and chemical industries are in decline, and Middlesbrough has barely ever featured in literature. One of its early football clubs, Middlesbrough Ironopolis, went bust in 1894. Middlesbrough FC, founded in 1876 and in better shape now than for decades, however, remains a source of identity and pride. 'Other fans call us "smog monsters", "smoggies", stuff like that. And they say we never won anything, but we turn that round and say we're proud of that.' Rob insists: 'There is something tangible of value in football traditions once you've stripped away all the trashy commercial nostalgia rubbish.' Fans remember the club's 'golden age' in the mid-1970s when Boro had a team of evocatively named local men such as Craggs, Spraggon and Foggon.

At Ayresome Park an artist called Neville Gabie worked with local people to create a subtle memorial to the past in a series of little bronze sculptures. A scarf on a fence marks a corner flag, a ball identifies a penalty spot, the old touchline is a row of studs in the road. 'It's very subtle and an example of history and tradition enriching people's everyday lives,' says Rob. 'If you want, you can trace the whole ground as it was. Or you can walk past every day and never see it. You can ignore the artwork, or you can think: "Yeah, this is where my parents and grandparents stood on the terraces, cursing the team in the old days."'

But undue reverence for the old days can get in the way of living fully in the present. 'It's not that I'm trying to get back to a happy childhood,' explains writer and Leicester City nostalgist Derek Hammond. 'It's just that the older I get, the more I realise that the person I was when I was about seven or eight is the most authentically me.' Derek, a one-time musician, swims endlessly in an ocean of cultural trivia from his youth. His work is a kind of English version of Proust's *Remembrance of Things Past*. If Derek can only probe his memories of early seventies comics, football, TV shows and James Bond movies hard enough and long enough, he will finally understand the true essence of both himself and the human condition.

He was once lyricist and singer with the decisively named 'Yeah Yeah Noh', a neo-psychedelic band which was one of John Peel's favourites during the 1980s. More recently Derek has written nostalgia-fuelled books about London and school, and he's working on a 'creepy thriller' set in Rutland, near where Derek grew up and has recently returned with his Scottish wife and their two children. 'Twenty years ago, each village round here had its butcher, its baker, its thatcher. Now they have an accountant . . . and an accountant . . . and an accountant. What happened to all those other people?'

Derek's most enduring obsession is football. His *Big Blue Leicester City Scrapbook* is a collection of odd and obscure things Leicester fans might remember fondly: Peter Shilton and his haircuts; the young Gary Lineker; the *Leicester Mercury*'s prediction that Johan Cruyff would sign for City; 'Sniffer' Clarke; pages of homage to Alan 'the Birch' Birchenall and Keith Weller. Anyone who doesn't have deep feelings for the club might find all this incomprehensible. But for Derek, his friend

Gary and the dozens of fans who contributed, the book's evocation of the past is a rich, multilayered source of shared memories, totems of their personal and tribal identity. It's not official football narrative, but a kind of random total recall which puts fans' stray memories at the centre of history.

Meanwhile, the passage of time takes Leicester City ever further from how it was in the seventies, a process which upsets Derek deeply. When City moved to their new stadium, he was grief-stricken. 'The last time I ever went to Filbert Street it was like someone had died. I feel like I've become a foster child. The new stadium is a big plastic bowl. It doesn't mean anything to me. It could be anywhere. It could be Nottingham or Vladivostok. And it made me realise how much being a Leicester City fan was down to nostalgia. It's because I go to football with my dad. For many years the only time I'd see him was when I went back to Leicester to go to matches with him. We always sat in the same place in the Double Decker stand, and we always moaned in exactly the same way, because if you're a Leicester City fan, that's what you do. I'm a Leicester fan because I'm from Leicester and I've always gone there. I've always done the same things, but I've always enjoyed it and it always was the same. And all of a sudden all those memories have been knocked down and we're having to go to this big plastic stadium and it just . . .' His voice trails off sadly. 'Yes, I suppose in some ways the new stadium is better for watching football, but it isn't the place I went from when I was eight or nine years old. When the team in blue comes on to the field it's just not the same. It's similar, but it's not the *same*. I think a lot of people around the country feel the same way about their teams' new stadiums. That's why people talk about "gypsy curses" on teams who moved. Without being morbid, in a few years my dad will pass away. Will I want to go to the new stadium then?'

Even the new-fangled names in modern football disturb him: 'Why have players' names changed? People called David would never have been allowed to play in the seventies. It would have been *Dave* Beckham. *Bobby* Fowler. *Jimmy* Rednapp. When Harry Redknapp called his son James, he can't have wanted him to be a Jamie. He must have thought he'd be Jimmy or Jim because, after all, he's *Harry*-fucking-Redknapp!' No such problem in the Hammond household. Derek's daughter Frances was named in honour of his hero, Frank Worthington. And son James is the real deal. 'Jimmy Hammond, eh? With a name like that he has to become a footballer. The plan is obviously that Jimmy will play for Leicester City and England. But if he doesn't make the grade he's always got the option of playing for Leicester City and Scotland.'

So many aspects of English culture are steeped in the past that it must at times seem incomprehensible to outsiders. Just as a coral reef is built over aeons by the accumulation of layer upon layer of the dead, so English common law sees itself as the accretion of the wisdom of ages: layers of ancient precedents, slowly forming themselves into an edifice of unsurpassed beauty and grandeur. It's the same with popular culture, which is made even more subtle by layers of irony and self-mockery. How could an American ever hope to understand *Viz* or Vic Reeves? Fat Les's historically sophisticated World Cup '98 song 'Vindaloo' blended references to the Battle of Waterloo, hot curry, the Verve and knitting into an unmistakable (for those in the know) portrait of modern England. And in the long-running radio comedy show *I'm Sorry I Haven't a Clue*, most of the dazzling jokes require knowledge of at least a dozen much older dazzling jokes, some going back decades. The show's highlight is always the playing of a timeless, precedent-ridden game, which doesn't actually exist, and each week lugubrious chairman Humphrey Lyttleton ends with an absurd metaphor of time itself, loaded with English bathos: '. . . as the vanquished charwoman of time begins to Shake 'N' Vac the shagpile of eternity . . .', '. . . as the sand castles of destiny are washed away by the incoming tide of time, it is clear that the grim deck-chair attendant of doom will shortly be upon us . . .'

Writer and journalist Neal Ascherson spent part of his childhood in a Derbyshire village where there was an annual ancient game of folk football. 'I forget what it was called, but one end was uptown, the other end was downtown and hundreds of young men joined in on each side. I think there was a ball, but it soon got forgotten and there was an enormous fight. It wasn't much more than that. And it was abolished by the council. I remember a speech by a woman who said it was "no better than a cannibal orgy".' Intriguingly, although the game had been played for centuries, it was not seen as 'heritage': 'There wasn't a great deal of conscious hallowing going on, which is probably the hallmark of a genuine institution. When things are really, genuinely old, you don't talk about it much at all because you are expecting it to happen next year too, and the year after that. Whereas the real English genius is inventing "age-old" traditions which have always existed – except they haven't – such as the royal family and the "immemorial" customs of the House of Commons, and many "ancient" university traditions.' In Britain the illusion of historical continuity has been an important way to preserve privilege and order. In periods of rapid and painful social change, the emphasis on historical continuity becomes louder. The last such period was the 1980s.

Evoking history and tradition is meant to make change acceptable to large masses of slightly indifferent but resentful people: 'Oh yes, this has always been here, you know.' 'It was always like this.' That things are continuously adjusted and reinvented is often concealed. If football in that Derbyshire

village had been an invented tradition there would have been a
lot more going on about how ancient and important it was.
People would have handed out leaflets. It would have been
written into the county history – 'this immemorial game'.

Yet invoking the past is extraordinarily potent for the
English. How else to explain the astonishing impact of Baddiel,
Skinner and Broudie's song 'Three Lions' during Euro '96?
The history-drenched lyrics weren't quite Churchillian, yet the
song roused the English to unprecedented peacetime levels of
patriotism and tapped right into England's soul in a way no
football song ever had before. Anywhere else in the world
references to old football incidents ('that tackle by Moore',
'when Lineker scored', 'Bobby belting the ball' – 1970, 1986
and 1966 respectively) could hardly be expected to exhilarate a
nation. Yet the Wembley crowds roared the song with a
fervour rarely heard for the national anthem. The 'three lions'
reference was also interesting. The England team badge had
been in use since the first England–Scotland game in 1872,
borrowed initially from the English cricket team which in turn
had adopted it from an element of the British royal crest dating
back to Richard I.

Loads of lineage there! But until 1996, no one in football had
ever thought to draw attention to the lions as a defining icon of
Englishness. Suddenly, as the crowds sang, this ancient symbol
of authority became a popular emblem of identity infused with
new power. And as they sang, the people also waved an old flag
in a new way. Until 1996, England fans had always used the
red-white-and-blue Union Jack while the red-on-white flag of
St George was tainted by association with the far right. Now
the English – as opposed to the British – took to St George with
relish and plastered it on cars, houses and pubs. (One nice irony
of 'Three Lions' during Euro '96 was that the German team,
which beat England on penalties in the semi-final, adopted the

song as their own – and even sang it on the bus on the way to the final – totally oblivious to the fact that 'thirty years of hurt' referred mainly to them.)

Both the song and the flag have gone on to become enduring symbols (for now, anyway) of an Englishness derived in large part from football history. During the last World Cup, journalist Sarfraz Manzoor, born to Pakistani parents, brought up in England and a supporter of the Pakistan cricket team, bought a St George T-shirt and went for a night out in Luton. 'In the bar where I spent most of the evening one man was wearing a huge England flag as a cape; an Indian friend had on his head a white plastic bowler hat painted with a red cross. At a certain point in the evening the opening bars of 'Three Lions' floated across the bar, and within seconds we were a sea of smiling faces and linked arms. Whites, Asians and blacks joined together, tunelessly and passionately, in this modern anthem to England's dreaming. This, I thought, must be how it feels to be patriotic; to be English. I could sing the lyrics to a song about English football with more conviction than I could ever muster singing about my hopes for the monarch. Sometimes football reaches the parts that politics cannot reach.'

Nevertheless, all this nostalgia, heritage and memory can be a trap. Ian La Frenais's theme song from *Whatever Happened to the Likely Lads* asks: 'Tomorrow's almost over, today went by so fast/Is the only thing to look forward to the past?'

The British enjoy condescending to Americans over their lack of history. In 1992 there was contempt in Britain for President Clinton's 'vulgar' inauguration ceremony. Neal Ascherson saw matters differently. Yes, Clinton's party was unlike the Queen's Opening of Parliament. But this was because British official ceremonies are as dusty and archaic as possible while American ones are vibrant and alive. The basic difference was that American rituals are fertility rituals, while British ones are acts of ancestor worship.

In September 1999 an old red-cotton football shirt with long sleeves was sold in London for £91,750. Six months earlier a pair of second-hand football boots had gone for £13,000. The prices had nothing to do with the items' craftsmanship, of course. These objects auctioned at Christie's in South Kensington were more like medieval holy relics. The shirt was that worn by Geoff Hurst in the 1966 World Cup Final. The boots had once graced the blessed feet of David Beckham. Such items are headline grabbers in a surging multimillion-pound business that thrives in Britain as nowhere else on the football-playing earth. So far, the record price paid for such an item was £250,000 for a replica of the Jules Rimet trophy. Pelé's shirt from the 1970 World Cup Final went for £157,000. Last year the football memorabilia trade in the auction rooms was worth £26 million. At the bottom end of the market, but driven by the same impulse, some 25,000 arcane objects of football memorabilia are offered for sale every day on eBay. Bits of kit, scarves, photos, posters, key-rings, videos, ashtrays, beer mats, mugs, mirrors, postcards – you name it, if it has a connection to football, someone somewhere in England will want to buy it. Who could resist the allure of:

* Pair of shorts 'draw-strung so as to be worn baggy for extra mobility' used in a match by Burnley's Matt O'Neil 'would make a special gift to any Burnley fan or an excellent addition to any football memorabilia collection. Comes complete with certificate of authenticity.' £6.05

*Grimsby *v* Sheffield Wednesday programme from March 1983 ('nr Mint condition'). 'Will be sent in a new stiff envelope.' 50p (plus £1 P&P)

* 'Unopened greetings card with a fridge magnet of Ray Parlour in England kit.' £1.25

* Ticket stub. Blackburn Rovers *v* Walsall, 1999. 'Mint condition.' 20p

One of the men behind the top end of the business is David Convery, Christie's head of football memorabilia, a warm, enthusiastic Glaswegian with unruly hair and paperclips for cufflinks. He helped organise the first big auction back in 1989. 'We'd been seeing football things selling for nothing. FA Cup-winner's medals going for £50, just scrap value. Something wasn't right there. We had very limited experience at that time. There was an old Arsenal Cup Final winner's medal from the thirties, George Male's from 1930, I think it was. We thought it might go for £1,000 and the opening bid was five and a half thousand quid. I remember thinking: that's unbelievable! There's something going on here. Since then it has got busy, busy, busy. Every sale has made more than the last.'

The market is almost entirely British – the French, Spanish, Germans, Dutch and Italians are less interested in such relics. 'It's just the British psyche. Maybe it's because we invented the game. The continentals are up to date with football, but they have no sense of history,' says Convery. A Christie's sale of Dutch memorabilia in Amsterdam 'was a complete and utter flop'. And while Geoff Hurst's shirt from 1966 fetched £91,750, Alessandro Altobelli's from the 1982 World Cup Final, where he scored Italy's third goal, went for £5,500. French star Raymond Kopa won the European Cup three years running with Real Madrid in the fifties, but French and Spanish fans weren't interested when his personal collection was auctioned by another company. 'Sweeties, we call them: European Cup medals given away like sweeties – six or seven hundred pounds.

Unbelievable! If he'd been English, you'd have been talking £10,000 a medal.' Even then, 95 per cent of buyers were Brits.

Most collectors are working-class supporters who only collect memorabilia from their club or England. 'These guys remember their team in "the good old days". They've grown up, got themselves some spare cash. These are clever men who know what stuff is worth, but are prepared to pay seven or eight times over the odds purely because of their passion for their club. Working-class people love football and if they can't get to an FA Cup Final, or play for their country, the next best thing is to own an FA Cup-winner's medal or an England cap. Take me, I'll never play for my club, Celtic. But at home I have a little shrine, just some shirts and bits and bobs, couple of caps, photographs, my first scarf. My wife doesn't like it of course, but that's my part of the house.' Is that what collectors do with their relics? 'They go on the wall usually. Sometimes I ask them: "Do you put this in a frame and hang it above the wife's bed, sort of thing, to annoy her?" I've seen photographs of some people's lounges and they're like a museum. Everything behind glass: shirts, pennants, pictures, programmes. Not beautifully laid out, but with gaps where stuff is missing. The 1934 Cup-winner's medal isn't there yet, so they leave a space.'

Revealingly, only objects linked to happy memories sell. 'The classic one is Steve Hodge, who has Maradona's shirt from the 1986 game against England – the "Hand of God" shirt. We'd sold Pelé's shirt [from the 1970 World Cup] for £157,000, so Steve Hodge called me up and said: "I've got Maradona's shirt – what's it worth?" He was looking for something like £200,000. I said: "With all due respect to you, you are crazy." The problem is not what is it worth but who is going to buy it? There is no Argentinian market. There is no Argentinian money. And why would an Englishman buy that shirt? To hang it on his wall? To burn it?'

Heritage – or nostalgia – is the essential ingredient in the success of TOFFS (The Old Fashioned Football Shirt Company) – 'established 1990' – which makes exquisitely accurate replicas of old-style cotton football shirts. To flick through the company's 24-page catalogue is to view a history of shirt design since the days of the Wanderers and the Royal Engineers. Through specialist shops and the internet, TOFFS now sell more than 800 designs from all over the football world, none more recent than the early 1980s. The company employs twenty-two people and operates in Gateshead, quite close to Nike's headquarters in nearby Washington. Alan Finch, who founded TOFFS with his wife Michele, explains: 'Our philosophy, which we don't always broadcast, is that we are not actually selling a football shirt. We are selling a piece of history. Our shirts spell history, emotion. When people talk to me about our T-shirts, I say: "Excuse me, but these are *football* shirts. Those things with a Nike sign on the chest are T-shirts. But this is a football shirt." They say: "What's the difference?" I say: "Well, that's it. You don't know because you're not a football fan. *That's* what the difference is: a Nike shirt has no history."' The company has shops in Italy, but most of its customers are English, many of them expats. 'Having lived in England all my life and having spent a little time in Italy, I know that there are people there who might be just as passionate as English people, but there are more passionate English people than there are Italians. The Germans don't give a monkey's toss about their bloody history. The Dutch are a bit the same. And the French haven't got so much football history. The Spanish have a good history, up to a point, but not as much as the English.'

'Nostalgia is a British thing, isn't it?' says Michele. 'Look at all the websites selling typically British things to expats abroad, like Bovril and HP sauce. People write us such beautiful letters:

"You should have been there . . ." "His face just lit up." One lady came in. Her two sons' grandfather had played for Sunderland many moons ago. Raich Carter, I think it was, and she got the two shirts he had worn: England and Sunderland. We found out what games he'd played in, and she got the shirts framed so she could say: "This is what grandpa wore when he played."'

An appeal to future nostalgia is the essence of the speech in *Henry V*, where the warrior king rouses his troops for battle:

> He that shall live this day, and see old age,
> Will yearly on the vigil feast his neighbours,
> And say 'To-morrow is Saint Crispian.'
> Then will he strip his sleeve and show his scars,
> And say 'These wounds I had on Crispian's day.'

And a few lines later:

> This story shall the good man teach his son.

Alan teaches his nine-year-old son, Tom, football. 'I've got a room in my house full of Arsenal memorabilia. When Thomas goes in there, he just sits down and looks at all the programmes and says: "Dad, do you remember that?" And he'll look at the date of the programme and say: "Did you buy this yourself?" And it'll be from, like 1961. And you can see, the history of the club is already beginning to sort of lay its seeds in his mind. And as he gets older, he will remember. He'll want to remember.' Tom is named after his maternal grandfather, who was buried in a coffin draped with the shirt of his beloved Newcastle United. 'My little Thomas said the other day: "How many times have you seen Arsenal, Dad?" I said: "God, let's work it out." I've been going since 1952, not that I remember much about it because I was three at the time. In those days, there were forty-two games a season, which would be twenty-one games at home, so you add all those years plus all the cup runs and the European games. You get a round figure of about 2,500. So I said: "I've probably seen Arsenal close to a thousand times, and you're just coming up to double figures" – cause he's seen Arsenal eight times. So I said to him: "You've got a lot of games to go to be part of that club." '

The past, though, comes in many flavours. Memory is not quite the same as sentimental nostalgia and we shouldn't confuse history with heritage.

History is perpetually reinterpreted and rewritten, and, in big and small ways, perceptions of the past change and are continually adapted to meet new circumstances. One of the sharpest observers of this process was Raphael Samuel, founder and leading light of the History Workshop movement. A brilliant essay in his book *Theatres of Memory* (1994) explored the shifting meanings of British brick. Brick-built Victorian workmen's cottages were the least desirable dwellings of the age in which they were built. And during the 1950s, brick, which was seen as labour-intensive and 'the enemy of light and space', was held in low esteem. Yet by the 1980s the cultural meaning had been reversed, and to the conservation movement brick became almost sacred. Brickwork – the older the better – now symbolised warmth, integrity, authenticity and heritage. House builders were anxious to include 'traditional' brick features; new, concrete office buildings were clad in brick façades, and a lucrative market developed for 'reclaimed' and 'antique' Victorian bricks. Unfortunately, there wasn't nearly enough of the old stuff to meet the demand, so factories in Telford and elsewhere used computer technology to make brand-new 'antique' bricks – designed with built-in flaws and

then 'distressed' (chipped, burned, discoloured and even enhanced with a little mildew) to make them look old.

In the late 1980s what the writer and journalist Robert
Hewison scornfully called the 'Heritage Industry' was thriving.
Neal Ascherson was also a vehement critic: 'As Britain declines
in the world, and as the traditional industries run down, the
search begins for new resources. And the most tempting of
these resources turns out to be the past. Unlike coal, North Sea
oil, ironstone or oak forests, the past is an inexhaustible raw
material which will never run out and never go out of fashion.
In Britain, after all, the deposits of recorded history are more
than 2,000 years thick. No wonder that there is now such a
rush to mine it. This country, which once manufactured real
goods for sale, now returns to its deserted mills and plants to
manufacture heritage for the tourist industry. Britain now offers
itself as a place of pilgrimage, a mall for shoppers of the
imagination, a long green theme park.'

Football, too, changes its approach to the past. In the 1940s,
1950s and 1960s, former heroes, now celebrated, were dis-
carded. Dixie Dean, the most prolific of all goalscorers, spent
the last years of his working life moving furniture in a Liverpool
warehouse; today there's a statue of him in the city. In the early
nineties, Wembley Stadium discovered its heritage, long taken
for granted, could be useful and turned itself into something of
a living museum. Built for the British Empire Exhibition in
1924, for decades it was, as any collector of ticket stubs knows,
The Empire Stadium, Wembley. But now it was marketed as
'the venue of legends' and heritage tours allowed the public to
visit its dressing rooms and 'hallowed' turf and climb the stairs
to the Royal Box where they would be presented with a cup to
hold aloft while loudspeakers blasted out the roar of the absent
crowd. In 1999, when the increasingly decrepit stadium was
finally closed, the event was marked by a flood of nostalgia

including an interview with John Motson, the TV commentator who is more obsessed with history and trivia than any other (and who, according to the BBC website, is now himself a 'legend').

There is the comfort of cosy slippers in English remembering. And, just as imperial nostalgia, perceptions of national decline and the memory of the Second World War stopped Britain embracing the future with relish, so in English football the temptation to seek comfort in past glories is often irresistible.

North London's rivals provide an interesting contrast. In the early sixties, stylish Spurs won the Double and were the first British team to lift a European trophy. While Spurs were the most glamorous team in Britain, dull local rivals Arsenal lived in the shadow of Herbert Chapman and the club's glorious 1930s and 1950s. By the early 2000s, positions had reversed. Gorged on (mainly French) beautiful football, star players and two recent Doubles, Arsenal fans now dreamt of winning the European Cup and supplanting Manchester United. They had largely forgotten Chapman and didn't think about Spurs very often. Spurs fans, disgruntled by their team's mediocrity, adopted Celtic's song 'If You Know Your History' and took refuge in the past. At White Hart Lane, the team once led out by Danny Blanchflower took the field to black and white images of Blanchflower while the loudspeakers blared the club song of his era, 'Glory Glory Tottenham Hotspur'. Spurs fans and their many websites love to talk about the club's 'glorious history', but it's not history that any self-respecting academic historian would recognise. In Spurs' case, 'real' history might involve exploring the boardroom scandals of the past twenty years or looking at the underlying causes of the club's failure to win the championship since 1961. The websites – at Spurs and at just about every other club in Britain – offer a steady diet of 'legendary' old players, historic triumphs and happy memories.

The historian Raphael Samuel, quoting Aneurin Bevan, said ancestor worship 'is the most conservative of all religions. It invites us to take a sentimental view of our weaknesses and a heroic view of our strengths. It is also a bounty on what Marxists call "false consciousness". Offering us a retrospective sense of belonging – what used to be called "lineage" and today is known as "roots" – to compensate for the uncertainties of here and now. It gratifies our needs for household gods, offering us a source of symbolic gratification and a transendence of, or escape from, ourselves. Ancestor worship usually involves a double misrecognition, both of our own qualities and those of our predecessors; each, by a process of osmosis, is apt to take on the idealised character of the other. Ancestor worship is premised on a necessary falsification of the past. Nothing is more chameleon than tradition. We all have half a dozen possible ancestries to chose from, and fantasy and projection can furnish us with a dozen more. It necessarily involves selectivity and silence – valorizing a prestigious great uncle, forgetting the family black sheep.'

Both in football and in wider culture the public, which prides itself on its collective memory, actually forgets important things and people all the time. In 1999, for example, fans at tradition-conscious Middlesbrough were asked to vote for the club's 'Player of the Century'. They completely forgot post-war giants such as Mannion, Clough and Hardwick and voted instead for Juninho, their Brazilian flavour of the month. This wasn't history; it was amnesia. Indeed, the British public regularly reveals it has the memory of a fruit fly. In the mid-nineties Oasis were voted the 'Best Band of All Time', far ahead of the Beatles. In a 2002 BBC poll Cliff Richard, Julie Andrews, David Beckham and John Peel were among the '100 Greatest Britons of All Time' and Princess Diana finished at number three, ahead of Shakespeare, Wellington, Darwin, Newton and Elizabeth I. As Groucho Marx observed: 'Time flies like the wind. Fruit flies like bananas.' He also said: 'I've had a great time, but this wasn't it.' Groucho had lots of great lines, but nobody remembered him either in a '100 Greatest Film Stars of All Time' poll for Channel Four. Viewers put Jackie Chan, Cameron Diaz and Ewan McGregor near the top of the list and forgot completely the likes of Olivier, Guinness, Cooper, Dietrich, Cagney, Welles, Mason, Garbo and Lancaster. The broadcaster Michael Parkinson has pointed to a similar defect in football memory: 'The trouble with nostalgia is it starts with the invention of video tape. Everything that went before is left to old men on park benches and granddads telling stories. The major misconception of the television generation is that if it isn't on video it didn't happen. "The 100 Best Goals Ever Scored" is a misnomer. It is, in fact, "The 100 Best Goals Ever Seen On Television", a different proposition altogether.'

Heritage is closely aligned with myth-making – but that doesn't necessarily make it a bad thing. Historian David Lowenthal has explored the murky connections between heritage, nostalgia and history. 'History seeks to convince by truth, and succumbs to falsehood,' he writes. 'Heritage exaggerates and omits, candidly invents and frankly forgets, and thrives on ignorance and error. Heritage is . . . not erudition but catechism – not checkable fact but credulous allegiance. Heritage is not a testable or even plausible version of our past; it is a declaration of faith in that past.' On the other hand heritage buttresses the deep needs for building group identity and for ritual devotion, not least when other faiths have declined: 'Like the medieval cult of relics, heritage today is a popular cult, almost a religious faith.'

A good example might be Manchester United. United are England's biggest and best-supported club because they have

the best history. Not the longest, richest or most intriguing for
historians, necessarily, but the narrative with the widest popular
appeal. This wasn't always true. In the early decades of the
game, the 'Invincibles' of Preston North End, and Aston Villa
basked in the glow of historic achievements and, later, Arsenal
were revered because of their pre-war grandeur. In the late
forties Manchester United were nothing special – a decent top-
division team, but with less resonant history than Manchester
City, Everton or Newcastle. Then in the 1950s Manchester
United had a terrific young team, nicknamed the 'Busby
Babes', which won two league championships and was just
beginning to fulfil its potential when, in February 1958, eight
members of the side were killed in a plane crash in Munich on
the way home from a European Cup match.

As far as building an appealing historical narrative's concerned, death is an unpredictable ingredient. On its own, it
doesn't do a club much good. A minor reliquary cult has grown
up around the memory of 'the club that died' – the badly run
and poorly supported Accrington Stanley, which went out of
business in 1962. But no one actually lost his life because of the
'Accies'. A more revealing comparison is the Superga air
disaster of 1949 which wiped out Vittorio Pozzo's remarkable
Torino team (seventeen players died, including eight interna-
tionals) which had won the four previous Italian championships
and is still seen as one of the best club sides Italy ever produced.
Despite much short-term sympathy, the disaster never had any
kind of silver lining. Torino's status as Italy's top club died with
the team. Since then they have won only one championship
and been left far behind city rivals Juventus who were carried
less by history than by their connection with Fiat and the
wealth of the Agnelli family.

Air disasters have wiped out other teams. But who weeps for
Alianza Lima of Peru, or the fourteen Surinamese players killed

in a 1989 crash, or the Zambian national team destroyed in 1993? Mass death in stadium disasters never led to anyone falling in love with Bolton, Bradford City, Sheffield Wednesday or Liverpool, though the status as innocent martyrs of Liverpool's ninety-six dead fans of Hillsborough did add gravitas to a club damaged four years earlier by Heysel. The sight of Anfield as a vast carpet of memorial flowers touched a deep nerve and the Hillsborough disaster led to the transformation of English stadiums. A plaque bearing the fans' names has become a place of pilgrimage. Yet the thirty-nine Italians killed in 1985 as a result of Liverpool fans' aggression at the Heysel stadium are relatively forgotten.

No. The key to the enduring appeal of Manchester United's story lies in its happy ending. The young players killed at Munich are still mourned, though few recall the names of the fourteen other people who died. But the club's status was ensured by the drama of redemption which followed the crash. Jesus rose from the dead on the third day, but it took thirteen days for Busby's assistant, Jimmy Murphy, to pull together a scratch team which, amid scenes of extraordinary emotion, beat Sheffield United in the FA Cup and went all the way to the final, where they lost to two goals by the unsentimental Nat Lofthouse. United's romantic appeal was secured by that Phoenix-like achievement. Even more compelling was the longer-term rebuilding which became simply the greatest football story ever told. In Munich, manager Matt Busby had had the last rites read over him while nineteen-year-old Bobby Charlton, a relatively minor member of the Babes, missed death by inches. Busby bravely recovered and went on to build a new, great side, one made noble by the presence of Charlton and sexy by that of George Best. Ten years after Munich, on a balmy evening in London, Busby and Charlton hugged each other through tears of joy as the club finally won the European Cup.

The perfection of the club's narrative was for many years an insupportable burden. After Busby, Manchester United had more history – and fans – than any other club. Yet they languished. When Busby retired, no other manager could live in his shadow. The 1968 team grew old together, Charlton retired, and United fell briefly into the Second Division. By the early nineties, the club had gone more than twenty years without winning the league championship. In 1989 journalists Michael Crick and David Smith in their book *Manchester United – Betrayal of a Legend* invoked the memory of Busby's teams to castigate the 'clan' around chairman Martin Edwards who 'put profit above all else'. 'The magic of Manchester United is fading rapidly,' wrote Crick and Smith. 'It is a hard thing for loyal supporters to admit, but arch-rivals Liverpool have now become what United was for more than a generation – the team with the aura and artistry, the side that everyone wants to watch.' In 1992 United choked on the run-in to the championship, beaten not so much by Leeds United as by the weight of their own history. The turning point came the following year with the liberating arrival of Eric Cantona, the Frenchman who loved the taste of English history but was immune to its toxins. The rest, as they say . . .

Since then, United have concentrated on making and marketing history rather than living in it and the club has changed beyond recognition, as its directors moved ruthlessly and radically to create an entirely new type of club. As a corporate entity, United have moved a long way indeed from Busby's day. Where the club was once based on local fans and home-reared talent, it is now a ferociously marketed, astutely positioned global product with a large staff of world players. Its domination of the English game – seriously challenged only by Arsenal and, more recently, 'Chelski' – has at times seemed monopolistic. And since the early nineties, United's restless commercial innovation and marketing strategies have left domestic rivals far behind. Other clubs may have copied the selling of high-priced replica kit, enlarging their stadium or becoming a public company, but United did it first, bigger and best. Manchester United's transformation has been astonishing and its domination of the English game on and off the field unprecedented. The long-term consequences of all this for the structure of the English game can only be guessed at.

The club has been careful to cloak all this momentous – and, for many, unnerving – change in the guise of history. As Neal Ascherson points out: 'In Britain, the illusion of historical continuity has been an important way to preserve privilege and order. An illusion of immutability and tradition is supposed to be reassuring.' At first, in this new era, United's exploitation of their heritage was sometimes clumsy. The 1992 'third strip', supposedly honouring United's humble beginnings as a railway workers' team called Newton Heath, was widely seen as a shabby device to sell garish shirts. Soon the club's touch became surer. A TV commercial of 1994 used special effects to make winger Ryan Giggs play alongside United stars of the past. The commercial opened with nostalgic images of fans in the 1950s and Bobby Charlton – now Sir Bobby – urged the audience to imagine United's 'greatest side'. Giggs then becomes the star of a move involving Gregg, Stiles, Viollet, Law, Coppell, Best and Charlton. Giggs scores brilliantly, gets hugged by Best and Charlton. Charlton's voiceover: 'Their greatest ever side. Giggs would be in it . . . And he'd be wearing Reebok boots.'

The story of United in the Busby era remains an affecting one. The best accounts, such as Eamon Dunphy's *A Strange Kind of Glory* (1991), are peopled by flesh and blood individuals coping with extraordinary circumstances. Dunphy, who joined United briefly as a player two years after Munich, had seen the Babes as a fan when they visited Dublin a year before their destruction. What struck him then was not how historic they were, but how new they seemed. 'The "Red Devils" were different from those who'd come before them. No baggy shorts, but neat, white pants, hitched up to show the perfect muscles on thighs of unimaginable power. They wore V-necked red shirts without the old collars of Matthews and Finney, trim and dashing, an emblem of those lithe bodies they adorned. Football never came to life so vividly, with such awesome beauty.' In the book, Dunphy describes the tragic events of Munich in detail, principally through the eyes of goalkeeper Harry Gregg. He also quotes Busby's close friend Paddy McGrath on his first meeting with the manager after Munich: 'He was always very careful with his emotions, you wouldn't know what he felt. I'd gone to his house to see how he was one afternoon. It was a nice spring day and Matt was sitting out in the garden. He was still in a bad way. But he got up as I came across to him. We just hugged each other. There were tears in his eyes. But he said nothing. Never did talk about the crash. But it was always there. In his eyes. Always.' At that time, Manchester United were not an international marketing phenomenon, but a club where many had suffered personal loss. 'By the time I arrived in 1960 Munich was history. Nobody mentioned it. The clock on the wall over the fore-court bore the words February 6th 1958. That was all. This was a modest and, it seemed, entirely appropriate memorial. There was no need for an ostentatious memorial, the grief was profound. But it was not our grief, rather Bobby's, "The Boss's", Jimmy's, the grief of those who'd belonged to another club.'

These days, United are rather less reticent, systematically turning history into a commodity and using it to promote their image. Actually, the word 'image' is far too small: United seem to be trying to turn the club into a semi-religious cult. In place of grief and modest memorials, fans are encouraged to 'worship' at the shrine of United – and buy into the club's hubristic new vision of itself. Historicity and myth-making are the key ingredients in the tireless promotion of the club's 'legendary' status by its own TV station and megastore. Old Trafford is now the 'Theatre of Dreams', whose reputation is burnished by stadium tours (one every ten minutes) and a £4 million museum. There are more than 100 videos and books about the club's history and current stars. One such is *Access All Areas – Behind the Scenes at Manchester United* by Adam Bostock and Roger Dixon, a glossy picture book published by Manchester United Books in 1998. The 'behind the scenes' tour of a club has long been a staple of football journalism. Bostock and Dixon have updated the formula in line with the new ethos. A chapter about supporters makes it clear the fans' job is to 'worship' and buy merchandise: 'Supporting Manchester United is a lifelong occupation.' 'Old Trafford stirs the soul of all its occupants, one and the same,' and visiting the stadium is like making the hajj pilgrimage: 'Ever since 19 February 1910, when Manchester United played their first league match here, Old Trafford has been a footballing Mecca, a place where people of all walks of life come together and worship one of the world's finest football teams . . . Today it's not unusual for fans to travel hundreds, or even thousands, of miles. But no matter how arduous or expensive the journey, once the supporter passes through the turnstile, he or she will tell you it was all worth it.'

By now, according to the book, United have become such an awe-inspiring institution that almost everything that happens there must by definition be historic. 'Capturing the very moment when history is made is a fine art. Just ask the many photographers who spend their lives at Manchester United. Some concentrate solely on the football action, snapping away pitchside on a Saturday in all weathers, whilst others spend the whole week ready to drop everything and race across Manchester at the drop of a transfer cheque whenever a new player is signed.' In the club museum, 'Fans of all ages can reflect in the glory of United's victories', and the names of all the players who ever turned out for United are inscribed on a large black marble wall – just like the Vietnam war memorial in Washington DC. The club's trophies are 'like the Crown Jewels', and 'To see them lined up, shining from the same museum cabinet takes the breath away.' Perhaps the book's most revealing image is a photograph of a small boy in the street below the large bronze statue of Matt Busby, wearing a suit and carrying a football, which stands at Old Trafford. Football-loving boys playing the game together in the street have long been a part of the game's heritage, but this new kind of football-loving boy is alone – and he has no need of a ball. Togged out in Man U trainers, sweatshirt and sweatpants, he happily swings a bag full of merchandise from the United megastore.

When United won the European Cup again in 1999, courtesy of two late goals in the final against Bayern Munich, hype and kitsch religiosity flowed unstoppably. The victory was commemorated in an official documentary film called *Manchester United: Beyond the Promised Land*. The poster featured the faces of three players blending into one – the Trinity of Giggs, Keane and Beckham – and a fan was wheeled out to explain that United's comeback against Bayern Munich was due to the dead players of 1958, who were present in spirit and joined the final attacks.

Nobody ever made such a claim for the late Bobby Moore, but the moment with which he is most closely associated – England's single World Cup success of 1966 – continues to lay a clammy hand of nostalgia across all English perceptions of the game and their own status in it. In *Ignorance*, his novel about the painful effects of false memory and aching nostalgia, Milan Kundera observes that 'The English are privileged to have had no important dates since 1945, which has allowed them to live a delightfully null half century.' But the way the English see it, 1966 nulls out all other dates. Never mind that England haven't reached a single major final since then, while the Germans they beat that day (with a little help from a Russian linesman) have appeared in ten finals and won five of them. The Jules Rimet trophy (permanently owned by Brazil) still gleams in English memory.

Former England and Wolves centre-forward John Richards has come to detest this attitude. He wishes the entire English game would follow the example of Manchester United and Arsenal and move wholeheartedly to embrace the foreign and the new. 'You have to move on in life. Lots of supporters don't do that. We still crack on about the "good old days" and there's nothing wrong with that, except the good old days can stop you from moving forward. And those good old days weren't really all that good. It's just that time makes them seem pretty. In a world team over the last ten years there's not one English player you'd pencil in. There are players from around the world playing in our league; they show us how it should be done. I like talking about the past, and you've got your memories. But the game is better now than it was in the seventies. And the game in the seventies was better than the game in the fifties. And the game in the fifties was better than the game in the thirties. There is no doubt about that. Everything about the game. It just keeps moving forward, and I'm sure in another twenty years' time the game will be even better than it is now. We've got to make sure as a nation that we embrace all the techniques and developments going on in all the other parts of the world and make sure we are not left behind because of our outdated attitudes, our reluctance to change. I want us to actually get to a European Final or a World Cup Final. I don't want us to be saying twenty years from now: "Fancy Zambia winning the World Cup and we haven't got any better." '

Eric Cantona once wrote (in one of those Manchester United books, funnily enough): 'English football represents all that football ought to be. The game in England is steeped in history. There's a rivalry between the clubs that stretches back for generations. The football stadia are always full. The game is alive with passion and energy here.' But he also allowed himself to be used in a famous poster which attempted to puncture the cult of 1966. At the height of Cantona's fame in 1994, an ad for Nike appeared on billboards across the country. It featured a stunning image of the haughty Frenchman, collar turned up in his trademark fashion, in front of the flag of St George, and staring down at the camera. Underneath were the words: ' '66 was a great year for English football. Eric was born.'

Copywriter Giles Montgomery, who came up with the line, says now: 'The ad was trying to burst that cycle of nostalgia. It was saying: "It's now that matters. Yes, it was good back then, but this is just as good, if not better." The ad was meant to be funny, and people took it that way rather than as a provocation. But when I think about 1966, I wonder if it would have been better if it hadn't happened. If we hadn't won, maybe we wouldn't be looking back, we'd only be looking forward. But then it's in our nature, isn't it? It's that *Daily Mail* thing of shaking your head and saying: "Where did it all go wrong?" My mum says: "I feel so sorry for you young people today with all the terrible things happening in the world." And I say to her: "But, Mum, you grew up in the Second World War!" It's all a matter of perspective.' For most of the last decade Montgomery has lived in Amsterdam. 'One thing about living in England that always got to me was that there seems to be this constant battle between looking back to the past, moaning about the present and then beating ourselves up for doing that. What I like about here is that people say: "It's a sunny day, let's go to the park," and get on with it. They don't say: "Yeah, it's a really nice day. But it's not quite as sunny as last year." '

A wild yell went up from the crowd as the long native, intercepting the pass, sprang in between the astounded forwards, and went tearing up the field like a greyhound, with the ball at his feet.

# THE PHANTOM LIMB

When Sven-Goran Eriksson became the first non-English manager of the England football team, Jeff Powell of the *Daily Mail* denounced 'this insult to our national pride' in sumptuously morbid terms: 'The mother country of football, birthplace of the greatest game, has finally gone from the cradle to the shame. England's humiliation knows no end. All that is left for the football men of England is to pull the sackcloth up over our heads and let the grave-dancers pile on the ashes.' England, he declared, had been 'lowered into the ranks of football's banana republics' and the 'rest of the world would be laughing at us'. 'Welcome to third-world Britain. One rainstorm and south-east England resembles Bangladesh, trains halted in a country which once refused to stop for the Blitz. One more week and we shall be stockpiling petrol and hoarding food. And now, to cap it all, we have a Swede managing our national team.'

Admirably, Powell held to his anti-Eriksson line even when it became clear foreigners weren't laughing, English football hadn't died and Sven was quite good. Powell is often mocked for his jingoism, but his writing fizzes, and this passage in particular is wonderfully revealing. It's not that he was right, or even wrong. It's more that he so precisely and evocatively captures the essence of something which is never far from the surface in England: the almost biblical sense of loss, of a nation gone to the dogs. 'Mother country' . . . 'shame' . . . 'grave-dancers' . . . 'humiliation' . . . 'laughing at us' . . . 'banana'. . . . As the psychiatrist said of Basil Fawlty: there's enough material there for an entire conference. But the notion of English football as a vehicle for national degradation is widely held. And it's really not Jeff Powell who's the basket case, it is the English themselves, or at least the side of them which loves to wallow in the idea that they are, collectively, one giant washed-up basket case.

As we shall see, such feelings are shared to a large degree across the spectrum. The writer John Le Carré observed: 'We have gone down the slide of materialism into something close to self-hatred. We're in a national psychological condition. When you come back from abroad, you are aware of how unhappy and dysfunctional our whole country has become. It's like visiting a much-loved old relative who has fallen on hard times. It isn't just the weather. We look like a nation in mourning. Coming here from affluent Europe to me is reminiscent of arriving in Eastern Europe from Western Europe.'

During Euro 2000, the *Guardian* columnist Catherine Bennett reflected on the near-universal 'preoccupation with the awfulness of being British'. When hooliganism off the field and defeats on it had – as so often before – triggered a 'season of self-loathing', the tabloids took some ironic comfort in a new book which seemed to claim that on average, the sex act in Britain lasts twenty-one minutes – seven minutes longer than in Italy. 'We're Champions of Europe – at Nookie!' the *Mirror* rejoiced. Closer reading of the statistics showed this wasn't quite true. Brazilians were the world's sex champs (more than thirty minutes on average) and the French had sex more often than us. In fact, the only sexual arena where Britain really scored was in its huge numbers of unmarried teenage pregnancies. Bennett asked mournfully: 'Considering the current scale of our national indignities, what is one further failure? Compared with the embarrassment of sharing the same nationality as English football supporters, as most of us do, further evidence of sexual mediocrity is no more than a pinprick.' Almost every day, she noted, media reports confirmed the British sense of being useless and depraved. Various recent surveys had shown Britain to be the worst country in the world for kissing, asthma, social inequality and having smelly homes; the worst in Europe for heart disease, pay inequality, fertility treatment, children killed by cars, divorce rates and traditional cooking. And British children were the laziest, least healthy, greediest and most selfish in Europe. 'What can be done?' she asked. 'Nothing, seems to be the despairing consensus . . . The only way is down. Except, of course, in self-loathing. When Penguin gets round to publishing an Atlas of Self-flagellation, the British will undoubtedly come top: for frequency, longevity and, most of all, accuracy.'

Ian Dury sang about his 'reasons to be cheerful' and, viewed through foreign eyes, there's little reason for the English to feel so bad about themselves. They live in a mid-sized, rather successful country that has enviable political stability, the most successful economy in Europe and a rich and ancient culture. Britain has more international status and influence than most, and its unusually vibrant and multicultural capital ('the world in one place') is one of the greatest of all cities. English football isn't entirely loathsome either. The passionate, exciting English league is at the very least one of the three best in the world (only Italy and Spain are rivals), and its polyglot, multi-talented top club teams are universally admired. Even the much-maligned England national side consistently reaches the quarter-finals, and sometimes the semis of major tournaments. With a bit of luck it could even win one day. As the Hugh Grant prime minister says in *Love Actually*: 'We may be a small country but we are a nation of Shakespeare, Churchill, the Beatles, Sean Connery, Harry Potter, David Beckham's right foot . . . David Beckham's left foot, come to that . . .'

Yet none of this makes the English happy, and a nagging sense of national mediocrity and despair is never far away. (Indeed, for most British critics, the very sweetness of *Love Actually* made it insufferable.) And in football, even in the relatively successful era of Eriksson, it doesn't take much to trigger tidal waves of self-disgust. At the time of writing, the most recent example was the amazing moral panic which swept the country after a peculiar week when two stories of rapes involving footballers (one an alleged gang rape in a London hotel which was investigated and dismissed by police) coincided with a rare – and inept – display of player power in the England team. The players threatened (without really meaning it) to strike in support of a colleague, Rio Ferdinand, who they thought was being unfairly treated over his failure to turn up for a drug test. Distasteful the incidents may have been; but it's hard to see how they could trigger the national tsunami of self-disgust.

In the midst of the crisis the still, small, perfectly sensible voice of Gary Lineker said: 'I do not agree that football as a whole is in terminal moral decline.' But lots of people were in no mood to listen. 'Surveying the wreckage of the Beautiful Game gives you some idea of what it must have been like to witness the last days of ancient Rome,' said the columnist Richard Littlejohn. 'No one in soccer can now doubt that the once-great game is deep in crisis,' said the *Sun*. Michael Parkinson reckoned the game 'needs fumigating, sterilising, and purifying, not to mention deodorising, disinfecting and decontaminating. Most of all it needs and deserves a good kicking. Taken in isolation the drinking, the whoring, the racism, the violence, the cheating, the lying, the false pride, the arrogant self-interest masquerading as team spirit, the conniving, the failure to admit blame and to accept responsibility, the fatuous excuses, the utter dumb, gormless stupidity of the players would be enough for grave concern. Put it all together, join up the dots, and what you have is Dodge City without the sheriff . . . It is what happens when men and money come together in an unregulated and unprincipled mayhem and all normal rules governing human behaviour are treated with contempt.'

How did English football become a vehicle for deeper anxieties about England's standing in the world? The answer is rooted – inevitably – in attitudes to the past.

A sense of calamitous decline – real or imagined – has been a key theme not only in football but in British culture as a whole since some time after the Second World War. Just as English journalists and fans continually bewail the lack of English football success in world and European tournaments, so other areas of British life have been coloured by the idea that something, or perhaps many things, have gone horribly wrong. Dwindling international status, combined with perceived economic woes, has been at the root of it, yet this sense of decline has been based at least as much on a 'vague sense of unease' as on hard facts.

Academics have spent decades wrestling with the subject, exploring post-imperial decline, post-war decline, even post-

Crimean War decline, usually from economic and strategic standpoints. But the topic has proved surprisingly slippery, and few widely agreed conclusions have been reached about precise causes or consequences. How should British decline be defined and measured? Could it have been reversed? Is it relative economic failure that bothers us? Or loss of the Empire? It's not even generally agreed when decline started. Some date it to the end of the Second World War, others to just after. Some scholars see the First World War as the turning point. Still others cleave to a kind of declinist version of original sin: the rot set in while Britain was at the very peak of her power and global influence in the 1860s and 1870s. This view is to be found in the influential 'cultural critique' of books such as Martin Wiener's *English Culture and the Decline of the Industrial Spirit, 1850–1980*, and it has been reflected in most modern history textbooks written in the last twenty years. Meanwhile, a parallel search for cultural clues has been a feature of debates about why England's footballers have slid from their original status as world top dogs to the second rank. As long ago as 1955 Brian Glanville opened his book *Soccer Nemesis* with this bleak analysis:

> The story of British football and the foreign challenge is the story of a vast superiority, sacrificed through stupidity, short-sightedness and wanton insularity. It is a story of shamefully wasted talent, extraordinary complacency and infinite self-deception . . . the second world war only hastened a deterioration which had been evident since the end of the first. Its causes are various; many immediate, a few fundamental, all of them avoidable. Foreign football has indeed grown into a strong man during the past fifty years, but the fact that British football has long since lost its supremacy is as much through its own failings as through foreign improvement.

In the wider world, has Britain really declined? Well, obviously yes. And clearly no. After 1945, Britain lost its Empire and ceased to be a superpower; on the other hand, the British standard of living has improved enormously. Queen Victoria may have been Empress of India, but how many of her subjects owned two cars and took holidays in Florida? Anyway, Britain's colossal lead on points in the league table of world affairs wasn't whittled away by losing matches: it was more that other nations won their games in hand.

Militarily and economically Britain is arguably stronger now than at the end of the Second World War; it's just that previously weaker and poorer rival nations got stronger and richer in the same period. The historian David Cannadine summed it up well. In an essay in his book *In Churchill's Shadow* on the futility of Joseph Chamberlain, Winston Churchill and Margaret Thatcher's attempts to reverse what they saw as grievous national decline, he observes:

> Much of Britain's international decline has been relative rather than absolute. It took – and is still taking – a long time, and it has been sometimes halted, though rarely reversed. Meanwhile, on the home front, changes have been in precisely the opposite direction: emphatically for the better rather than visibly for the worse. During the last hundred years, levels of output, income and national wealth have increased unprecedentedly. Today, for most people, life in Britain is more rich, prosperous, varied, abundant and secure than it was for their late-Victorian forebears over a hundred years ago.

The end of the Empire, he argues, wasn't the moral, economic or military catastrophe it is often painted but a necessary, and perhaps even belated, return to the normal state of affairs. A country as small and lacking in natural resources as Britain could never hope to be top dog for ever.

> The economic, naval and imperial dominance which Britain had enjoyed in the heyday of 'Pax Britannica' was in many ways a fluke – the accidental result of early industrialisation, and Empire run on the cheap, and a lack of credible continental rivals. Once the other, bigger nations caught up, once the empire became harder to defend, and once military equipment became more expensive, it was inevitable that, sooner or later, Britain would revert – and is, today, still in the process of reverting – to being what throughout most of its history it has always been: a small group of islands off the coast of Europe. Given the size and natural endowments of other countries and other empires, it was (and is) inconceivable that Britain could persistently play a very significant or autonomous part in international affairs, however much it may try to 'punch above its weight'.

In recent years academics have begun to look afresh at the whole question of decline. If they couldn't agree what it was, when it started, or why it happened, then maybe they'd been asking the wrong questions. Perhaps Britain wasn't a nation in decline as such, or at least not in the way politicians and others expressed it. Maybe it was more that we just liked *thinking* of ourselves as being in decline, which is a rather interesting phenomenon in itself. So now, instead of looking at decline itself, historians have begun to switch their attention to 'declinism'. Instead of asking: where did Britain go wrong? (because maybe it didn't), they have started to look instead at the state of mind which has interpreted things as having gone wrong. Moreover, why was Britain's fall imagined to be someone's *fault*? Why was it always assumed that something could be done to stop the rot and restore the nation to its rightful place at the top?

This goes to the heart of modern, post-imperial Britain's sense of itself in the world. And it goes to the heart of modern English football too. Perceptions of English football decline – like Jeff Powell's – are clearly linked to questions of wider decline. But has English football really declined? Or has its history been much like that Cannadine described for the nation? As Britain's early Industrial Revolution gave it an economic and military jump on its rivals, so England's invention of football (and, indeed, of most modern sport) inevitably gave it a big lead over everyone else. But as other nations took up the game, and got serious about it, it was simply a matter of time before they caught up and overtook us.

In matters of diplomacy and economics, evidence of decline can be a matter of perception and interpretation, but in international football, results provide a pretty incontrovertible picture of who's up and who's down. Brian Glanville reckoned England's status as the world's undisputed footballing top dogs didn't last much beyond 1914. As early as the 1920s England were regularly outplayed and defeated on foreign tours and by the time of the Second World War, England could realistically claim to be no more than 'first among equals'. In the modern era – with the odd, brief hiatus for 1966 – the idea of the English naturally dominating the football world seems simply daft.

English football and the English press and its soccer-loving public, however, never quite reconciled themselves to the new realities. Hence the (what is it now?) . . . forty years of hurt; hence the extraordinary manic-depressive mood swings triggered by success or failure of the England team. Euro '96 provides a fascinating example. Winning the World Cup in 1966 had been a relatively low-key affair, partly because, as we shall see, English football declinism didn't set in until later. 'Everybody cheered, a few thousand came out to say well done, and within a week everybody had disappeared. That was the end of it,' recalled Jimmy Greaves. But by the time England staged its next major tournament, exactly thirty years later, the country and football had changed.

In the run-up to Euro '96, the jingoistic English press was remarkably nervy and lacking in confidence. The 'beef war' raged; fear of hooliganism was widespread; there was much nostalgic wallowing in memories of 1966. Just before the tournament, outrage greeted reports that drunken England players had damaged a plane. The team was the 'laughing stock of the whole world', said the *Daily Mirror*. When England played badly and drew 1–1 with Switzerland in their first game, the *Daily Mail* demanded: 'Gazza must go' and the *Mirror* claimed: 'We are sinking in a sea of booze.' All was forgotten when Gazza scored a terrific goal and David Seaman saved a penalty in the 2–0 defeat of Scotland. 'Forget Bannockburn and forget Culloden,' said the *Sun*. 'In years to come students will be schooled in the precise moment Scottish forces were so heroically repelled by Lord Admiral David Seaman at Wembley.' A few days later, to everyone's astonishment England played brilliantly and thrashed Holland 4–1. *The Times*:

> In 90 minutes, and four goals, football has done what a thousand speeches by government ministers, and a hundred election promises by Tony Blair, have all failed to do. England feels great about itself, almost invincible not just on the football field, but in business, the Olympic Games, politics, you name it. A David once anxious about its economy, its sporting prowess, its beef, has turned overnight into a Goliath. If you're looking for a fight, look elsewhere. Plunge your thermometer any-

where into England's psyche today and it emerges glowing red
with patriotic fever.

Alan Clark, the former Tory minister, noted that English
triumphalism reflected 'a very deep-seated emotion that no
amount of politically correct brainwashing will eradicate that
we are better than anyone else, and that the more often we can
demonstrate that the better. It illuminates a very strong and
deep-seated sense of patriotism. The people have got it very
deep in their veins.'

A few days later England were outplayed in the quarter-final
by Spain but survived to win on penalties, thanks again to
Seaman. Now the euphoria became uncontrollable. *The Times*:
'Those feet that may have walked upon England's mountains
green have done it again. The countenance divine of William
Blake's "Jerusalem" shone through the clouds at Wembley to
give England a sensational victory over Spain.' Politicians were
desperate to join in. Prime Minister John Major broke away
from an EU summit in Florence to watch the match: 'It was a
tremendous result, a wonderful result,' and opposition leader
Tony Blair chipped in with: 'England showed once again they
had the skill and determination to win. They deserve this
memorable victory.' With a semi-final against Germany to
come, English patriotism was 'puffed up like a bulldog on
steroids' and doing a pretty good impersonation of James
Cagney as Cody Jarrett in *White Heat*: ecstatically astride a
giant petrol tank, insanely blazing away with his handgun and
screaming 'Made it, Ma! Top of the *world*!!' In the movie, the
cops shoot back with machine guns, the petrol tank explodes
and Jarrett dies in a huge fireball. At Wembley, despite being
slightly the better team in a 1–1 draw, England couldn't survive
the Germans' perfect shootout penalties. Just as quickly as
euphoria had erupted, the nation imploded back into bleak

anguish, small riots broke out across the country and, in Sussex, a Russian student was stabbed to death by English fans who thought he sounded German.

Perhaps football defeats are especially difficult for the English to accept because losing to foreigners transgresses what was almost a founding principle of the game. As historian James Walvin observed:

> The key issue [was] not that the British played games but that they were *better* than others at those games. British athleticism – original, manly and pioneering – was but another illustration of the superiority of the British. Sports and games seemed to confirm the abundant evidence which is available on all hands – economic ascendancy, imperial prime, diplomatic assertiveness – that Britain was the world's pre-eminent power. Moreover, that global pre-eminence was to be found in the personal and collective qualities of her people. If Britain was the world's leading power, it was because the people were superior. There is . . . a welter of evidence to illustrate the fact that the British *believed* themselves to be superior.

It's been a long time since the heyday of empire and one would have expected us to have got over the problem by now. Instead, free-floating anguish about the state of the nation and the game didn't diminish the further we got from the nineteenth century. It got worse. The contrast in reactions to England's two famous defeats by the USA is revealing.

In the early nineties the misfortunes afflicting the England manager Graham Taylor and Prime Minister John Major seemed to flow together. Defeat by Holland stopped England reaching the 1994 World Cup, but Taylor had suffered his worst week in June 1993. First, England lost a World Cup match 2–0 in Norway, partly because Taylor played Gary

Pallister out of position in a bizarre defensive formation. ('Norse Manure!' screamed the *Sun* headline as the paper superimposed Taylor's face on a pile of horse shit.) Five days later England 'plumbed new depths' by losing 2–0 in a friendly in Boston, and *The Times* asked: 'How low is it possible to sink without drowning?' Actually the Americans were skilful, super-fit and had experienced players from the German, English and Spanish leagues. Their second goal was headed by Alexi Lalas who went on to become a minor cult figure as a player in Italy. But for England to be *outplayed* by the Yanks was considered scandalous. It was a full decade before the comedian Ricky Gervais joked to a Hollywood audience: 'I'm from a little place called England – we used to run the world before you did.' But the declinist awareness of lost power was similar. At the post-match press conference Taylor was asked whether he felt responsible for 'the ultimate national disgrace'.

Three months later, *Viz* chipped in memorably: 'England have not won a match in three months. The fact we have not played one is irrelevant. Graham Taylor should be hung, and so should his successor.'

In 1993 it wasn't just football that was making the English miserable. The effects of the ERM crisis the previous September were still felt. After Black Wednesday a *Times* vox pop had caught the mood. 'Considering we're meant to be a great nation, it's funny how we always end up at the tail end of everything,' said one interviewee in Newcastle. 'I cannot see how anybody looking at recent events will say that Britain is great. Once again we are the weak nation of Europe,' said a man in Derby. A student from Nottingham observed: 'I am sure that the way things have gone we must be the laughing stock of Europe.' Seven months later the start of the 1993 Grand National was botched and the race annulled. 'We will be the laughing stock of the world,' said jockey Peter Scudamore.

Meanwhile, the strange case of a cliffside hotel which was collapsing into the North Sea was making headlines. The hotel had been built on an eroding cliff and each day, as a little more of the cliff was washed away, TV pictures showed hotel rubble crashing to the rocks below. In the House of Commons the Leader of the Opposition blamed the Prime Minister for everything: 'No wonder we live in a country where the Grand National does not start and hotels fall into the sea.' The *Sunday Times* observed:

> The motorways are cracking up in the heat, our cricketers have lost six Tests in a row, our footballers are unable to beat even the Americans. We are disgusted with our leaders and uninspired by those who seek to replace them. Isn't life marvellous! Baleful introspection is not a singularly British pursuit – the French and Germans are at least as self-obsessed as we are – but nowhere else is the cult of misery so entrenched and nowhere else is so much pleasure taken in a zeitgeist of gloom. The British are not merely miserable, they are brilliant at it. There seems no event, no matter how trivial, that cannot arouse us to a new frenzy of self-mortification.

If losing to a professional American soccer team was traumatic in 1993, imagine how apocalyptically demoralising it must have been to lose to them in 1950 when the USA were the rankest of amateurs. If ever a football result merited the rending of English garments, it was surely what Brian Glanville later called this 'cataclysmic' defeat.

In Portuguese, *belo horizonte* means 'beautiful horizon' and the Brazilian city of Belo Horizonte, built according to utopian architectural visions, is famous for its grand plazas and huge diagonal avenues. In modern English football parlance, the words have come to signify 'premonition of the Fall', the

moment when it became clear that England was on the point of
expulsion from its imagined pre-war soccer paradise of eternal
dominance. For the city was the venue for what is still seen as
England's most 'humbling', 'shameful' defeat. England, having
stood aloof from the competition in the 1930s, were taking part
in their first World Cup. Even though Stanley Matthews was
rested, the cream of English football, including Billy Wright,
Tom Finney, Wilf Mannion and Stanley Mortensen, resplen-
dent in blue shirts, took on an oddball team of outsiders
representing the United States. The USA were genuine no-
hopers who had lost 9–0 to Italy in a warm-up game. The
American team of amateur players also expected to get ham-
mered, and some were out dancing until 2 a.m. the night before
the match; some even played with hangovers. Yet, on a bumpy
pitch before 30,000 amazed Brazilian spectators, the Americans
scored first – a lucky headed deflection off their Haitian centre-
forward, Joe Gaetjens, who worked as a dishwasher in a
restaurant. England pressed, at first calmly, later more urgently,
for an equaliser. But they kept hitting the post, missing sitters and
seeing the goalkeeper Frank Borghi make a string of fine saves.
The Americans hung on to win 1–0 and were carried off the
field as heroes by the Brazilian crowd. Belo Horizonte remains
the single most unexpected upset in World Cup history.

If ever a British sporting mishap merited the full 'Where have
we gone wrong?' treatment, this was surely it. If decline was a
problem in the 1990s, then surely the Britain of 1950 was
slipping faster and further than it ever did forty years later. For
those who cared to see it, Britain's prestige had taken a
battering – militarily, economically and diplomatically. India
had been lost in 1947, and a year later Churchill would claim
that the period since the war 'marked the greatest fall in the
rank and stature of Britain in the world, which has occurred
since the loss of the American colonies 200 years ago'.

In this context, how did the British press and public react to their 'cataclysmic' football defeat? They barely noticed it. The World Cup was still regarded as a faraway competition of which we knew little and cared less. Only a handful of English reporters attended the game and when the news reached London by telegram, newspapers assumed there was a glitch on the line and the true score was 10–1. For the players involved it was traumatic, but for the public at large, the story made barely any impact and was swiftly forgotten. Coverage in the *Daily Telegraph* was typical. The big story of the day was West Indies' first ever win at Lord's (which, unlike later Windies victories, was greeted with widespread approval and was not interpreted as a disaster for England). Events at Belo Horizonte merited just four inches of a single column report a long way down the page – roughly the same space as that devoted to a preview of a cricket match between Eton and Winchester. Under the headline 'England Lose Cup Match – One of Worst Soccer Games', the report said the match had been 'probably the worst display ever by an England side'. The English forwards 'were particularly at fault, blazing the ball wide or over the bar and hesitating in front of goal'. But there were no photos. The report appeared instead underneath a picture of 'Gorgeous Gussie' Moran ('graceful as a ballet dancer') in action in the ladies' doubles at Wimbledon.

Belo Horizonte could perhaps be dismissed as an eccentric, distant, one-off oddity, but what of those even more unmistakably catastrophic failures of English football in the early fifties – the awesome thrashings inflicted by the 'Magical Magyars'? England had been losing away matches to foreign opponents since 1929, but they had never lost on home soil. At Wembley, on 25 November 1953, that record was ended as Hungary, a team promoted by the Hungarian government as a symbol of the virtues of communism, won 6–3. The Hungarians didn't just beat the mother country, they crushed it with a hitherto undreamed-of combination of brilliant teamwork, fantasy, skill and speed. On the day of the game Frank Coles of the *Daily Telegraph* had put his faith in downright English blows, predicting: 'Hungary's superb ball-jugglers can be checked by firm tackling.' But, in football terms, the game was as epoch-defining (and as much a mismatch) as the military contest at Omdurman seventy years earlier between charging Dervishes and British Maxim guns. It was England's turn to be annihilated by a thin red line of mercurial, cherry-shirted 'wizards'.

'It was like cart-horses playing race horses,' England's winger Tom Finney commented later. Defender Syd Owen said that facing Hungary 'was like playing people from outer space'. Hungary scored after just fifty seconds – their 'deep-lying' centre-forward Nandor Hidegkuti shooting in from 25 yards. Unlike a traditional English centre-forward, Hidegkuti operated from deep midfield, surging forward when the mood took him, and spraying lethal passes at strange angles. Coaches and journalists knew his style and there was even an article about it in the match programme. Yet England manager Walter Winterbottom neglected to take counter-measures and Hidegkuti was left free to wreak havoc while England's centre-half Harry Johnston floundered, not knowing whether to mark him or hold his line. At one point, Johnston turned to captain Billy Wright, and asked: 'What do I do, Billy?' Wright answered: 'I don't know, Harry.' Just before half-time, Wright himself was famously embarrassed. As he charged in to tackle Hungarian captain Ferenc Puskas near goal, Puskas dragged the ball back with the sole of his boot and left Wright charging at thin air ('like a fire engine on the way to the wrong fire', as Geoffrey Green of *The Times* put it) and Puskas lashed in Hungary's third goal. 'Now the World Is Really Upside Down' said the *News*

*Chronicle* the next morning above a picture of Gyula Grosics, the Hungarian goalkeeper, walking on his hands. The *Daily Mirror*'s headline was: 'Twilight of the (Soccer) Gods'. In the *Observer*, Alan Ross said the difference between the Hungarian and English teams had been that 'between artists and artisans, strategists with a flair for improvisation and stumbling recruits bound by an obsolete book of words'. Six months later, in the return match in Budapest, England proved incapable of changing their ancient tactics and were humiliated 7–1. Throughout the match, as England stumbled ineptly to the heaviest defeat they have ever suffered, listeners to the BBC commentary heard summariser Charles Buchan, who didn't realise his microphone was open, muttering and groaning constantly as things went wrong.

Nothing so humbling had happened to an England team before or has happened since. These reverses were genuinely momentous, a death knell for an insular and outmoded English game, and triggered furious debate in football circles. Brian Glanville, one of the few journalists to warn years earlier that the English had been left behind by developments in Latin America and Europe, wrote: 'The result of this match gave eyes even to the blind who had ignored all those defeats which had taken place abroad. All at once . . . everyone was wise, everyone casting round for scapegoats and explanations, everyone, in short, had discerned the crisis which had existed for over thirty years.' Yet, reading contemporary reports, instead of blame, anger or any sense of national crisis, what is most evident is the extraordinary English warmth and generosity towards their conquerors. The huge Wembley crowd applauded the Hungarians off at the end of the match and thousands of Londoners turned out to cheer them when they left Victoria Station. Puskas's 'drag-back' was regarded as a thing of wonder and beauty. Puskas and Wright became firm friends and Puskas would later remark in his memoirs, *Puskas on Puskas: the Life and Times of a Footballing Legend*, edited by Rogan Taylor and Klara Jamrich: 'I know the Wembley game must have been a painful experience for English players and fans alike . . . [but] they were one of the fairest groups of people I've ever met. I'll never forget the way everyone we encountered in England hailed the victory without resentment.'

Travelling on a train to France that week, Neal Ascherson ran into a group of amiable, leather-coated men – the victorious Hungarian team on their way home. 'Puskas Ferenc! He was there. They were all very friendly, but most of them didn't speak anything but Hungarian, so it was difficult to communicate.' Ascherson vividly remembers the general reaction. 'The English people took a lot of pleasure from the idea that these people were so good. You could call it sporting. Or you could call it inconceivable complacency. Or you could call it a rather healthy attitude. It turned on the idea that we had taught them, and they had become rather good at the game. "The people we taught have grown up and can actually beat us at it now! Well done chaps!" It was like that with Tiger Khomich too [Moscow Dynamo's charismatic goalkeeper in their 1945 tour of Britain]. Everyone fell in love with Khomich. At that time the English were still in a sort of magnanimous glow from the war. I don't think anyone thought being beaten by Puskas or Khomich was the end of anything, that it punctured an illusion.'

Memoirs and books on the subject all convey the same impression of fondness. At the official banquet after the London match, FA chairman Brook Hirst said Hungary had 'given a display which everyone must admire' and promised England would in future 'try to cultivate the style of football which the Hungarians had demonstrated so wonderfully'. No British newspaper called the players, manager or selectors a 'national disgrace', no one told Winterbottom 'In the Name of God, Go', or printed pictures of him as a vegetable, hardly anyone even mentioned his tactical errors. After the Festival of Britain, the Coronation and the conquest of Everest by a British-led team, English national confidence was high, and 1953 was a year when the English felt good about themselves. 'The shock of defeat stayed within football and was containable,' says historian Dilwyn Porter. And the Hungarians inspired a new interest in tactics which led to new coaching methods. The defeats arguably paved the way for modest reforms and England won the World Cup thirteen years later.

Losing to the USA and Hungary revealed the decline of English football much more dramatically and shockingly than anything since. So why didn't the nation curdle into anger and despair? Perhaps it was because the population of Britain had not yet got their heads around the notion that Britain was in decline at all.

Amputees often continue to 'feel' parts of the body which no longer exist. These phantom limbs can be the source of great pain; sometimes they produce neutral or pleasant feelings. In all cases, the most striking sensation is that they are still present. A classic case of the phenomenon was that of the brilliant Viennese pianist Paul Wittgenstein, brother of the philosopher Ludwig. Paul lost his right arm in the First World War, yet his mind retained an incredibly vivid memory of the vanished limb. One of his former students, Erna Otten, recalled: 'I had many occasions to see how involved his right stump was whenever we went over the fingering for a new composition . . . He felt every finger of his right hand. At times I had to sit very quietly while he would close his eyes and his stump would move constantly in an agitated manner. This was many years after the loss of his arm.' One theory as to why this happens is that the brain works to an ineradicable 'map' of the body and this continues to operate even when part of the physical reality has changed.

Is this how it is with the English? Their status as the dominant great power in the world was amputated long ago. The Empire no longer exists. But Britain's national nervous system is still wired to feel as if it did.

The traditional view of the impact on Britain itself of the end of Empire was that there was almost no impact. Numerous books have explored the cultural and political consequences on once-colonised countries after the British left, but few have seen the British themselves as a subject for 'post colonialism'. David Cannadine suggests: 'The British Empire may have been won "in a fit of absence of mind", but as far as the majority of the population seems to have been concerned, it was given away in a fit of collective indifference.' The American commentator Michael Kinsley observed:

> The British handled their decline pretty gracefully. In just a couple of generations Britain sank from economic and political superpower to second-rank member of a second-rank regional bloc. Yet the transformation happened without much domestic rancor, despite Britain's supposedly bitter class divisions. At worst, the general attitude was a certain sullen resignation. At best, there was a jolly, fatalistic insouciance. The Brits almost seemed to enjoy their ride down.

But Australian historian Stuart Ward doesn't see it that way. He thinks Britain's post-war fall from power was – and still is – a massive cultural trauma for the British, one which continues to resonate and goes to the heart of Britain's sense of itself and its place in the world. In 1999 he edited a pioneering collection of essays on the subject, *British Culture and the End of Empire*.

Economic historian Jim Tomlinson has suggested there could be a relatively simple, technical explanation for declinism, namely that it was caused by new kinds of economic statistics. Before the war, politicians didn't discuss 'standard of living' because such a thing was impossible to measure. From the 1950s, though, new kinds of statistics became available and politicians used them as sticks to beat their opponents, claiming, for example, that Britain was falling behind European rivals economically. Tomlinson says: 'The declinism invented in the 1950s proved to be long-lasting. For the next forty years, except perhaps for a brief period in the late 1980s, the assumption that Britain's economic performance was inferior to its competitors, and that this was a symptom of secular malaise, dominated much of both popular and the academic discussion of the economy.' But there is surely much more to it than that. Ward: 'The economy is so complex and economic data is just data which can be read in many ways. The average Briton has been better off year after year from 1901 until now. So to interpret statistics as meaning: "there is something inherently wrong with the economy" and the country going economically down the googler even in years of economic growth is very strange.'

Ward thinks declinist post-imperial trauma might explain Britain's unnecessarily bleak view of its economy and international standing in the world; it could also account for its odd reactions to sporting disappointments. (And the very fact that the trauma is largely unacknowledged just makes it worse.) 'The self-loathing doesn't seem to abate. It can be traced back in various ways to the fifties. But it seems to intensify. The eighties was a particularly nasty era, when the tabloids in particular just seemed to lose any sense of perspective. It carried on through the nineties. And it's still going on. I happened to be in the UK in 1993, which was a particularly bitter year. I remember one of the tabloids had a huge front-page headline: "Losers at cricket! Losers at football! Losers at Rugby! Let's face it – WE'RE AWFUL!" You couldn't get a headline like that in Australia, no matter how bad the team was going. We don't have that same perpetually punctured expectation of the national self. Australians expect a lot of their sporting heroes, but they don't risk this kind of vilification if they don't perform. So the question is: what lies beneath these English expectations that are so bitterly disappointed seemingly time and time again?'

Some have taken issue with Ward. 'I've taken a fair bit of stick for it, especially from the older generation. I gave one lecture in London, and you wouldn't believe the reaction. It boiled down to: "What would you know about it, sonny? You weren't even born then!" A number of people told me: "I remember that era very well and we did *not* feel *any* kind of anxiety about the loss of Empire. It wasn't even thought about in terms of loss. It was thought of in terms of gain. And we did a jolly good job, thank you very much!" That orthodoxy is still around, but you're seeing more and more people beginning to realise that this is a trauma which continues to manifest itself in various ways. People are now saying: why is there this delayed reaction? We are clearly looking at a major long-term trauma that has its roots in the imperial condition.' Ian Budge makes a similar point in an essay on the political dimensions of decline: 'It is the nagging perception that Britain has lost out as leader of the West, together with a strong but unexamined sentiment that it *should* still be top dog, that forms the stimulus to national soul-searching.'

Another historian, Dilwyn Porter, who co-edited a recent book on *Sport and National Identity*, has explored the impact of the England–Hungary games and the emergence of declinism in football. He broadly agrees with Ward's approach and suggests Britain's post-imperial angst derives in part from the deceptive and hidden nature of the nation's fall from power after the Second World War. In the twenty years after 1945, the gradual destruction of Empire was disguised from the British public. Politicians of both parties were keen to project as powerful an image of Britain as possible. The post-war Labour government, for example, was desperate for its 'nuclear deterrent' to be seen as independent from the Americans. Referring to the Bomb, Foreign Secretary Ernest Bevin said: 'We've got to have the bloody Union Jack flying on top of it.' It was not said that former colonies had thrown the British out; rather, it was suggested, British influence had 'civilised' countries such as Uganda and Nigeria to the point where it was now in the interests of all – especially the mother country – for the British to 'grant' independence. The fiction that the Empire was not disintegrating but merely evolving into the Commonwealth – a friendlier, family version of its old self – helped to anaesthetise and disguise British pain over the process. When France lost its Empire, says Porter, it suffered OAS bombs in Paris, the disaster of Dien Bien Phu, bloody war in Algeria and the fall of the Fourth Republic. Such cataclysms made it clear to the French public that the country's imperial days were over. But, in Britain, there were no such dramatic endings, and even the Suez Crisis of 1956, often seen as a turning point, provided no clean break. Porter explains: 'It is all very delayed and dragged out. You don't get the catharsis you had in France. In England, even after Suez, "the regime holds" as it were. Anthony Eden leaves office but the Conservatives win the election three years later under Macmillan with "you've never had it so good". When the subject comes up again in the early sixties, the end of Empire is a factor in politics but it's always containable.'

Declinism simply didn't exist until the very late 1950s. Then it arrived with a bang as books began to appear on the theme 'What's Wrong with Britain'. Hugh Thomas's *The Establishment: A Symposium* paved the way in 1959, and soon titles such as *The Stagnant Society* and *Great Britain or Little England?* were essential reading. Time and again, observes Ward, these writings convey 'a potent blend of trauma, nostalgia, and resentment towards the ruling establishment converged around a deep sense of loss at the core of British civic culture'. In the influential *Anatomy of Britain* (1962) Anthony Sampson evoked the sense that:

> A loss of dynamic and purpose, and a general bewilderment, are felt by many people, both at the top and at the bottom in Britain's today . . . It is hardly surprising that, in 20 years since the war, Britain should have felt confused about her purpose – with those acres of red on the map dwindling, the mission of the war dissolving, and the whole imperial mythology of battleships, governors and generals is gone forever.

In *A State of England* (1963), Anthony Hartley worried: 'In the past, loss of power in the world has often been accompanied by a period of national decadence, by a decline affecting not only the external relations of a society, but also its own intrinsic quality . . . shall we, too, be added to the ranks of those countries on whom the loss of empire, the loss of purpose, have had a crippling effect? Or shall we manage to escape the descent into limbo?'

The issue of British decline became a major theme as numerous politicians began to take up the question in the late fifties. The 1964 general election, the first fought on explicitly declinist ground, was won with Harold Wilson promising to revive Britain using the 'white heat' of the technological revolution. Over the next two decades a potent declinist sensibility – mournful, elegiac, confused and hankering for former glories and certainties – emerged right across British culture. Even the Beatles, in 'Nowhere Man', were touched by it.

In The Clash's 'Something about England' we meet a gloomy old man impervious to the erosions of time. The Kinks' 1969 album *Arthur – or the Decline and Fall of the British Empire* is full of ironic, wistful reflection on the mid-twentieth-century English condition and the propaganda of war and imperialism. When England were knocked out of the 1980 European Championship by a goal scored by Italy's Marco Tardelli, the disappointment was promptly celebrated by a punk band calling itself Marco Tardelli. These days, there is the witty, ironic 'retro claustrophobia' of the Brighton-based indie band British Sea Power (two of whose members used to be in an outfit called 'British Air Power'). On stage, British Sea Power, who have been compared to The Smiths, have performed in football shirts but usually wear bits of old military uniforms. They are obsessed with agriculture and are the only pop act in history to cite Field Marshal Bernard Montgomery as a major influence. Their first album was called *The Decline of British Sea Power*. Their early single, 'Fear of Drowning', was about little England, whose only way was down.

The spy novels of John le Carré are melancholy, labyrinthine distillations of post-imperial English disappointment. Football writer Simon Kuper says that a national football team is 'the nation made flesh', but le Carré suggests that it is the secret services that reflect the true essence of a country. Le Carré's darkly moral stories, mixing philosophy, betrayal, murder, politics and disillusion, explore much deeper, murkier terrain than anything in sport. While his enigmatic hero George Smiley might be a symbol of an older, dying England, the

'Circus' – M16 – is clearly, among other things, a metaphor for England itself in decline. American academic Myron Aronoff sees novels like *Tinker Tailor Soldier Spy* and *Smiley's People* as 'allegories of Britain's loss of a sense of direction, unwillingness to face new realities, and failure to adapt to them', a Britain 'bewildered by the changing international environment'.

Le Carré's sense of Britain's post-war loss is vividly expressed in the stories of the betrayal of the Circus by one of its leading lights, the elegant, upper-class Soviet 'mole' Bill Haydon. Haydon is a fictionalised version of the real-life Cambridge spy circle – Burgess, Maclean, Philby and Blunt – whose unmasking through the sixties, seventies and eighties was a potent focus of English post-imperial angst. Le Carré felt this distress more keenly than most because he'd worked for British intelligence. *The Honourable Schoolboy* resonates with the consequences of betrayal: 'There were those who seriously believed – inside the Circus as well as out – that they had heard the last beat of the secret English heart.' There's even a biblical metaphor: the unmasking of Haydon's treachery becomes 'the Fall' and Circus history is divided into before the Fall and after it.

Le Carré's friend, the playwright David Hare, is another elegant chronicler of national disappointment. In *Plenty*, decline is seen through a young English woman who fought with the French Resistance and later finds it impossible to move on from the intensity of her wartime experiences. As Britain becomes increasingly wealthy, she slides ever further into disillusion and mental illness. A Foreign Office mandarin observes: 'As our power declines, the fight among us for access to that power becomes a little more urgent, a little uglier perhaps. As our influence wanes, as our empire collapses, there is little to believe in. Behaviour is all.'

As an idea, then, decline had taken root in Britain from the late fifties onwards, but, with England winning the World Cup, football was hardly an ideal vehicle for free-floating anxiety about the state of the nation. That began to change on 14 June 1970.

'What happened on June 14th 1970?' asks Bob three years later in an episode of *Whatever Happened to the Likely Lads*.

> TERRY: *What happened??* I would have thought that date was printed indelibly in the mind of every Englishman worthy of the name. England TWO! West Germany THREE!! That's what happened!
>
> BOB: Oh, my God. Of course! I've only just learned to live with it myself.

It was worse for Terry because he watched the game in Germany, surrounded by the German family of his now ex-wife Jutta. In the blazing Mexican heat of León, England had taken a 2–0 lead in the World Cup quarter-final and seemed to be coasting. Then a mistake by goalkeeper Peter Bonetti, standing in for food-poisoning victim Gordon Banks, allowed a shot by Franz Beckenbauer to creep into the net and the Germans were inspired to stage their famous comeback. Terry blames the game for destroying his marriage:

> TERRY: I was standing on the sideboard singing 'Rule Britannia', 'Land of Hope and Glory'. Their faces! And then . . . The shame! The humiliation! To have them all leaping up and down, eyes glazed with national socialist fervour. It was the old '*Deutschland über Alles*' all over again. The old jackboots. I thought they were going to rush out and invade Poland. You can realise how I felt about it at that moment. I just got up and left. Quite unnoticed. Just got me bag and walked out of her life forever.

León was a genuine shock. England were reckoned to be an even better team than the winners of '66. After the previous match against Brazil Bobby Moore and Pelé had exchanged shirts as equals and (it was assumed) had said to each other: 'See you in the final.' Prime Minister Harold Wilson always claimed the wave of national gloom which followed the German defeat cost him the general election four days later. Attendances slumped at league matches the following season, and for the rest of his career, Bonetti was subjected to chants of 'You lost the World Cup'. Even so, at the time the result was seen more as a sporting calamity than as a symbol of national failure. 'It was a conspiracy of fate more than a footballing defeat,' wrote Hugh McIlvanney in the *Observer*.

Sir Alf Ramsey's team are out because the best goalkeeper most people have ever seen turned sick, and one who is only slightly less gifted was overwhelmed by the suddenness of his promotion . . . Those who ranted smugly in distant television studios about the tactical blunders of Ramsey were toying with the edges of the issue. Errors, there were, and Ramsey in private has acknowledged one or two but the England manager is entitled to claim that his side were felled by something close to an act of God.

When England were beaten by the Germans again two years later – outclassed 3–1 at Wembley in the first leg of the European Championship quarter-final – the tone got a lot darker. Football is so unpredictable. The Wembley match saw the remarkable Gunter Netzer give his greatest performance. To the English, it seemed almost as if the new, post-war Germany had unveiled a footballing miracle to go with the almost frighteningly successful revival of their economy. Yet it was the Germans who had expected the worst. In the tunnel

Netzer had turned to Beckenbauer and predicted the score would be 5–0 – to England.

In the event the English press rounded on Ramsey. Even the generous McIlvanney complained:

> Cautious joyless football was scarcely bearable even while it was bringing victories. When it brings defeat there can be only one reaction . . . What is happening now we always felt to be inevitable, because anyone who sets out to prove that football is about sweat rather than inspiration, about winning rather than glory, is sure to be found out in the end . . . [Ramsey's] method was, to be fair, justifiable in 1966, when it was important that England should make a powerful show in the World Cup, but since then it has become an embarrassment.

Declinist legend has it that Ramsey's team selection further disgraced the nation in the 0–0 return leg in Berlin. Most of the British press demanded the inclusion of attacking 'flair' players like Peter Osgood. Instead, Ramsey's plan to reduce the two-goal deficit meant keeping the game tight and hoping for an early goal. Instead of flamboyant attackers, he chose Peter Storey, who kicked Netzer out of the match. Journalist Ken Jones believes Ramsey was probably right, and cites in evidence the phone call he received before the game from his friend Helmut Schoen, the German manager. Schoen wanted to know if Ramsey would bow to media pressure and field an attacking team. 'Oh, you know Alf,' said Jones. 'He'll just do what he thinks is right.' 'Pity,' said Schoen. 'If England come to attack, we will win 6–0.' Ramsey's tactics nearly worked, but Roy McFarland missed the single good chance that came his way in the heavy rain. In the grey concrete bowl of Hitler's old Olympic Stadium, England and Germany fought each other to a standstill.

Most commentators were in no mood to be generous. As the Germans had built their 'economic miracle' from the rubble of 1945, so German football had apparently learned from their '66 defeat and developed much further than England. As Peter Wilson put it in the *Daily Mirror*; 'As is so often the case, we have been content to dwell in the past and rest complacently on past triumphs until events – and other nations – overtake and surpass us.' This view – and the belief that England's football had lost its way – was dramatically reinforced by the 1–1 draw with Poland at Wembley in 1973. The result put England out of the following year's World Cup, and the game is chiefly recalled for Tomaszewski's inspired goalkeeping and a defensive mistake by Norman Hunter which led to the Polish goal. That night, when the Polish team went to a London disco to celebrate, they found England supporters in tears as the DJ played a string of old hit songs from 1966. Late in the game Roy McFarland had rugby-tackled Poland's winger Lato to stop him scoring. Brian Glanville commented bitterly: 'Once you have reached this stage of cynicism, games aren't worth playing at all.' A reader of the Polish newspaper *Zycie Warszawy* said: 'The British Empire tried to save itself by pulling the pants off Polish footballers.'

Dilwyn Porter says that from the early 1970s the game was increasingly 'written and talked about in a way that implied a sense of cultural bereavement, an awareness that something important had been lost or damaged beyond repair'. The idea of England as a once-great nation incapable of living up to its past or competing with its rivals took hold. 'English football and those who reported on it . . . contributed to the prolonged angst about British decline and to the sense of crisis that it engendered.' The idea spread that 'something should be done' about the England team, even if it was only to sack the manager. Donald Saunders of the *Daily Telegraph*, for example, after the Poland game: 'Now England have been relegated to a place among soccer's second-class powers . . . the long difficult task of rehabilitation must begin immediately.'

Yet, at club level, it would not be impossible for a rational person to interpret the late 1970s and early 1980s as something of a golden age for English football. English teams – Liverpool, Nottingham Forest and Aston Villa – won the European Cup seven years out of eight between 1977 and 1984. No other country ever had such a run of success. But as we shall see in a later chapter, England failed to qualify for the 1978 World Cup too, and a profound sense of melancholy and unease settled on discussions of the game. Laments for the passing of former greatness became commonplace, and the decline in technical and moral standards was the source of much angst.

In 1978 the writer Tom Stoppard took the game as a metaphor for his TV play *Professional Foul*, in which dim-witted members of the hopeless England national football team collide with a group of philosophy dons in a Prague hotel. The academics are in town for an ethics colloquium, the footballers for a World Cup qualifying match, which they lose by four goals ('There'll be Czechs bouncing in the streets of Prague tonight as bankruptcy stares English football in the face'). The play takes its title from the moment in the game when an English defender commits a McFarlandesque foul to stop the Czechs scoring. After the match, one of the professors tries to engage the player responsible in a philosophical discourse about the new 'yob ethics of professional footballers'. Why, he demands, do players appeal for throw-ins when they know they put the ball out? 'Is it because they are very, very stupid or is it because a dishonest advantage is as welcome as an honest one?' Why do footballers celebrate goals 'with paroxysms of childish glee', whereas in rugby a score is acknowledged 'with pride but with restraint'? The philosopher speculates: 'The reason footballers are yobs may be nothing to do with being working class, or with financial greed, or with adulation, or even with being footballers. It may be simply that football attracts a certain kind of person – namely yobs.' The England defender responds by punching the philosopher in the face.

Economically, Britain was now seen as the 'sick man of Europe', supposedly on its knees because of militant trade unions and incompetent management, and declinist politicians urged drastic changes to revitalise the nation and its economy. Margaret Thatcher came to power by promising to 'reverse national decline' and put the 'great' back into Great Britain. On the eve of the 1979 election she said: 'Unless we change our ways and our direction, our glories as a nation will soon be a footnote in history books, a distant memory of an offshore island, lost in the mists of time, like Camelot, remembered kindly for its noble past.' Meanwhile, as Martin Wiener had traced Britain's current economic problems to the anti-entre-preneurial culture of the 1860s and 1870s, so football pundits now tended to blame 'the assorted butchers, bakers and candle-stick-makers to be found in the boardrooms of every club in England' for every England failure. Where Britain's perceived economic problems were blamed on 'sclerotic tendencies' in the country's institutions, critics of the football establishment such as Malcolm Allison railed against 'the dim, bland men whose voices were most powerful in English football'. When things began to go wrong for Alf Ramsey, he complained that 'the amateurs are back in charge'. In 1973 and 1977, the FA refused to appoint Brian Clough – 'a moderniser frustrated by a football establishment displaying all the symptoms of institu-tional sclerosis' – as England manager. Later, Clough called the FA selection panel old men who had 'bungled a few things in their time'.

In 1966 Alf Ramsey's innovative 'scientific management'

had seemed a football version of the scientific modernisation Harold Wilson promised in 1964. From the new deep pessimism, even winning the World Cup was interpreted as a disaster, and 1966 became just another peak from which England had since fallen, 'another item in the collection of cultural clutter symbolic of lost national greatness'. In 1994 Rob Steen argued in his book *The Mavericks* that 'the 1966 World Cup was the worst thing ever to happen to our national game'. By the late 1990s it was 'the fatal victory' which reinforced ideas of English superiority, making it difficult to adapt to or learn from development of the game elsewhere. Peter Allen's book *An Amber Glow* told the story of the lost ball used in the 1966 Final: 'a symbol of England's lost greatness, as prime ministers and international managers presided over a period of devastating failure on and off the field'.

Away from football, David Cannadine sees the country's fall from great power status in quite benign terms:

> Britain may indeed have fallen in the world rankings of prosperous and powerful countries. But it is still, despite everything that has happened during the last hundred years, one of the most prosperous and powerful countries in the world. And there seems no good reason to suppose that it will cease to be so in the foreseeable future . . . Moreover, compared with earlier nations and empires on the wane, Britain's retreat from greatness has been remarkably stable and trouble-free – no barbarians at the gates, no enemy invasions, no civil wars or revolutions, no end to civilisation. Britain's decline has not only been relative, in a contemporary sense; it has also, in historical terms, been relatively gradual and relatively gentle.

The balance sheet of English football is open to positive as well as gloomy readings. The national team's record in major tournaments over the last four decades – one tournament win, three semi-final appearances and six quarter-finals – is only a 'disgrace', only makes us a 'laughing stock' if you think like the Victorians that England has a divine right to dominate. English football hooliganism rose – but then it fell. English fan culture is rich, deep and vibrant. English club football is not just fast and thrilling but (thanks to all the talented foreigners who play and coach here) increasingly sophisticated.

Perhaps it would help if we all sat down together and watched *Groundhog Day*, the movie in which a bitter, cynical, sarcastic man is doomed to live the same day over and over again. Eventually he breaks free by accepting his history and adopting a more open-hearted, positive approach. When the forward-looking England rugby coach Clive Woodward guided his team to victory in the Rugby World Cup in 2003, some commentators wondered aloud what it might do to our by-now deeply ingrained (and frankly comforting) English pessimism and self-denigration. Like Sven-Goran Eriksson, Woodward is a pragmatic, open-minded modernist and a skilled technician. He scours the world for new ideas, makes a virtue of never invoking 'thud 'n' blunder' rhetoric about pride and commitment. He seems downright American in his devotion to winning. There are only half a dozen good teams in world rugby; the football World Cup is a much tougher proposition. On the other hand, England were just a game away from winning in Japan (had they got past Brazil, would Turkey or Germany have stopped them?).

Football has been a potent carrier of English declinism for the last thirty-five years. What might winning the football World Cup do to the psychology of the nation? Would it be greeted as if it was a belated return to the natural, ancient order of things? Or would it be seen as a symbol of a new way of being English, one which fused the old strengths with fresh

optimism and openness to new ideas? The prospect is not
unthinkable. Foreigners often take a rosier view of England
than the English themselves, and one of Italy's most respected
football writers, Mario Sconcerti, (whom we shall meet again
later) suggests England may be just one great player short of
being world or European champions: 'It is my conviction that
the next force in world football will be England because
England is no longer the team of twenty years ago. You are
very strong and very rich and you are moving forward and
researching. You will have to know exactly how to use this
research. If you don't use it well you will not become powerful.
But I can imagine very easily that in another five or ten years
England will be a serious power which wins the European
Championship and the World Cup. All over the world we will
see a multiracial culture in football. France became powerful
with a multiracial team. England was one of the first to put
together black and white players. It is a great strength. England
now lacks only great attackers. You have many good midfield
players, but no great attackers. Michael Owen? There are many
Michael Owens in the world. If England had Van Nistelrooy
you would be very near to being the kings, the number one.'

Joe's left flashed out ; it caught Grogan on the side of the jaw. The football manager pitched sideways to his desk, cannoned off it and crashed to the floor. Rene, watching, was torn between pride in her sweetheart and terror at the struggle.

# IT'S COLD AND WE'RE RUBBISH

It's a long time since English football enjoyed the presence of anyone as relentlessly, fantastically positive as Bill Shankly. 'You haven't broken your leg. It's all in the mind,' was a typical Shankly line. When the ebullient, granitic former Scottish miner took over at Anfield in 1959, Liverpool were a mediocre Second Division outfit in a city dominated by their neighbours, Everton. By the time he left in 1974, he had made Liverpool the most powerful, admired and glamorous club in Britain. Under his protégé Bob Paisley, over the next decade the Reds extended their rule to Europe and the world. No club in England has ever dominated the game as did the Liverpool that Shankly created.

Much has been written about Shankly's socialist principles, his on-field tactics, his charisma and rapport with the fans, but perhaps his most potent weapon was his remorselessly im-modest, thoroughly un-English humour. 'There are two great teams on Merseyside,' he would say, 'Liverpool and Liverpool Reserves.' When Alan Ball, then the hottest property in the game, signed for Everton in 1966, Shankly quipped: 'Don't worry, Alan. At least you'll be able to play near a great team.' When Shankly failed to sign Lou Macari in 1973, he claimed: 'I only wanted him for the reserves anyway.' When he recruited the original 'Big Ron', Ron Yeats, it was: 'With him in defence, we could play Arthur Askey in goal.' After a 5–4 match: 'We massacred them.' 1–1: 'The best side drew.' In fact, pretty much everything Shankly ever said was geared to building up his own side and belittling or psyching out the opposition. Just before a Cup Final, he offered his rivals' goalkeeper some friendly advice: 'Aye, watch it, Bob, it's very greasy and treacherous out there. Very difficult for goal-keepers.' Performed by less twinkly men, Shankly's shtick might have sounded loathsomely bombastic. Brian Clough made less audacious claims, but got himself a reputation as 'Old Big 'Ead'; Alex Ferguson is considered sour. Even Bob Paisley's Shankly-derived 'Mind you, I've been here during the bad times too – one year we came second' doesn't dance like a good Shanklyism.

In his *Memories, Dreams, Reflections* Carl Gustav Jung told the story of how he once had a dream in which he saw Liverpool as the centre of the life force. Although the great psychoanalyst had never visited the city and quite possibly never even heard of Anfield, Liverpool appeared as a place of darkness except for its central point: 'A single tree, a magnolia, in a shower of reddish blossoms. It was as though the tree stood in the sunlight and was at the same time the source of light . . . I had had a vision of unearthly beauty, and that was why I was able to live at all.' Shankly seems at times to have been impelled by similar visions. On one famous occasion he met a young fan from London who had travelled specially to stand on the Kop: 'Well, laddie,

how does it feel to be in heaven?' Shanks could even make the
club's perennially muddy pitch sound lustrous: 'It's great grass
at Anfield, professional grass.'

Shankly's role models were not Austrian psychoanalysts but
the kind of Hollywood gangsters portrayed by James Cagney,
George Raft and Edward G. Robinson. When Liverpool
travelled to away matches, Shankly made sure the team reached
their hotel in time for him to watch Robert Stack playing
Elliott Ness in the TV show *The Untouchables*. In team talks,
instead of discussing tactics, opponents or even football, he
often tried to inspire his players with tales of screen mobsters.
He once challenged Tommy Smith: 'You think you're a hard
man?' and threw down pictures of Cagney and Raft. 'These
guys were hard men. If they did something wrong they got
shot!' Shankly was a 'man's man', a former boxer and he never
gave an inch. He once rounded on his captain who appeared at
training with a bandaged knee: 'Take that poof bandage off!
And what do you mean your knee? It's *Liverpool's* knee!'
Shankly got some of his best material from America. His
most-quoted quip about the centrality of football ('People
say football is a matter of life and death. I'm very disappointed
with that attitude. I can assure you it is much, much more
important than that') was a better version of a line also used by
the famously witty American college football coach Duffy
Daugherty, who said: 'When you're playing for the national
championship, it's not a matter of life or death. It's more
important than that.'

Raising a smile, of course, was never Shankly's central
objective. He saw humour as a weapon; his jokes were 'bombs',
and his central objective was supremacy: 'My idea was to build
Liverpool into a bastion of invincibility. Napoleon had that
idea. He wanted to conquer the bloody world. I wanted
Liverpool to be untouchable. My idea was to build Liverpool

up and up until eventually everyone would have to submit and give in.' It seemed to work. As he explained: 'A lot of football success is in the mind. You must believe you are the best and then make sure that you are.' Away from Merseyside, English fans were never quite sure what to make of Shankly. Certainly, he was considered admirable, but he was also seen as an eccentric, a 'character'. His fervent belief that 'If you are first you are first. If you are second you are nothing' sounded slightly odd and fanatical. American sport is full of such bons mots. In the USA, fans quote football coach Vince Lombardi's line 'Winning isn't everything, it's the only thing' all the time. Leo 'The Lip' Durocher's baseball dictum that 'nice guys finish last' is standard wisdom. As baseball writer Jerome Holtzman observed, 'Losing is the great American sin.'

Losing is not quite the great English sin. In England, football humour, like wider attitudes to the game and the country, is laced with cheery masochism. In England, it's rather stylish for a relegation-haunted manager whose team has just lost again to say: 'Well, that's football. Some games you lose. Some you draw'; for England fans massed in Trafalgar Square to greet their team's failure against Brazil with the song 'We're shit and we know we are'. Club fanzines wallow in their dogged, wry irony and exult in their melancholy titles: *When Skies Are Grey* (Everton), *Those Were the Days* (Ipswich), *A Load of Bull* (Wolves), *Fortune's Always Hiding* (West Ham), *Tired and Weary* (Birmingham City). English fans' favourite adjective about themselves is 'long-suffering'. Humiliation, defeat and degradation aren't seen as perils in English football; they are essential, intrinsic elements of the pleasure taken in the game.

As comedy writer Andrew Nickolds, creator of the bitter and mediocre cricketer Dave 'Pod' Podmore, observes: 'As Englishmen, we like to lose because melancholy is the default

setting for an Englishman. Americans don't get this. Australians don't get it at all. I've been over there, busily self-
denigrating, and it just goes right over their heads. They call
us "whingeing poms" and completely miss all our lovely
negativity. Did you ever see *The Gambler*, the Karel Reisz
movie with James Caan? It's about the whole psychosis of the
gambler, which is that he *wants* to lose. There's something in
that. I back horses quite a lot and when you have two or
three winners in a day you feel "there's something wrong
about this". One doesn't like to acknowledge it, but there is
dissatisfaction there. I think that's how it is when we watch
football. That's why Graham Taylor was the ultimate England manager. It's why the English press has never really been
comfortable with Sven. He comes into our simple, straightforward game, and somehow it doesn't go according to plan
any more. I'm sure the press will try whatever they can to get
him out somehow. He just doesn't understand the way we
like to play and react to the game.'

As Bill Shankly neared retirement in the early seventies, a
much more authentic voice emerged to express this spirit.
Where Shanks offered uplifting triumph, the satirical magazine
*Private Eye* created a comic vision of ineptitude and squalid
delusion. And how we loved it! Neasden Football Club was
football's greatest, longest-running and probably most influential joke. For more than twenty-five years, the cliché-drenched,
scandal-racked world of 'ashen-faced' 'supremo' Ron Knee
(aged fifty-nine) and his fellow grotesques provided a pitiless
satire of English footballing inadequacy. Whatever went wrong
in the English game (and something always did), it was reflected
in the distorting mirror of competitions such as the North
Circular Relegation League, where Neasden always lost by
huge scores to teams like Gunnersbury Park British Legion
Under-70s and Ayatollah Academicals. Every fortnight, the

world of football would be 'rocked to its foundations' by events at Neasden where the cast of absurd characters was tiny but somehow included all the important stereotypes of the game: one-legged 'net-minder' Wally Foot; troubled prima donna Bert O'Relli (often in prison); own-goal hotshot 'Baldy' Pevsner; dodgy chairman (launderama magnate Brig. 'Buffy' Cohen); 'controversial' referee Sid Himmler; and the club's vicious hooligan crowd (Sid and Doris Bonkers).

Above all, the column mocked the clichés of sports journalism. Reporters such as Dud Fivers (Soccer's Mr Football) and E. I. Addio were lazy, incompetent, seedy, alcoholic purveyors of pure nonsense. Their delicious spoof bylines alone probably constitute a kind of social history of Britain. In the early years their names appeared with tags like 'Our Man in the Car Park Listening to the Results on the Radio'. Later, the tone darkened: 'Our Man in the Director's Box with the Black Coffee and the Alka Seltzer', 'Our Man in the Gents' Toilet with the Pale Face and Trembling Hands', 'Our Man in the Casualty Ward with the Enlarged Liver and the Fractured Elbow'. By the nineties, alcoholism had been replaced by a fantastical obsession with snack-food: 'Our Man in the All-Seater Stadium with the Spaghetti-Carbonara-Flavoured Crisps', 'Our Man in the Press Gallery with a Can of High-Cal Coke and a Colonel Sanders' Combination Special of Peppermint-Flavoured Nachos and Extra Onion Rings', 'Our Man on the Terraces with the Neasden Fried Chicken Special (Includes Nuggets, Diet Shake, Onions 'N' Fries) and a Paperback Copy of *Fever Pitch*'.

Where Shankly's humour sprang from his own irrepressible dynamism, Neasden reflected wider disillusion and burgeoning self-loathing. After England's 3–1 home defeat by West Germany in 1972, Alf Ramsey was satirised as a defiant Knee, saying: 'Don't write us off yet by any means. My message to the knockers is this: get stuffed! We are still a great club as our past history shows.' It may have been his 181st defeat in a row, but Knee insisted: 'We are just going through a bad patch. It happens to all teams about this time in the season.' A year later, when Poland stopped England reaching the World Cup and the England players stuck up for Ramsey, the story was reworked as Neasden stars backing their boss: 'He has at all times commanded our total respect and was in no way to blame for the shock 15–0 defeat on Saturday against the Polish league-losers Warsaw Wanderers who in our opinion dis-played midfield mastery and this unsettled our back four and brought about a goal riot which Wally was totally powerless to prevent.'

We'll meet its creator, Barry Fantoni, presently, but before we do, it's worth looking at Neasden in a wider context. Neasden FC coloured modern English football humour from the fanzines to TV shows such as *They Think It's All Over*. Without Ron Knee, how could there have been a Ron Manager on *The Fast Show*? But Neasden also had its pre-decessors and it derived in part from the peculiarly English post-war phenomenon of intellectually superior, mocking self-laceration.

Before the Second World War, the idea of Britain or the British establishment as inherently laughable simply didn't exist. Neal Ascherson observes: 'In the First World War [working-class soldiers] didn't laugh at their young officers very much, alien, weird and ridiculous as they often were. But by the Second World War they *were* laughing at the funny accents and the funny attitudes, particularly at the command-ing sort of voice which would be used to say something particularly untrue and preposterous, which was what the Goons were so good at. It was the same with John Cleese and funny walks. Who are the people with funny walks? They're people *in authority* with funny walks. They walk funny, and they're different. They are physically different. They talk a different language and think different thoughts. And the thoughts they think so differently are . . . *ridiculous*! And not only ridiculous but, if you let them get away with it, dangerous. They will destroy us all.'

The first eruption of this new spirit in comedy came in the early fifties with the wild and surreal *Goon Show*, written by Spike Milligan, which changed the way the English laughed. John Cleese reckoned that Milligan's genius underpinned the wider cultural revolution which transformed Britain in the 1950s and 1960s. 'It was a time when people were getting fed up with the stuffiness of England and asking: surely this can't be what life is all about? Writers like John Osborne and John Braine dealt with it through fury . . . the Goons challenged the stuffiness with joy. They created a sense of liberation which went beyond laughter, evoking a strange, insane energy from people who suddenly found themselves breaking through the glass ceiling of respectability that had haunted them all their lives. In the 1950s, all the other performers were doing perfectly standard, sometimes quite decent, comedy, full of doors opening and people coming in with catchphrases. Spike threw all that out . . . We all loved *The Goon Show* in the Monty Python team: it ignited some energy in us. It was more a spirit that was passed on, rather than any particular technique. The point is that once somebody has crossed a barrier and done something that has never been done before, it is terribly easy for everybody else to cross it.'

Milligan was also the first to fuse an absurdist, declinist view of the British establishment with an absurdist, declinist view of British football. This once-radical idea would be nurtured by the satirists of the early sixties and would reach a baroque maturity in the pages of *Private Eye*. Later, it would become a comedy commonplace from 'alternative comedy' to sitcoms, fanzines and news quizzes.

*The Goon Show* took the form of weekly adventure stories which, among other things, served as fantastical repudiations of the boys' yarns Milligan had grown up with in imperial India. The stories simultaneously mocked the old values and gave them a new lease of life in comedy form. Others would follow Milligan's ambivalent model, and football would usually be somewhere in the mix. A first glimpse of what would become standard modern English footy humour came in *The Goon Show*'s 'The Whistling Spy Enigma', broadcast in October 1954, four months after England lost 7–1 to Hungary in Budapest. 'Throughout the civilised world, and America, British prestige has fallen very low,' says the sinister Hercules Grytpype-Thinne, played by Peter Sellers. 'One thing killed Britain, and that was our defeat by the Hungarian football team.' To help restore the nation's pride, Grytpype devises 'Operation Explodable Boot' and sends Neddie Seagoon to Budapest to put dynamite in the toecaps of the Hungarian players' football boots. Everything goes according to plan until the day of the match:

BBC COMMENTATOR: And the teams are just coming on to the field now, Hungary versus England . . .
SEAGOON: Ha-ha! This is the end of the Hungarians, lads!
COMMENTATOR: . . . The match was nearly called off because the British team forgot their football boots, but the Hungarians sportingly gave them theirs.
SEAGOON: No, no! Stop the match! Stop! No!

Two years later another *Goon Show*, 'The Nasty Affair at the Burami Oasis', broadcast on the eve of the Suez Crisis, had a

British desert garrison under constant night-time attack from Arab warriors loyal to 'Sheikh Rattle and Roll' who hope to tire the British sufficiently to beat them in a football match. To save the day, Britain's high command sends a gunboat to the desert – dismantled and disguised in six-inch packets marked 'date fertiliser, this end up'. Milligan's detestation of British imperialism and militarism was instinctive, fuzzy and derived from his traumatic war experiences and his childhood as the son of a servant of Empire in the 1930s. Milligan, Sellers and Harry Secombe were working-class lads who had met in the army; their comedy successors were younger, Oxbridge-educated who brought a sharper, more political focus.

Big claims have been made for the satire boom which began in 1960 with *Beyond the Fringe*. The Peter Cook, Dudley Moore, Alan Bennett and Jonathan Miller show is remembered for being subversive and dazzlingly original. Its witty assault on previously sacrosanct authority figures such as politicians, vicars and the royal family inspired the TV show *That Was The Week That Was* and led to the creation of Cook's short-lived comedy club The Establishment and *Private Eye*. Historian Stuart Ward argues that satire was 'overwhelmingly preoccupied with Britain's dwindling role in the post-war world'. Mocking declinism was at the core of the new comedy from the beginning; it held old values such as sacrifice and devotion to nation to ridicule. One particular target of *Beyond the Fringe* was Prime Minister Harold Macmillan.

Of the Fringe four, only Cook, son of a colonial adminis-trator, had any interest in football. In one sketch he played a Whitehall mandarin ludicrously turning to the recent memory of Roger Bannister's four-minute mile to suggest Britain could cope with Armageddon: 'Now we shall receive four minutes' warning of any impending nuclear attack. Some people have said "Oh my goodness me – four minutes? That is not a very long time!" Well, I would remind those doubters that some people in this great country of ours can run a mile in four minutes.'

Most famously, he played an RAF officer invoking the spirit of soccer to send pilot Jonathan Miller on a pointless suicide mission:

> COOK: War is a psychological thing, Perkins, rather like a game
>     of football. You know how in a game of football ten men
>     often play better than eleven?
> MILLER: Yes, sir.
> COOK: Perkins, we are asking you to be that one man. I
>     want you to lay down your life, Perkins. We need a futile
>     gesture at this stage. It will raise the whole tone of the war.
>     Get up in a crate, Perkins, pop over to Bremen, take a shufti,
>     don't come back. Goodbye, Perkins. God, I wish I was going
>     too.

Satire is said to have destroyed old habits of deference and paved the way for the sixties. But Stuart Ward, who explored the subject for his book about post-imperial Britain, views the satire movement more as a symptom of après-Empire anguish. 'If *The Goon Show* was so "liberating" and "subversive", how come Spike Milligan's number one fan was Prince Charles? If this was social revolution, then why did it not have any discernible social consequences?' Ward's research involved spending weeks in the basement of the British Film Institute watching old shows. 'The archivist said to me: "First couple of days when you're in there you were giggling away and having such a marvellous time. But by the end of the first week I could tell you weren't laughing as much." At first I couldn't get beyond "God, these guys were funny." But it really started to wear on me. I started to think: "there's a complacency about this, a self-congratulatory tone. It's very cliquey, and they're saying: "We have the right way of thinking." It gradually started to dawn on me: *this* is the establishment. If you look at the backgrounds of these people, most of them are members of the establishment in one way or another. They're a very molly-coddled generation. So what's their problem? Deep-seated, deeply rooted bits of the national self have been shaken to their very foundations and now these guys were *disappointed*! When they ridicule Macmillan, they're not ridiculing what he represented, but rather his failure to live up to what he represented. They're saying he ought to have been able to project a more commanding vision of Britain's role in the world.'

The heady days of early sixties satire ended in late 1963 when the BBC took *TW3* off air, but *Private Eye* survived and, in its pages, the comedy of national self-mockery slowly began to turn to football as a symbol of Britain's ills. Initially, sport rarely came up and the 1966 World Cup was barely mentioned, but the first stirrings of violence on the terraces offered the magazine a worthy target. On the eve of the 1968 Olympics, the *Eye* celebrated a new area of British excellence: 'Having watched our lads in action at the specially built bullet-proof stadium on the Essex marshes, I say this. Britain's soccer hooligans are in a class of their own.' A year later, 1966 had become a symbol of lost British greatness. When decimalisation arrived:

They used to say that John Bull could see anything through . . . Remember Dunkirk, the Blitz . . . In those days, when we had our backs to the wall, we could take it on the chin. But . . . you would have to go back to the days of the Black Death to find a similar tale of woe and misery on every side, such as we have

seen in recent days . . . Wake up the entire nation! The spirit
that won the World Cup is not dead yet.

By the time West Germany beat England in Mexico in 1970,
the spirit of Ron Knee was beginning to move upon the waters
of the *Eye*:

> Whatever the scores may say – Britain's 12–0 defeat by plucky
> little San Marino admittedly looks on paper like a defeat – there
> is no doubt at all which was the best team in this Mexico
> marathon. This morning the world's press gave their verdict –
> and Sir Alf and his men must thrill with pride at what the battle-
> hardened newsmen are saying about them in every continent
> . . . Yes, make no mistake about it – the verdict of the world is
> 'Hats off to Alf Ramsay and his lads – you may have lost but
> you're still the champs.'

The *Eye*'s writers, mostly public-school men, were generally
uninterested in football. Editor Richard Ingrams, a former
Shrewsbury boy, had gone into the army expecting swift
promotion and been asked: 'What do you play?' When he
answered 'The cello', his career as an officer was over before
it began. Now one of the few working-class men on the
staff, Barry Fantoni, a decent amateur footballer who
once scored twelve goals in a single match against a pub team
in the Croydon League, persuaded Ingrams football was
simply too important a subject to ignore. The resulting
creation – FC Neasden – would bring to perfection the
comedy idea from which the English have since derived
much pleasure: our players, managers and administrators are
stupid, graceless, deluded and doomed to fail. As the club song
goes:

> I belong to Neasden
> Good old Neasden Town
> There's nothing the matter with Neasden
> Except she's going down and down.

Fantoni recalls that Neasden was founded on theatrical principles. 'Football is show business. It's a form of theatre and it represents real drama, except, unlike a play, the characters are themselves. "Becks" is Becks playing himself playing football. He's not invented – only he's invented himself *totally*. At Millwall, Harry Cripps would put his "Harry Cripps" mask on each week and go out to play as the person people wanted him to be. I thought: as a dramatist, can I invent a whole team of characters who are ludicrous in the extreme? Can I use all the clichés like "finding the back of the net", "wizard of the wing", and all that bollocks? Neasden somehow encapsulated all that: the game as it is presented, and all the people who present it. In theatre, names are everything. *Othello* wouldn't work if he was Riccardo.' 'Baldy' Pevsner got his name from architecture guru Nikolaus Pevsner, who Fantoni and Ingrams both 'just disliked for some reason'. Bert O'Relli, named after an Italian restaurant, was loosely based on Peter Marinello, the reputed 'new George Best' whom Arsenal signed for a huge fee in 1970, kept mostly in the reserves, and then sold to Portsmouth three years later. Neasden FC itself was based on the club Fantoni had supported since his East End childhood: 'Neasden was just my melancholic view of being a Millwall supporter. Millwall are the only team in London never to have played in the First Division. Ever! We lose everything. We're no good. 0–0 draw at best. It was always a crap, shit team. Still is.' (This was a few months before Millwall reached the FA Cup Final for the first time.)

Neasden also reflected Fantoni's belief that 'footballers are thick cunts, all of them', and that few journalists understand the game. 'Middle-class journalists have a very different view of football from that held by those who play it and by the vast majority of those who watch it. And working-class journalists who write for the red tops are essentially secondary-school boys who managed to learn to write but not necessarily how to think. As a journalist, all you can really say is: he scored, and then he scored . . . he passed the ball, then he passed the ball . . .' The professional player and all the things that surround him – his team, his manager and his aspirations – are very seldom understood by anybody outside the game.

'Football is better to watch or play than read about, but I do find the aftermatch commentaries very entertaining,' Fantoni says. 'What interests me about all those people is the *unbelievable* tedium of what they're saying! The predictability of it all! The "experts" are all monstrously self-created, and they know they're talking bollocks, because the truth is that it's *mayhem* backstage.' Thanks to his friendship with Millwall chairman Reg Burr, Fantoni had plenty of access behind the scenes. 'It was very different from what I imagined. I couldn't believe the laziness or the lack of concern of the footballers for the job that they had. For training, they turned up at ten o'clock, eating toast, half pissed. Did a bit of bodywork. Kicked a ball about. Shouted a lot. And went home at twelve. They couldn't have run a marathon to save their lives; they couldn't even run ninety minutes to save their lives. They were poorly educated. Most weren't much more interesting to talk to than the average postman. They had access to lots of sex and booze, and a bit more money than the average postman, but very few of them could see further than their nose. Eamon Dunphy, who was there, was an exception. He wrote a very entertaining book about it. Harry Cripps was an exception. But the rest just didn't care. We even had a manager who was off shagging some bird on match days. He wouldn't be at the game. He'd say "I've got to go and look at this winger" and go off to see his bird!'

The violence surrounding FC Neasden was also based on Millwall: 'We invented soccer hooliganism. If you want any kind of record for bad behaviour, worst football, anything, Millwall will be near it. The first person murdered on a football field was in Uruguay in the 1930s when a man ran on and shot the referee. The referee had given a decision against his team and, quite rightly, the man blamed the referee. No point blaming the other team. If something goes wrong, blame the referee. Now in England, no one has ever done anything like that, except at Millwall. I think he's out of prison now, but we had "Mad Harry". A decision went against us, so Mad Harry tore a piece of guttering from the North End stand, ran on to the pitch and hit the referee with it. We had to play behind closed doors for four weeks after that.' When Millwall fans set fire to an opposition team coach, the police tried to reduce the violence by banning away fans. With no rival fans to beat up every week, the Millwall supporters attacked each other. 'It was sort of like binary fission. They like fighting, so the East and North stands just started fighting. They even had two fan magazines: *The Lion Roars* and *No One Likes Us*. It's kind of unique.'

For all its comic distortion, Fantoni insists, Neasden remains an accurate portrait of the English game. For such a warm and engaging man, he takes a spectacularly bleak view of the nation. 'As an Italian living in Britain, what I notice most is that almost everyone here thinks their team will win. In my country, we all think our team will lose. We have no confidence, though history has shown Italy is one of the three best. We know our failings. All Englishmen think they are the best, but there is no evidence to support it, so life is a constant disappointment to them. In cricket, the Australians and Indians are better. In football everybody is better. Everybody! Because England have won fuck all. They didn't even win the World Cup. They got *given* the World Cup by a shit linesman and the fact they were hosts. Everywhere else they've lost. Semi-finals is the nearest they get. So, what good are they? For a country of 52 million people? Can you give me one example where England is better than everybody else? Hopefully, you'd stutter Shakespeare, and maybe Turner. And then I'd tell you that Shakespeare copied it all off the commedia dell'arte, and Turner would have been no one without Claude Lorrain. Now where're you going? Stanley Spencer? Nat Lofthouse? Really? What have you fucking got? Nothing! Nothing! It's a shit-arse fucking dump! That's what it is. Nothing! Some Scots inventors. Some Scots physicists. I'll stick Newton in, just to be generous. And some thinkers. And some good scientists, who were ignored. Sportsmen? Tennis players?' (He laughs.) 'Even the great footballers are all Scottish and Welsh.' I protest: surely this is melancholic declinism to the point of absurdity. Isn't Neasden just too miserable? After all, foreigners rather admire the Premiership; they like our traditions. Men like Wenger, Houllier and Ranieri speak fondly about England and its football. 'Well, they speak fondly about everything. They are very diplomatic people. But I think Neasden is spot on. About the national team too. What can you say about the England team? Every pratfall in the business, it does it.'

The gulf between delusions of grandeur and pitiful reality is at the core of most post-war British comedy. It's the basic joke underpinning sitcoms from *Hancock's Half Hour* to *The Office*. Basil Fawlty, Captain Mainwaring, Patsy and Edina and Alan Partridge suffer from the syndrome. While Neasden was working its way towards a kind of comic perfection, *Monty Python* fused the wild imagination of *The Goon Show* with satire and introduced a surreal intellectual edge. Python's football jokes turned on the notion of thick, brutal footballers getting mixed up with the world of ideas. The typical Python footballer was 'midfield cognoscente' Jimmy Buzzard. When a pretentious interviewer compliments him on his 'almost Proustian display of modern existentialist football', all Jimmy can do is blankly repeat stock phrases like: 'I hit the ball first time and there it was in the back of the net.' In the 'Billy Bremner version' of *The Importance of Being Earnest*, Chopper Harris fouls Algernon from behind, and attacks Lady Bracknell with a series of short left jabs to the head. 'The Philosophy Football Match', narrated by a BBC-style commentator, pits 'Chopper' Sophocles against 'Nobby' Hegel. In the 'Communist Quiz Show' sketch, Karl Marx and Che Guevara know all about dialectical materialism but trip over a question about Coventry City and the FA Cup.

The only Python who really liked football was Michael Palin. The best of his 'Ripping Yarns' was 'Golden Gordon', about a Neasdenesque Yorkshire team called Barnstoneworth United. Every week, Gordon Ottershaw, the club's biggest (and only) fan, smashes up his front room in disgust at the latest defeat, but when the directors try to sell the club and its players to a scrap dealer, he persuades former centre-forward 'Baldy' Davitt to come out of retirement. By 1988, Neasdenesque and Pythonish themes were standard. Marcus Berkmann's radio series *Lenin of the Rovers* (produced by Peter Cook's future biographer Harry Thompson), starred Alexei Sayle (leading figure of 'alternative' comedy) as 'balding midfield maestro' Ricky Lenin, 'a superbly trained athlete, blessed with ball skills comparable only to the great Jeff Astle'. Lenin stages a coup at Felchester Rovers (geddit?), ousts Ray Royce (gedd that too?), and turns the club into Britain's only communist football team. The show featured Chopper Harris jokes, journalistic clichés

and Kenneth Wolstenholme as a football commentator called
Frank Lee Brian.

The last acclaimed TV performance of Peter Cook's alco-
holism-shortened life was as football manager Alan Latchley –
a Ron Knee made flesh – interviewed by Clive Anderson on
his chat show in 1995. 'Dare to Fail' was Latchley's motto; his
coaching was based on 'the three Ms: motivation, motivation,
motivation'. He also believed in 'equal playing facilities': 'If
you had skilful players on your team, that was no excuse for
them playing better than the others. 'Cause it makes the other
ones feel, you know – inferior . . . Some of them are worse
than the others, and my tactic was to get them all down to
exactly the same level.' Latchley's inspiring vision for English
football was: 'Let us work our way up from the bottom – and
stay there if we can.' By the year 2000 the assumption of
English footballing inadequacy and post-imperial impotence
were so firmly intertwined that no one thought it the least bit
odd when Blackadder (Rowan Atkinson) performed a sketch
(written by Ben Elton) for Prince Charles at the Royal Variety
Performance:

The sun, they say, never set on the British Empire. Now what
have we got? The Channel Islands . . . So what is to be done?
Well, the answer to my mind is very simple. If we are to re-
establish our position in the world, the army must return to its
traditional role, the very reason for which it existed in the first
place. We must invade France. Why France? Well, that's a very
good question. But I can think of three reasons. Firstly,
whenever we try to speak their language they sneer at us
and talk back to us in English. God, they are so irritating.
Secondly, they deliberately won the World Cup by maliciously
playing better football than us. And thirdly, simple political
strategy. Look at the history books, whenever Britain fought

the French we were top dog. For 500 years from Agincourt to the Battle of Waterloo, Britain went from strength to strength and gained the greatest Empire the world has ever known. The minute we start getting chummy with the garlic chewers, within three short decades we're buggered.

They say there are just seven stories in the entire world, so having two basic types of English football joke – melancholy Neasden variations and one Happy Shankly Heresy – probably constitutes healthy diversity. Meanwhile, humour published by and for football fans themselves emerged, drawing heavily on the idea that the game was 'going down and down'. The first fanzine was launched in 1972 by two Cambridge undergraduates, Steve Tongue and Alan Stewart. *Foul!* ('the alternative football magazine') was modelled on *Private Eye* and ran for four years before a threatened libel action closed it down. Like the *Eye*, *Foul!* was iconoclastic, satirical and obsessed with football journalism; like the *Eye*, it featured amusing bubble-captions on the cover (fanzines still do to this day). Where early sixties satire focused on 'What's wrong with Britain?' and blamed those in charge, *Foul!* bemoaned a decline in football standards and decided that the man who'd won England the World Cup was a menace. 'There is no longer any question of whether Sir Alf Ramsey should go, only of when,' the magazine wrote in late 1972. 'If England should suddenly "come good", the effect would be as disastrous for world football as our 1966 win, because it would once again assert Ramsey's values as the ideal . . . The whole underlying philosophy of Ramseyism must go when its founder does: the sooner the better.'

Named to avoid confusion with teenagers' magazines like *Shoot!* and *Goal!*, *Foul!* denounced the sports media with venom: Jimmy Hill was 'no more than a symptom of the diseased state of televised soccer'; Desmond Hackett 'has single-handed done more damage to British sports writing than anyone else'; Peter Batt of the *Sun* was 'The Biggest Mouth in Soccer'; Frank McGhee of the *Mirror*, 'living proof of the Fleet Street maxim that if they're old enough they're good enough'. Ironically, many of those connected with *Foul!* – Harry Harris, Chris Lightbown and Peter Ball – went on to successful media careers themselves.

*Foul!* is remembered for being daring and searingly funny, though leafing through old copies it's not always apparent why this should be so. Where *Private Eye* mocked the Prime Minister in 'Mrs Wilson's Diary', *Foul!* taunted the England manager with the clunking 'Lady Ramsey's Diary'. After Mick Channon (pronounced Shannon) starred in a 5–0 England thrashing of Scotland at Hampden in February 1973, the column had Mrs Ramsey writing:

> He's terribly worried about this Mr Shannon. 'You see, my dear,' he told me (it's amazing how different he sounds after those elocution lessons), 'we just can't afford to have individuals playing so well. It undermines the whole team effort. Besides, people will start expecting to score five goals in every game, and we can't have that.' 'But,' I said, sticking my neck out, 'I thought you were meant to score a lot of goals.' And I knew I shouldn't have because I always get one of those withering 'you stupid women don't understand football, it's a man's game' glances. 'That's what the Brazilians thought,' said Alf, 'and look what happened to them: we nearly beat them in Mexico.'

'Oh God! It's awful, isn't it?' recoils Andrew Nickolds, who worked on the magazine. 'I don't remember who wrote that, but Alan Stewart did like to dip his quill . . . Poor lad, he got killed by a landmine. I did a piece for *Foul!* that still causes me to shiver every so often. It was about the press and I think now: "Who *was* that self-righteous little prick?" What can I say? We were young and cheeky. There was some very funny stuff in *Foul!*, though. My favourite was a parody of Brian Glanville's kids' book *Goalkeepers Are Different* called "When the Press Box Roared" about a lad getting his first job in the press box and being taken under the wing of a paedophile.'

Mordant laughs were an equally essential ingredient when two friends from a Soho record shop, Mike Ticher and Andy Lyons, launched *When Saturday Comes* (*WSC*) in 1986. The self-styled 'half-decent football magazine' helped to inspire a wave of fanzines, most of which continue. Pessimism was an essential ingredient from the start. Under the headline 'England Expects', the 'European Championship Special' in 1988 featured a picture of the *Titanic* sinking and former players Ray Wilkins and Norman Hunter covering their faces in shame. In its early days *WSC* looked a good deal like *Foul!*, which had in turn looked a lot like *Private Eye*. Where *Foul!* had 'Foul of the Month', *WSC* mock-gloried in 'Great Own-Goals of Our Time'. Ticher, now in Australia, was a *Foul!* fan and later edited a collection of its highlights, but says music fanzines were more important early influences. Lyons, who still edits *WSC* and does most of its jokes, also acknowledges a debt to *Private Eye* but says the magazine's humour was shaped more by the 'wry' style of the *New Musical Express* and *Melody Maker*.

*WSC* mellowed after some 'quite angry, fairly ranty stuff', says Lyons. Over the years the magazine has nurtured some fine and original writing but never lost its miserablist edge. 'The idea of things being a bit dismal and denigrated is a fundamental part of British life which goes back to the end of Empire and people not knowing what Britain's place in the world is,' says Lyons. 'We are good at doing dingy. The country remains relentlessly third-rate in certain ways. I suppose, up until the 1960s, and buoyed up by 1966, there was a belief that football was still one of the things we could do properly. And then disillusion set in. If there were any last vestiges of optimism, they were pretty much wiped away by 1973. I often think of 1966 as being a bit like the Crucifixion: the further we get away from it, the more mystical it becomes, the more incredible it seems that we ever produced a team capable of winning the World Cup.' But what about the star-studded Premiership, the passionate crowds and exciting games? 'Why does Sky say the Premiership is the best league in the world? That's just PR bullshit. It's not a thing you can quantify. It's just a marketing slogan.' The magazine's attitude to the England team is ambivalent. 'Scepticism generally is part of our thing. We aren't ever going to say: "Come on, England." We don't refer to England as "we". There are plenty of other places where you can read unquestioning clenched-fist patriotic stuff. I'm pleased when England do well if they play well. But there are so many negative associations. It's not just the hooliganism but the jingoism that's brought out when the national team plays. At England home games there's been an effort to get more people in wearing face paint and behave in the way fans are supposed to behave according to Sky television. But I can't imagine why anyone would want to be at an away game stuck in a ground with a load of England fans. It's a bit like being a psychiatric social worker. I know some people are prepared to do it but I wouldn't.'

The notion that English football is 'a bit crap' has hardened into comedy orthodoxy, but TV impressionist Alistair McGowan is far from impressed. He observes: 'Miles Kington wrote a very good piece a few years ago about how certain jokes become jokes and survive even though they're not funny or true any more. His example was the "stale British Rail sandwich". A very long time ago, British Rail did make sandwiches, and they were awful. But British Rail no longer exists. It no longer makes sandwiches. The sandwiches you can buy on a train are made by Upper Crust. And they're very good. So the joke doesn't work on any level. Yet you still hear boring old stuff about things being "as stale as a British Rail sandwich". It's the same with British tennis. On *They Think It's All Over* the idea that British tennis is rubbish always gets a laugh and Tim Henman is still the butt of jokes. Actually, Tim Henman has surpassed the achievements of most tennis players in history. He hasn't won Wimbledon but he has reached – whatever it is – four Wimbledon semi-finals and four quarter-finals in nine years. That's better than almost anyone in history except Borg and Sampras. Even John McEnroe was never so consistent. Henman's been in the world top ten for seven years, which is an immense achievement and a better record than Philippousis or Hewitt. Yet you still hear the same tired old jokes.'

In the early nineties *Spitting Image* sent McGowan to a pub in Soho with a camera crew and a life-sized puppet of Graham Taylor. The idea was to tap popular feeling against the England manager for some laughs, but the experience convinced McGowan that vicious satire was not a style of comedy he wanted to do. 'As an impressionist you tend to embrace sports people more than you want to make fun of them. But this was one time I noticed it could be quite powerfully negative. The hatred that came out was incredible. At one point, this fellow turned to me – or rather he turned to the Graham Taylor puppet I was standing behind – and he was very aggressive and he said: "I don't know how you got the *nerve* to pick an England team! You dunno *what* you're doing! You're a *joke*! An *absolute joke!*" All I could think of to say was: "Well, you're the one who's talking to a puppet, young man." But really we'd paved the way for that sort of vitriol by going in there like that. *Spitting Image* was much more that kind of programme than my show is, or Rory Bremner's ever has been. It was cruel.'

Cruelty isn't McGowan's thing, and he deplores it in others. David Baddiel and Frank Skinner's persecution of Nottingham Forest striker Jason Lee, for instance, was 'inexcusable'. Instead, McGowan draws more from the *Two Ronnies*/Harry Enfield school of sharp observation and fantasy. He mocks accents, linguistic idiosyncrasies and personal foibles, but rarely deploys malice. With his partner, Ronni Ancona, he was also responsible for the best long-running Sven-Goran Eriksson gag: Sven knows nothing about football and it's his ambitious, domineering girlfriend, Nancy dell Olio, using him as a front, who runs the England team. This constitutes a significant variation on Neasdenism. The joke isn't that Sven is a rotten manager; it's that his impression of competence is a brilliant deception. 'The minute I saw Sven I thought: "You don't look like a football manager," ' says McGowan. 'When England trained, you'd see him in the background, hands behind his back just sort of wandering around. He looked like an accountant. I kept thinking: "OK. You're an accountant. You're not a football manager. What's going on?" Then Nancy suddenly came to the fore, and we thought: "Oh yes, let's do that! Where *she's* the one in charge!" ' In one show, when Nancy is kidnapped, Sven has to select an England squad without her and, because he hasn't a clue, picks Joely Richardson and the Bishop of Durham.

On the other hand, the English habit of self-mockery does have something going for it. McGowan says: 'We do like to moan. In February you hear the weather forecasters saying: "Tsk . . . tsk . . . it's really terrible weather . . . it's going to rain . . . oh dear, it's very cold." Well, of course it's cold! It's February! The great thing about football is that you can moan like mad, and we take comfort from that. We crack a joke about ourselves to bring ourselves out of something. I think that's probably uniquely British.' He backs this claim by citing the reaction of a Belgian girlfriend to Matt Lucas's show *Little Britain*. 'She couldn't get over the fact that there was a programme on television which made so much fun of our own country. I said: "Don't you have that in Belgium?" They don't. She's lived in lots of countries and travelled all over the world. She said: "No one else in the world makes fun of themselves the way you do." I said: "Well, we're allowed to run our country down if we want to." It's like I can make jokes about my family. *You*'re not allowed to, but *I* can say what I like.'

Conversely, McGowan was in Belgium when the country was knocked out of the 1998 World Cup, and he was shocked by the TV commentator's reaction to defeat. 'He was just incredibly angry: "*C'est un désastre!*" . . . It was a disgrace . . . It was an insult . . . It dishonoured the memory of the great team of Ceulemans . . . everything you can think of. An English TV commentator would never do that. The tabloids might do it the next day and, in the studio, one of the panellists might. But the commentator would say: "[John Motson voice:] England are out. They expected to go further, but they haven't. It's a great shame . . . Look at Sven's face . . . Ooh, he's upset . . . Back to you in the studio." Then the general policy at the BBC would be to lift people. Lineker would probably be told: "If England lose, after the game you've got to say: 'Well, England are out – but Scotland are still there' or 'We've gone out, but the boys have played well . . . We'll see you tomorrow.'"'

McGowan's comedy was an important part of the BBC's coverage of the last World Cup. Just before England played Brazil, he received a phone call telling him that executives had decided to put one of his shows on immediately after the match. 'They told me: "If the game's gone well, people can enjoy the show, and if it goes badly, it will cheer them up." I thought: God . . . it's going to be *my* responsibility, even on tape, to cheer the *nation* after the Brazil game. I watched the match and, afterwards, I just switched the television off. I couldn't believe we'd capitulated like that. But ever since, I've had so many people tell me: "It was a stroke of genius to put your show out after the Brazil game. It cheered me up no end." Or "We kept the TV on after the game, and suddenly we were laughing." I wasn't making jokes about the game we'd just lost. It was about football in general. But it was about football. And people were happy to laugh straight after the game, about the game. I wonder how many countries would have thought to put that on. For a long time we've used humour to buttress disappointment. That's what the fanzines do; you take crumbs of comfort. You laugh at your situation. But sometimes it's beyond laughter.'

No one mined this seam of humour more effectively than Nick Hornby. His book *Fever Pitch* was a fresh, touching, self-deprecating and very funny account of his life as an obsessive, depressive Arsenal fan. The book's most striking – and most fervently copied – premise was that a fan's devotion to a team is essentially masochistic. 'The natural state of the football fan is bitter disappointment, no matter what the score,' he declared. Or: 'I go to football for loads of reasons, but I don't go for entertainment, and when I look around me on a Saturday and see those panicky, glum faces, I see that others feel the same.' As a child of divorced parents in the late sixties, Hornby was drawn to a club where the relationship between team and fans seemed to resemble a hideous marriage: 'one partner was lumbering around in a pathetic attempt to please, while the other turned his face to the wall, too full of loathing even to watch'. Hornby was even strangely relieved when, in the early 1990s, Arsenal suddenly declined after having briefly threatened to become the country's dominant team. 'Highbury became a place for discontented players and unhappy fans once more, and the future began to look so dismal that it was impossible to remember why we thought it looked bright in the first place. I began to feel comfortable again.'

Actually, the book's miserablism was leavened by a yearning for beauty, grace and success: Liam Brady was adored for his intelligence and subtle skills; an unexpected cup win over Spurs lifted years of depression; George Graham, who turned Arsenal into a winning team, was embraced as a father figure. And the stupendous drama of Michael Thomas's last-minute championship-grabbing goal in 1989 is simply 'the greatest moment ever' (better than sex). The scene even provided a happy ending for the film of the book with Colin Firth. (Oddly, a downbeat ending is planned for a new American film version, about a fan devoted to the supposedly cursed Boston Red Sox, but Hornby is only distantly involved with the project.)

*Fever Pitch* remains a delicious book. It helped make Hornby a literary superstar, persuaded publishers there was a huge market for football books and was part of a shift in the wider culture of the game. But Hornby also became a target for sneers. One journalist bizarrely accused him of 'launching a million prawn sandwich-eating locusts on the game'. Hornby remembers: 'First of all it was about being a yob. Then it was about middle-class people "slumming it". Then I was somehow responsible for the Premier League. But in America, people accept baseball for what baseball is. A smart person like Roger Angell in the *New Yorker* can write his stuff about baseball and use any words he wants, and no one thinks it peculiar. I think it's partly because the glory of American culture is popular culture, whereas here, anyone who takes an interest in popular culture has to watch out. It's assumed there must be some pose involved.'

In truth, the only bad thing that can really be said about *Fever Pitch* is that its slew of imitators weren't as good as the original. Even now the fanzines strain to achieve a Hornbyesque air. The man himself, though, has emphatically moved on: 'I never look at that stuff. I'm sick of it. It was a very thin vein that I tapped into. Between us, *When Saturday Comes* and me took all there was out of it. It's just one joke: "it's cold and we're rubbish". There's only so many times you want to read that joke.' Nor has he been tempted to write again about the game he still loves: 'I just thought I'd said everything in the one book and I didn't know where I could take it after that without repeating myself. I've had a couple of recent offers from France to write about Arsène [Wenger] and Thierry [Henry] and there does seem to be a fair bit to say about them. But that's about something else: excellence, intelligence, winning.'

In *Fever Pitch* the quintessential Arsenal experience was 'a nil-nil draw, against a nothing team, in a meaningless game, in front of a restive, occasionally angry but for the most part wearily tolerant crowd . . .' At that time Hornby couldn't even *begin* to imagine what it might be like to support a really good team. Then Dennis Bergkamp and Arsène Wenger arrived, and Arsenal became beautiful, exciting and widely loved. They've won two Doubles and an FA Cup, and, a few days before we meet, they wrapped up the championship again, this time without losing a single match. I suggest to Hornby that he must be feeling pretty awful about this turn of events. The eyes of the high priest of wry melancholy light up. His whole face lights up. 'It's *fantastic*! At Highbury the whole thing has changed, obviously, in all sorts of ways. One of the ways is that people are shocked to think about what they used to tolerate. We know we'll never ever see anything as good as this again (and by that I mean probably what the next few years hold as well). But even when Wenger leaves, Arsenal aren't going to appoint Micky Adams as the next manager. Or Martin O'Neill, come to that. People have become used to watching something good, and that is a very important shift in the mind of a football fan.'

Hornby recalls that for the first three or four years after his book came out, the team was still a 'pretty perfect' reflection of its tone. 'Really, Arsenal were terrible. It was as bad as it has ever been, I think, just before George [Graham] got sacked. The one triumph was the 1994 Cup Winners' Cup in Co-penhagen, and it was hilarious. I think Kevin Campbell was in midfield with Ian Selley and Ray Parlour, who was still drinking at the time. And we were playing Parma who had Brolin, Asprilla and Zola. Arsenal had one shot – the Alan Smith goal – and then it was the Alamo for the rest of the game. You couldn't help but appreciate it as comedy. It was comedy that *this* team beat *that* team. It was a fantastic night, just hilarious and joyful, but joyful despite really what had taken place on the pitch.' A year later, tedious, mediocre Arsenal lost the cup in Paris and the team looked decrepit. 'To think that three years later we'd be winning a Double with an amazing team, with Overmars, Anelka, Bergkamp, Vieira, Petit . . .' His voice trails off, still lost in the wonder of it. 'And that was it. All that old humour finished then. All those jokes. And it will never come back. Not at Arsenal. I can't see it.'

Isn't there just a tiny part of him that misses the old misery? 'Oh God, no! Absolutely not. When Dennis arrived, he exposed something about England. It's as if you're watching a film with special effects where everything is very small, and it's fine as long as they keep the cameraman out of the picture . . . but then: "Oh, they're only an inch tall." The players, as far as we can tell, were drunk all the time, and the only reason they went training was to sweat everything out. And you saw what happened over the next couple of years: the only players who survived were the ones who shaped up, as opposed to shipping out. What happened with Ray Parlour was incredible. He got serious. He stopped drinking. So did Tony Adams and the defence. There's still a lot of affection for Parlour for that. People sort of hang on to him as a symbol of the lost old ways. I went to the pub on Sunday night in Holloway Road and they were singing a song about Victoria Beckham. I can't remember the first line but at the end it's: ". . . she wears a Wonderbra / And when she's shagging Beckham / She thinks of Ray Parlaaaahh." His Englishness, his *slight* ineptitude, compared to the others, is cherished, I think, in disorienting times.'

On a recent edition of *They Think It's All Over*, Lee Hurst joked that London shouldn't host the Olympics 'because we're crap and we don't want the rest of the world to know'. But London isn't crap, and Wenger's new Arsenal is the perfect marriage between stylish foreign stars and the aggression and drive of the city. Hornby reflects on why the old jokes persist: 'It's a difficult thing to imagine in England: a humour of excellence. It's difficult anyway, generally. I think most comedy is based on being incompetent. But it is an extraordinary feature of English football that the lower divisions dominate all aspects of football. In the past, they dominated the game's decision-making processes. They still dominate the ethos of support. Most clubs out of the ninety-two are rubbish. If you support a team that is not rubbish, but plays well and wins, you feel that you are somehow missing out on the spirit of English football. You're outside the culture, or you certainly were outside the culture. You still hear that stuff about "Fancy Dan" foreigners too. That's not just xenophobia. I think it's a sort of protectiveness towards the poverty of what there was before. I'm sick of it.

'One doesn't want to end up like Jeffrey Archer who always says: "In America they celebrate success; they don't knock it." One is always hesitant to get drawn into that position. But I do think optimism and soul are very difficult English positions. Take food. When you go to an American game people buy hot dogs, and enjoy them. They're not very symbolic of anything except what you do when you go to a baseball game. Whereas here . . . I'm guessing that an English meat pie at a stadium is of similar quality to an American hot dog in terms of nutrition and taste. Yet the symbolism here is: that's another crap thing to do when you go to an awful football match, you eat a horrible pie. There can't be that big a gap in quality between the pie and the dog, but it does seem typical of an attitude that we take to football. The worse things are there, the better it will be for us, and the more fondly we remember it.'

It was two American writers, Anne Tyler and Lorrie Moore, who showed Hornby that it was possible to write simply, intelligently and with humour and soul. By contrast, he finds fashionable British cultural cynicism merely depressing. In his novel *How to Be Good* he listed cultural icons whom two characters, both hip Londoners, considered to be 'talentless, overrated or simply wankers'. The list goes on for nearly two pages and includes the likes of Shakespeare, Tony Blair, Dickens, John Lennon, Pelé, Maradona, all women tennis players, Homer (but not Homer Simpson), Coleridge, Keats and all the Romantic poets, and 'anyone they were at school or college with who is now making a name for themselves in the fields of journalism, broadcasting or the arts'. Hornby sees no sign of such attitudes disappearing. 'I think *Private Eye* has an awful lot to answer for, in that people are very scared of not being in on the joke. With *Private Eye* and *Have I Got News for You* the joke is that everyone is corrupt and everything's awful, so it's hard to talk seriously about Thatcher or Blair, or, in fact, any politician. It's unfashionable to think any of them might have any motivation other than cynicism, greed and corruption. The default "smart" position is: there's more to everything than meets the eye. I once got invited to a concert by Elvis Costello and afterwards there was a little bar backstage. It was a little bar and there were just a few people. And he said: "People always think there's another door where the proper party is going on. But there isn't. This is it."'

# A STRANGE FINISH
## A FINE FOOTBALL STORY

By some extraordinary means the Moore had suddenly overflowed her banks, and millions of gallons of water were pouring into the football field.

# COOLING THE BLOOD

The ball itself was a shapeless inert object that plumped listlessly from mud-patch to mud-patch and resisted all efforts to drive it any distance. When in the air, no one evinced the slightest desire to meet it with his head, and at times a shovel would have been a fit implement to dig the leather out of the mire. 'By gosh, I shall be danged glad when this is over,' muttered Ed Maddock as he dashed the rain out of his eyes and ballooned the ball a dozen yards with a mighty kick which, in the ordinary way, would have carried the leather three-parts of the length of the field. 'It's too much like hard work, more like booting a cannon ball around a ploughed field than playing soccer.'

The bedraggled players gave a hearty cheer as they squelched their way to the clubhouse where Ebenezer Squibbs had a plentiful supply of hot water, soap and dry towels waiting for them.

*Boys' Realm*

A small, soggy saga from the FA Cup reminds us how deeply English football has changed. It's not a question of globalisation, agents, media or foreign players; something much more fundamental in the game has shifted: the ground under its feet. In January and February 2004 the fourth-round tie between non-league Telford United and First Division Millwall was twice postponed because Telford's Bucks Head pitch was waterlogged. The Londoners claimed that the pitch was unplayable, and the referee agreed. True, after a week of heavy rain and the application of forty tons of sand, the playing surface did resemble a sticky toffee pudding garnished with a few blades of grass, but what was 'unplayable' about that? Not so long ago, most British football grounds, even at top clubs, were quagmires in winter. Telford's pitch was no worse than the famous bog on which Hereford thrillingly defeated Newcastle in 1972, or indeed pitches on which dozens of epic cup ties were played. When the game was eventually played on a dry pitch the higher division side won comfortably. But a match in the mire would have been truer to the history of the game than the pristine surfaces on which most ties are now played.

As life on earth first crawled from the primeval soup of the oceans, so the English game was born amid the clammy ooze of the English countryside in winter. For more than a hundred years English football revelled in its wintry wetness and adapted to suit the conditions. Traditionally, the game was played by sturdy men in ankle-high boots driving monstrously heavy leather balls over atrocious surfaces. At most grounds, drainage was agricultural and the assorted odd-job men and former players who served as groundsmen often made things worse. Heavy rollers pulverised grass. Frozen pitches were sometimes thawed with burning braziers or even salt.

Classic elements of the English style developed accordingly. Big, strong centre-forwards and centre-halves drilled to thump the ball rather than control it, sturdy wing-halves moving the ball on quickly and without fuss. Sliding tackles. Power preferred to finesse. Usually the only players on the team encouraged to be wizards were the wingers – and they played on the only firm part of the field. C. B. Fry, the Corinthian who played for Southampton in the 1902 Cup Final, enthused in his memoirs about 'great and gruelling' matches in appalling conditions. In one game against Aston Villa 'the ground was sodden; and there were pools of water in places . . . it was a heroic game'.

Mud was inseparable from fighting spirit. Historian Percy Young described a typical contest between Bolton Wanderers and Manchester City in 1960: 'Under scowling skies . . . the two teams played a fierce scherzo over the mud. Skill there was in plenty – if only in the way that twenty-two players contrived not merely to stand but also to move with speed and manipulate the ball; but skill engaged with vigour. The tackling was of a ferocity unknown in Barcelona, but regarded as axiomatic among other devotees at Burnden.' It was, said the *Guardian*'s W. R. Taylor, the sort of 'blood and thunder match that no one dared to leave early in case he missed the odd murder or sending off'. 'There was no point trying to play artistic football when the ground was muddy and the ball was heavy,' explains Bolton's full-back Roy Hartle. 'We didn't pull the ball down because if you stopped it, it was difficult to get it moving again.'

The renowned journalist Ken Jones remembers that mud even led to outstanding players being dropped. 'Little Tommy Harmer at Tottenham, for example: immensely skilful player, but when it got round to midwinter they wouldn't play him because they said he "couldn't cope" in the mud. There were quite a number of players like that. Because pitches were in such a bloody awful state we had to have the "sturdy" type of midfielder, who was often very skilful, people like Carter,

Mannion, Doherty and Bryn Jones. In awful conditions you could hardly play pattern-weaving football, so the English game became a longish ball game. You still find it now: look at England last week [against Turkey in Istanbul, 11 October 2003]: a lot of balls aimed wide and long and very little fluency in the play. But, Christ Almighty, you needed Wellington boots to play on some of the old pitches! Players today don't know they're bloody born! I just look at the pitches and I can't believe how good they are.'

The worst pitch in the country was probably Derby County's Baseball Ground, regularly inches deep in Passchendaele-style bog, where players like the huge Jackie Stamps, a centre-forward who resembled Desperate Dan's bigger brother, flourished. John Richards recalls scoring a goal there in about 1971. 'I came on with fifteen minutes to go. We were 1–0 down, but you couldn't run. You could barely move. You just stuck. The only style of play that could work was to hit the ball as far as you could in the direction of the opponents' goal, then try and contain it in that area. We had a corner, the ball was somehow hoofed into the area and Derby just couldn't clear it. One of our players headed it against the bar and it sort of looped down. I was about a yard from the goal line and just headed it. Any further out, it wouldn't have reached the goal because the ball was so heavy.'

Mud was also a potent and trusted weapon against foreigners. Prototypically, in 1934 a wet pitch helped England win the Battle of Highbury against Italy. Writing thirty years after the event, Italy's coach Vittorio Pozzo recalled with a shudder: 'Winners of the world championship, we now had to pass under the grim gallows of England.' It was an odd phrase, triggered perhaps by his memory of press reports about the last conversation of a young man executed on the morning of the match at Pentonville Prison, barely a mile from the stadium.

The last friendly face nineteen-year-old killer and Arsenal fan John Stockwell saw was that of his brother Horace. The brothers discussed football and weather and the doomed man made a perfectly accurate prediction: 'If it rains tomorrow afternoon, well, England will walk away with the match. My tip's England.' In 1954 Stan Cullis's Wolves beat Honved by watering the pitch until it resembled 'a cattle ground at the end of a four-day show in the rain'. The skilful Hungarians took a 2–0 lead but were soon exhausted. Wolves fought back and won 3–2 in a match hailed as a triumph for traditional English football ('English soccer, the genuine, original, unbeatable article, is still the best of its kind in the world,' said Desmond Hackett of the *Daily Express*). And at Elland Road in the seventies, Don Revic had the pitch watered when Leeds faced European opposition.

By the 1980s, though, such innate English wisdom was becoming obsolete and clubs began to see mud as a problem. One of the key arenas to change was Highbury. For decades the ground had been synonymous with midwinter mud, but in 1989 mud almost cost them the championship. As Nick Hornby relates in *Fever Pitch*, Arsenal won the title with almost the last kick of the season at Anfield. But it should never have been that close. The club's young groundsman, Steve Braddock, remembers: 'If you look at the video footage you see that towards the end of that season Arsenal were drawing and losing matches at home they normally would have won. Everyone was starting to say: "If they lose the championship it'll be down to the pitch." I was almost having a nervous breakdown about it.' In an interview after a particularly marshy home game against Sheffield Wednesday which Arsenal could only draw, winger Brian Marwood had menacingly joked: 'On Monday morning our groundsman is going to be picking up his P45.' The terrible pitch was hardly Braddock's fault. He had joined the club in 1987 and discovered drainage was almost impossible as undersoil heating pipes were just a few inches below the surface. 'I was only about twenty-two at the time. To go to a big club like Arsenal in your first season and say: "I want you to spend £150,000 to £200,000 on your playing surface" wouldn't have gone down very well. I did what I possibly could. But it got to the stage where we had to do something fairly major.'

In the summer of 1989 the club finally decided to invest in a complete reconstruction of the old pitch in line with new scientific principles of good groundsmanship. As a result, Highbury was transformed. Where the traditional, vigorous English style once reigned, Highbury now has an immaculate natural grass playing surface all year round and hosts one of the most elegant ball-playing teams England has ever seen. 'The secret is a good drainage system,' says Braddock. 'A good root system usually comes when you have good drainage, and that creates harder-wearing grass. If grass has good roots it will wear well.' At Arsenal's new training ground at London Colney, on Arsène Wenger's orders, muddy boots are even banned from the changing rooms.

Curiously, the first big stimulus to the scientific revolution which underlay this transformation came from the most un-likely source. Professor Bill Adams of the University of Aber-ystwyth remembers: 'When *Match of the Day* was in black and white you couldn't tell the state of the pitch. When colour came in, you saw how different grounds were on the same day. One would be good, another very muddy. We began to ask ourselves why.' The short answer turned out to be: bad drainage. 'In the early days,' says Adams, 'lots of clubs would thumb their noses at us and say: "We don't need any help thank you very much; we know what we're doing."' Bad practices were common and managers often added to the problem: 'It's just part of the psychology of the game. Teams at the bottom of a division often have the worst pitches because managers just need to win and always think there is added value in being able to train on the pitch.' Adams and his Aberystwyth colleague Vic Stewart worked out the principles of good drainage for sports turf. They drew on the work done in America to improve golf courses, and showed that football pitches could be improved by changing the structure of the soil. Dave Saltman, who now runs Pitchcare.com, a website for the profession, remembers: 'When I first started, a lot of grounds-men were ex-players. It would be jobs for the boys. "Grounds-man" just meant the bloke who rolled, mowed and marked the pitch. People thought rolling the pitch gave you a nice flat surface, which it doesn't. In the sixties and seventies, they'd use lime or creosote to mark out the pitch, which would be banned now. Where there were divots, they'd just roll them out. Pools of water didn't matter. They'd play on anything. It wasn't important to keep grass alive – you just needed a reasonably flat space for lads to go out and kick a ball.' When the first generation of plastic pitches failed in the early eighties, clubs began to experiment with new ways of constructing pitches, most often using sand instead of heavy natural soils. By the mid-nineties, tough new grasses, sophisticated equipment and a new generation of scientifically educated groundsmen had wrought a revolution. In the last ten years the culture shifted.

Mud is now doomed, and elements of the English style are disappearing with it. Football of a speed and dainty technical excellence unimaginable in the past is now routinely played on the smoothest, firmest, best-quality grass pitches the game has ever seen. The notion of football as 'the beautiful game' is a Brazilian import. English football was never meant to be beautiful; it was about something else. But there was a grace in that and, as the mud vanishes, something of the old spirit of the game drains away too.

Ironically, though, a gulf has opened between top-level football and the rest. Alex Vickers of Cranfield University observes: 'I don't think anyone ever sat down and planned to change the pitches to bring in a new kind of football. I think it was an accident. It was a result of other economic issues. There is no going back, but now there's a split between the highest level of the game and the lowest. The top clubs are spending £15 or 20 million on training-ground pitches because they want the same surface as in the stadium. They take kids at seven or eight years old to train them. But where do other kids play football? In local parks, which are like the way the first-class game was in the 1970s. The quality of provision at the local, general amenity level has declined massively. In the eighties compulsory competitive tendering was very damaging and the standard of council pitches has gone down terribly in the last fifteen years. Now, when you watch the Sunday League side in a local park, how do they play? Is it the Brazilian style? No. They still play kick and rush because it's the only game they can play on a pitch that's half under water. A second phase of development is needed because people will want the same kind of good pitches down at the park level.'

Meanwhile, a new threat has emerged which could rip the game from its ancient roots completely. The dawn of the problem can probably be dated quite precisely to August 1996, when the then European Champions, Ajax of Amsterdam, opened their 'futuristic' Arena stadium. The sliding roof was hailed as a technological marvel, but its downside became apparent within weeks: grass simply couldn't grow properly in a concrete bowl without natural airflow or light. The pitch rapidly deteriorated and Ajax's team, famous for their slick passing game, began to malfunction. Ajax laid a new pitch pronto, which also died. Then they laid another . . . and another . . . and another . . . Ajax now install four new pitches a season, which costs them £1 million a year. The sorry tale might have served as a warning to all other clubs considering building new stadiums, or putting up huge new stands which cut out light, air and water. But financial imperatives have made such stadiums the norm. Natural grass playing surfaces are consequently under threat. There have been imaginative solutions at some European grounds. Arnhem and Schalke have their pitches on giant wheeled trays which roll out of the stadium after the match, recover in the fresh air and get pushed back for the next game. At the Millennium in Cardiff, the grass is on concrete pallets moved in and out of the stadium by fork-lift truck. But at stadiums such as Dortmund, Milan, Chelsea and Manchester United high new stands were built to boost attendances – with predictably dire consequences for playing surfaces. For now, clubs in new stadiums with grass-growing problems have to pay the high costs of re-turfing several times a season. They and the game's governing bodies are attracted by a radical alternative: plastic.

In the early 1980s a handful of English clubs, including QPR, Oldham and Luton, sought to escape the problems of perennial mud (whose main drawback was expensive match postponements) by installing artificial playing surfaces. These early plastic pitches, hailed at the time as the way of the future, turned out to be terrible. Far from mimicking the best characteristics of grass, the carpets of hard green plastic, often laid on top of concrete, rendered matches farcical as balls sped over the slick surface or bounced freakishly high. A generation of players was traumatised by knee injuries and friction burns. Players hated them and Kenny Dalglish declared: 'An artificial pitch produces an artificial game.' The pitches were soon banned, and money and technological resources were switched to natural grass instead. Fans and players assumed they had heard the end of plastic. But in the last few years, a new style of plastic pitch has made an appearance. Synthetic turf manufacturers in Europe and America, who claim the new products look, feel and play like grass, sense a huge potential market. The technology has certainly improved since the QPR days: the new products have thicker carpets of softer plastic grass, laid on top of combinations of rubber and sand. Many such surfaces have been installed at Premiership training grounds, although plastic is still banned from top matches – but that could soon change. These so-called third- or fourth-generation plastic surfaces are viewed with enthusiasm by the game's two most important governing bodies – Uefa and Fifa – who are keen on the idea of using them around the world. But, although standardised playing surfaces everywhere from Saudi Arabia to Iceland might appeal to tidy-minded administrators, others will react with horror.

The new plastic fields would be Stepford Pitches, devoid of individuality, robotically standardised. But they could well be on their way, and it could have as big an impact on football as the death of grass courts and pitches had on tennis and field hockey. In 2003 Uefa began a two-year pilot study: six plastic pitches were installed at clubs around Europe. One is in Scotland at Dunfermline Athletic, where a Canadian-designed pitch was put in at the start of the 2003–04 season. Uefa insists that players' and fans' views will be taken into account, and that the effects of plastic on injury rates will be a key factor, but if the experiment is deemed a success, plastic will be cleared for use in World Cup, European Championship and Champions League games.

Senior Uefa official Rene Eberle hopes and expects it to happen. He predicts that in future natural turf will be used 'wherever possible' but in the closed arenas expected to dominate future stadium design, 'we are sure that it will go in the direction of artificial pitches, provided that the artificial turf industry will be able to come up with pitches of a quality that we can say yes, we can accept that'. In twenty years' time, he says, 80 or 90 per cent of top football will still be played on grass. 'For football, there is nothing better than a nice natural turf. That is quite clear. But the tendency we have with modern stadia today makes it more and more difficult in having an acceptable natural grass pitch in those grounds. Look at Dortmund. Look at Milan. It's horrible. Any second-category product of artificial pitch would be better. We hope the product will hold up and also be accepted by the players. If that is the case, it will be the future. It may be that the research we are doing and the input we receive is too negative. But I don't think you can stop the evolution.'

Eberle insists plastic pitches will improve the game. 'I have spoken to players right after matches and on several occasions I got: "Yeah, it's perfect to play, but it stinks!" This is because the rubber doesn't smell like grass. That is their biggest criticism. I remember when I used to play football as an amateur, when it was wet in the countryside and you had one of those bloody balls on your head, you were knocked out. I remember pitches where you had to be careful you didn't lose your boots in the mud. That doesn't happen any more today. The biggest negative aspect [of plastic] is the sliding tackle: you cannot do it the way you do it now. On the other hand, on artificial pitches we have noticed the game is becoming definitely faster, with less interruptions and it hugely favours technically good players because ball control is much easier.'

For clubs the main attraction of plastic will be financial. At a cash-strapped outfit such as Dunfermline, chairman John Yorkston points to the advantages of having a pitch which can be hired out and used for everything from training to rock concerts. 'What other business would have a 10-acre site which is used only twenty days a year?' He also claims plastic will improve the game itself. 'Last year we went to Motherwell and it was an ice rink. We went to Dundee United and it was like a ploughed field. You're not going to tell me that something like this is worse than that. If you like folks sliding around in mud and kicking a ball then fine, but I don't. I like seeing boys passing the ball about and tactically beating the opposition. I think the big teams and those who like good football will enjoy it. There will always be some players and managers who say: "We played at QPR and it was terrible." But that was the dark ages. All the problems they had in the past have been overcome. Uefa see this as the way forward. So many games are postponed or unavailable because of bad weather. We are not saying it is better than grass in the summer months but, over the year, it is the more even and consistent surface.'

At the time of writing, a debate about this has barely begun in English football, but in Scotland, where several Premier League clubs could follow Dunfermline's example, feelings are beginning to run high. Celtic's manager, Martin O'Neill, is one of the most passionate opponents: 'If this catches on, we might as well head for Siberia as they have the same kind of pitches there. The very best players will leave the country. I just disagree with it entirely. It is not football as we know it. If you are telling me that some other clubs are thinking of doing the same, well I am sorry, that will get the game done away with.' Among the groundsmen, plastic is viewed with equal dismay. 'Synthetics will kill the game,' says Dave Saltman. 'It'll take out a lot of the character. The best new artificial pitches are probably better than the average natural turf pitch, but not as good as the top-quality natural pitches.'

Like many, Saltman is bitter that Uefa and Fifa seem to be supporting synthetic surfaces so enthusiastically just when the natural turf industry has made the biggest advances in history.

'Scientific research over the last fifteen or twenty years into everything has improved everything,' he insists. Even in high-sided, roofed stadiums, natural grass can be supported: 'It's not outside the wit of man to solve these problems. We have under-soil heating, pitch covers, rain covers, frost covers, pumps to suck air through the pitch or suck moisture out of the pitch or pump warm air in and circulate it under the roots. New bio-sugars might help grass to produce sugars without photosynthesis, so you could even grow grass in the shade. In Japan they're looking at hydraulic systems to jack the pitch up to the roof. The next couple of years will see major strides using natural grass that will beat anything that the synthetic boys can come up with.'

At Arsenal Steve Braddock is also fearful: 'I reckon all it will take is one Premiership club to do it, or get permission to do it, and the rest of them will follow suit. It might be quite attractive for clubs like Man U or Chelsea. As long as Arsène [Wenger] is manager of the club, I like to think I could persuade him to keep a natural surface. He believes in everything being natural. I'm very excited by new light systems which can make grass grow in winter, though that's expensive and artificial in a different way. From what I've seen, the artificial pitches aren't that good, and aren't going to improve that much. I think the technology hit a ceiling. I can certainly see a role for them, in Third World countries or places like Iceland where it's hard to grow grass. Here, they should be used in indoor training halls, but not in a main stadium. I really don't understand why Uefa is pushing this. Plastic surfaces would take the spirit out of the game. Part of football is facing the challenges that lie ahead in a gruelling season. If you are playing on the same surface day in and day out it gets too predictable.'

Wolves and England player John Richards is equally scep-tical: 'Anything that moves the game forward has got to be applauded. But players prefer grass. It's as simple as that. Synthetics have improved a great deal since the eighties, but not to the extent where they are going to supersede natural turf. I just don't think that will ever happen. Synthetic technology may be improving, but so is the advance in turf science. It's staggering the way things have moved. You can now grow a pitch outside and roll it under the stand. Who would have imagined that a few years ago? You can replace a pitch in just a few days during the season in the middle of winter, and have it playable! Grass is always going to be able to keep ahead of the synthetics.'

Professor Adams, though, sees the issue as hanging in the balance. 'I've thought about it quite a bit. I think if there is a change it needs to be done for the right reasons, not because someone has built a stadium they can't grow grass in. I think it will be decided by commercial pressure. The game would change very quickly if synthetics were allowed at the top, as happened in hockey. If international matches could be played on synthetic surfaces, the whole thing would change overnight. I suppose there is no reason why the ingenuity of man shouldn't produce an artificial playing surface as good as the best natural turf surface. But you will lose something. Whenever and wherever football is played it would always be the same. Does that matter? It's a bit like eating chicken. If you've never tasted chicken with any flavour in it, you'd never know what you're missing.'

# ITALIAN JOB

In 218 BC, Hannibal and his elephants crossed the Alps and entered Italy on the first stage of a doomed attempt to destroy the growing power of Rome. The first place he reached at the foot of the mountains was the city we know as Turin. Hannibal politely asked the inhabitants to join his war. When they refused, he pillaged the place, burned it down and butchered the population. The Romans used to behave much the same way all over the ancient world, but modern Italians, aware that their country was a playground for invading armies over the last few centuries, still prefer to remember Hannibal's crime. Wryly, they quote Livio's line '*et Hannibal movit ex Tauriniis*' – and Hannibal left Turin – roughly meaning: 'invaders came from the north and brought misery'.

In April 1764, with Britain well on its way to becoming the world's greatest power, the historian Edward Gibbon retraced Hannibal's footsteps. A former captain of the Hampshire

Grenadiers, Gibbon was twenty-seven years old at the time and could have managed on his own feet, but that's not how English gentlemen expected to travel in the age of the Grand Tour, so Gibbon permitted himself to be carried in a litter over Mount Cenis by Italian peasants. His first stop on the plain was a city he found dreary: 'The architecture and the government of Turin presented the same aspect of tame and tiresome uniformity,' he wrote. After a brief stay he moved on towards Rome where the majestic ancient ruins inspired him to start work on his epic *The Decline and Fall of the Roman Empire*.

By 1969, the old winding mountain paths had been up-graded and the journey could be made by car. In the dying days of the British Empire, this twisting route was the one chosen by Cockney crook Charlie Croker in *The Italian Job*. Turin was now 'famed for its architecture', its footballers and its Fiat cars; Croker's gang, disguised as England football fans, planned to reduce the city to traffic chaos and escape under cover of an Italy–England match.

The history of Anglo–Italian rivalry is a tale of journeys and fluctuating fortunes. As one side's power wanes, the other's waxes; the balance swings from mastery to subjection and back again. For centuries, England's standing in the world could be gauged by its relationship to Italy. Two thousand years ago Roman conquerors first brought Britain into ambivalent connection with continental Europe. Fifteen centuries later Britain's surge to great-power status began with Henry VIII's break with Rome. During the Renaissance, the British were intellectually, commercially and culturally in thrall to Italy. By the nineteenth century the balance of power had been reversed and, over the last century or so, football has been as vivid a guide to this switching balance between the two nations as war, politics or the arts. Relatively untainted by the bitter political and cultural rivalries which colour England's relationship with, say, Germany or Argentina, the Italian connection provides a revealing case study of English footballing attitudes to 'Johnny Foreigner'. In *Gazza Agonistes*, his 1995 book about Paul Gascoigne's time at Lazio, Ian Hamilton explained Italy's central place in the British sporting psyche. 'Italy, although we beat them now and then, would always remain out of reach, the sinister, dark Other: a Brazil that was too close to home. Whenever our standing in Europe was discussed, Italy was the principal yardstick by which we measured our strengths and weaknesses.'

But few relationships have been defined so clearly by a kaleidoscope of commonplaces. The English have seen Italians as charming, warm-hearted, well-dressed, family-minded, cowardly, mother-fixated, bottom-pinching, stiletto-wielding assassins. Italy was the land of murder, corruption, hysteria, sex, beauty, good food, fine wine, warmth and sunshine.

A good place to start exploring this confusion is on the road to Turin with *The Italian Job*, the much-loved crime caper movie, icon of modern Englishness – which is largely unknown in Italy. The title itself spawned a thousand back-page headlines, and *Italian Job* was even the name of a short-lived England supporters fanzine. The city of Turin, where the main action of the film takes place, has also been the scene of some definitive Anglo–Italian football encounters. In 1948, for example, with England's post-war prestige high (and Italy still mired in après-fascism poverty), the England of Finney, Mortensen and Mannion crushed a fine *azzurri* side 4–0 in the sunny Stadio Comunale. For weeks afterwards in the city's cinemas the awed Italian public watched ninety-minute newsreels of the master-class. A decade later Italian design and food had begun to transform England domestic tastes, and a tactical revolution had turned Italian teams into champions of Europe. By the early sixties a handful of British football stars had been 'lured by the lira' to Turin. At Juventus, John Charles, '*il gigante buono*', 'the gentle giant', loved and was loved. But Denis Law hated his season with Torino and fled home as soon as he could. By 1973, *il sorpasso* – the economic overtaking of Britain by Italy during the 1980s – was presaged by the reversal of the footballing balance of power. After four decades of trying, the Italian national team finally managed to beat England, first in Turin, then again at Wembley. Three years later the Italians established football dominance over England in the year of the IMF crisis as Juve's Bettega headed England out of their second World Cup in a row. (England hasn't beaten Italy in a match of consequence since.)

In 1984 Bill Buford, for his book *Among the Thugs*, watched 'fat, sticky' Manchester United fans vomiting in the Piazza Castello and urinating through the doors of a café in the arcades used for the *Italian Job*'s car chase. In 1985 Liverpool fans caused the death of thirty-nine Juventus fans. But at the 1990 World Cup, a resurrection of sorts began as England's national team, inspired, it seems, by the sound of Pavarotti singing Puccini on the BBC, reached the World Cup semi-final at Turin's new Stadio delle Alpi (but lost the third-place match to Italy). In the early nineties, with Serie A matches now watched live in the UK, Italian clubs came to seem glamorous, rich and powerful almost beyond English comprehension. Again, Turin saw the tipping point as this perception was reversed. In 1999, once more at Delle Alpi, Juventus were astonished to find themselves out-thought and overpowered as Manchester United, playing a new brand of sophisticated British football, fought back from 0–2 down to break the Italian champions 3–2. In the last couple of years top English clubs have become the teams Italians fear most: Arsenal beat Roma 3–1 in Rome and Inter 5–1 at the San Siro; Chelsea thrashed Lazio 4–0 in the Stadio Olimpico; Man

U beat Juve again, home and away. Giovanni Trapattoni wasn't being polite when he said he was pleased to have avoided England in the draw for Euro 2004.

*The Italian Job* was made in 1969, about halfway through this sweep of history. England were reigning world champions, Italy had just won the European Championship and English hooliganism was still in its infancy. *The Italian Job* isn't always seen as a football film, but it surely is. The robbery takes place under cover of an Italy–England match (film of which was planned but eventually cut); the gang are dressed as England fans; their getaway vehicles are plastered with the names of England players. As they get nervous during the escape, Bill says: 'Look happy you stupid bastards – we won, didn't we?' Proto-laddism suffuses every frame and, back in Blighty, when news of the successful heist reaches criminal kingpin Mr Bridger, he basks in the acclaim of the prison crowd chanting 'England! England!' as Wembley did for Nobby and the Bobbies and Alf in '66.

There's even a photograph of the film's cast and crew (including the future Jesus of Nazareth, Robert Powell) posing like a Victorian football team at an Italian villa, under a banner which reads: 'European Crime Cup Winners'. Oh yes, it's a footy film all right, and one that captures part of the essence of modern English football-related patriotism. As one of the film's army of admirers put it on a website, *The Italian Job*:

holds a dear place in the heart of British filmgoers everywhere . . . Michael Caine's Charlie Croker leads a daredevil plan to steal $4,000,000 through a traffic jam – and more importantly, stuff one up the foreigners. In these days of properness, when only questionable types seem to be allowed to wave a Union Jack any more, it stands as a refreshing slice of patriotic tongue in cheekery – God Bless the Queen!

Or, in the words of the film's producer, Michael Deeley: 'The whole point of the movie was us against them. It was the first Eurosceptic movie. It was us showing the Italians a thing or two. It was our lads against their lads, us being terrific and them being silly.'

Not everyone likes the film. The *Guardian* recently called it 'stupid and insular': 'It feels like a blueprint for twenty subsequent years of football hooliganism, pissing in foreign fountains and all those things that prompt the French to call us *les fuckoffs*.' But Michael Caine understands the enduring appeal of his early movies for young Englishmen: 'I was Alfie, so that's all the women taken care of. *The Italian Job* we won the football and got the gold, even though we lost it in the end. And [in *Get] Carter*, you get your nose pushed down your throat. So there were the three iconic things for a young man to look at: an Englishman on the screen that was all those things.' Meanwhile, a line from *The Italian Job*'s song theme about the lads, being a '*self*-preserv*ation* soss-aye-a-*teeeeee*' has become one of the favourite anthems of England supporters who sing it round and round like a tape loop. It's rousing, boorish and self-mocking, and it's what England fans were singing when Ronaldinho scored in Shizuoka.

Irony swirls around *The Italian Job*, not least because foreigners contributed some of its best-loved bits. The patriotically dashing red, white and blue Mini Coopers that leave the plodding Fiats for dead were designed by Turkish-born Alec Issigonis. A Frenchman, Remy Julienne, did the stunt-driving. And Fiat, whose gold is Croker's target, supported the film much more than the Mini's manufacturers, the British Motor Corporation, who told Deeley that if he wanted Minis, he could jolly well buy them at full retail price. Gianni Agnelli, the Fiat and Juventus boss, put the resources of his company and the city of Turin at the film-makers' disposal and even let the crew shoot on the race track on the roof of the Fiat factory. (BMC later ceased to exist; Fiat prospered for three decades.)

Even more ironically, the film was first conceived as a satire of the Englishness it ended up celebrating. The line voted by English viewers as the funniest in film history ('You're only supposed to blow the bloody doors off') was ad-libbed by Michael Caine. But that was the least of the changes to the original script by Troy Kennedy Martin, creator of *Z Cars* and the stunning *Edge of Darkness*. In the film, Croker walks straight out of prison into the arms of his dolly-bird girlfriend Lorna, who whisks him to the Royal Lancaster hotel for an orgy. In the subsequent novel, which was based on Kennedy Martin's original script, Croker is greeted by his 'nauseating' dysfunctional family: 'They were all there, every last one. His spotty-faced brother, his cousin on a grimy old scooter, his sister and her brood of seven kids. It was horrible.'

While the Brits in the film are characters, the Italians are clichés: elegant, sinister *mafiosi*, wildly gesticulating officials or excitable locals, who drive on the wrong side of the road and are easily outwitted by superior British pluck and panache. The casting of Noël Coward as Mr Bridger, the royal family-obsessed crime boss who wants to 'help Britain's balance of payments', gave the film deep resonance. Off screen, the old faux-aristocrat Coward and sexy young working-class hero Caine became friends; on screen, something more profound occurs. As the writer John Lahr says: 'The very notion of the English that the English themselves have, is something that Coward created in art and was then adopted by the public . . . English cultural history between the world wars is, in some extremely large part, Noël Coward.' *The Italian Job* is where Coward hands on this baton of Englishness to Caine. The old Englishness meant duty and self-sacrifice; the new kind would be carried by football, pleasure and humour. The old

imperialism turned into a kind of jokey, postmodernist version
of the same thing.

It could have been different. In the original script, Mr
Bridger (a part written for Nicol Williamson) turns out to
be an unpatriotic hypocrite who cuts a deal with the Mafia to
give them the gold. But Coward's patriotism in the film was
not far from his personal stance. A few months after Suez he
wrote in his diary:

> . . . good old imperialism was a bloody sight wiser and heal-
> thier than all this woolly-headed, muddled, 'all men are equal'
> humanitarianism which has lost us so much pride and dignity
> and prestige in the modern world. British Empire was a great
> and wonderful social, economic and even spiritual experiment,
> and all the parlour pinks and eager, ill-informed intellectuals
> cannot convince me to the contrary. There is much to be
> deplored in the British character but there is also much, very
> much, to be admired and respected. We have done a great deal
> of good to a great many million people, principally by helping
> them towards common sense.

The film's cliff-hanger ending (getaway coach balanced on the
edge of a mountain) was the producer's last-minute idea and
was done with a sequel in mind. Kennedy Martin didn't write
the scene and director Peter Collinson hated it so much that he
refused to film it. When *The Italian Job* was re-released on its
thirtieth anniversary in 1999 Kennedy Martin still seemed a bit
baffled by its enduring popularity. 'I never thought the film
would be iconic. The reviews weren't that good . . . and of
course it didn't have a traditional ending. We didn't realise just
how good it was.' He seemed somewhat embarrassed by the
film's treatment of women and foreigners. 'It really is very
chauvinistic, even if the chauvinism wasn't intended seriously.

All the girls are dolly-birds, and when I see the way the women are treated it makes me wince.'

The sequence in the film when Croker's gang of asthmatic losers and incompetents suddenly turn into a brutally efficient fighting unit to smash into the bullion van and outmanoeuvre an army of dim-witted Italian uniforms celebrates English fighting prowess and plugs into an ancient tradition. Cheeky Charlie Croker is a throwback to the earliest British imperialists – swashbuckling patriotic Elizabethan buccaneers such as Hawkins and Drake (Sir Francis, not Ted). The robbery scene also evokes two decades of English jokes about Italian tanks having one forward gear and four for reverse. The overwhelmed Italians are not far from caricatures like the vain and cowardly Captain Bertorelli ('oh whatta mistakea I make') from *'Allo 'Allo*. Sneering references to cowardly Italians also appear in *In Which We Serve*, Noël Coward's wartime film, in which two sailors talk scathingly about 'the Macaronis':

'The Eyties will do anything for money.'

'Anything but fight.'

'That's why they were so lousy in the last war. That's on account of their warm, languorous southern temperament.'

In the eighteenth and nineteenth centuries, at the height of the Grand Tour, travelling in Italy was reckoned to be an important element of a young man's education. Aristocratic British travellers 'patronised a museum set in a picturesque landscape', and loved wandering around the relics, such as Roman ruins, beautiful architecture and plentiful art, left behind by earlier inhabitants. But their attitude to the Italians they met was stunning contempt.

'There are two Italies,' wrote the poet Shelley.

One composed of the green earth & transparent sea and the
mighty ruins of antient times, and aerial mountains, & the warm
& radiant atmosphere which is interfused through all things.
The other consists of the Italians of the present day, their works
& ways. The one is the most sublime & lovely contemplation
that can be conceived by the imagination of man; the other the
most degraded disgusting & odious.

However, there was genuine affection too. G. M. Trevelyan
talks about the 'passionate and many-sided devotion of the
English to the literature, language, art, history and civilisation
of ancient, of medieval and of modern Italy' and insists that the
English 'had always displayed a particular love for Italy'.

A large part of Italy's mystique lay in its alarming, contagious
feminity: Italy was dubious, unmanly. The summer heat, the
exotic, 'voluptuous' landscape and the beauty of Italian women
simultaneously excited and frightened the English. Venice and
Naples were the 'brothel of Europe'. (For the highly sexed Lord
Byron, who loved the place, merely speaking Italian was 'like
kissing'.) The peninsula was also regarded as deeply sinister – a
legacy of the religious wars and Protestant fear of the heartland of
Catholicism. Jacobean theatre's blood-drenched revenge dramas
were invariably set in Italy. Much later, Gothic horror, invented
in the 1790s by Ann Radcliffe, who never actually visited Italy,
was born, with novels such as *The Italian* and *Sicilian Romance* set
in a land of boundless violence and luxurious passions. By the
early nineteenth century this fictional Italy was the setting for
tales of highly sexed Latin lovers, evil counts and sadistic nuns and
inquisitors. This passage from Edward Montagu's 1807 novel
*Legends of the Nunnery* was typical:

Near the town of Friulo, towering high above the surrounding
forest, rises the immense castello of Signor Coloredo. Proud,

ambitious, haughty and despotic, he ruled with an iron sway over his numerous vassals and dependants . . .

The dark walls rose with a sullen horrific appearance from the rugged rocks erected by the overhanging battlements, where, through the loopholes, the deadly cannon stretched out of their murderous mouth.

Ambition, the spring of evil, had here held her usurping reign: Coloredo came into possession of those lofty towers by the purchased dagger of the assassin but his mind, inured to deeds of blood . . .

Few English writers (Dickens was an exception) engaged with the mundane, real life of modern Italians as Goethe did. By the late nineteenth century, the image of Italy was firmly established in the English mind: at best, Italians might be seen as cheery rustic peasants; at worst, as Machiavellian killers. Later, the bandits of these stories would be replaced by the Mafia. In football, the era of *catenaccio* would see many of these old English views slide across to a new discourse of football tactics.

When football was becoming England's national game in the 1880s, the old attitudes were summed up neatly by a student called J. Ross Murray in a prize-winning essay about the superiority of English writers over Italian ones in the sixteenth century. Italy, he said, was:

the land of Adventure, Intrigue, Sensationalism, Scandal, Crime. The courts were centres of refinement, gallantry and subtlety; the Academies were nurseries of learning, but also of evil theories; the towns were full of turbulent life and restless activity; the streets were constant scenes of strife and assassination. Mocking Atheism went side by side with devout Catholicism, cynical indifference watched the gorgeous processions of the pomp-loving Cardinals, while eager place-hunting and

passionate Revenge dogged their footsteps with the dagger and
bowl of poison ever at hand, and poets all the time went on
singing dainty melodies of Love and Beauty.

The Italians, he concluded, were 'unnatural and affected', the
British more like 'unvarnished oak'. And it was clear which was
morally preferable: 'Better the rugged majesty of the honest
Teuton than the voluptuous effeminacy of the doubtful
Tuscan.'

The English would often see Italian football through a haze
of suspicion, disdain and envy. Naturally, there was a benign
side to the relationship too. As the English had drawn much of
their modern civilisation from the Renaissance, so Italians later
drew their footballing traditions from the English. Football was
brought to Italy by expats who founded clubs with English
names such as Genoa, the first Italian club, and Milan. The
black and white stripes of Juventus came from Notts County.
Italy's first great coach, Vittorio Pozzo, who led the *azzurri* to
victory in the 1934 and 1938 World Cups, was a devoted
Anglophile who learned the game at the feet of men such as
Charlie Roberts of Manchester United and Steve Bloomer of
Derby. But the darker pattern laid down by the sulphurous
Battle of Highbury in 1934 defined the English view of Italy–
England games as moral conflicts: English manly decency versus
Italian elegance, hysteria and slyness.

In the build-up to the 1934 game, the *Times* correspondent
in Rome predicted that Italy, who had recently won 'the so-
called World Championship', would be no match for the
robust English. He explained how Italy's talented forward
Giuseppe Meazza could be stopped: 'Close marking . . . usually
damps his ardour, for he is not over fond of rough and ready
encounters.' In the *Daily Express* George Harrison said the
Italians 'can "work" the ball delightfully and shoot well. But I

do not think they will stand for the full 90 minutes the pace that England are certain to set.' Off the field, English reporters were dazzled by Italian beauty and impressed by 'the fire and excitement' of their fans. In the *Daily Mirror* 'A Woman Reporter' was much taken with 'these stalwart, olive-skinned Italian footballers . . . going about London causing many a flutter to feminine hearts'. Some 2,000 Italians travelled to London for the match and 10,000 expats (mainly from the 'knife and fork trade' as one paper sneered) also made their presence felt. The *Express* noted: 'All last night Soho was in such a ferment that it resembled the shaky ground around Vesuvius. The 2,000 excursionists were frequenting with the local Luigis and Carlos, and the run on chianti was phenomenal.' The *Daily Mail* reported excitement in the cafés and restaurants of the West End: 'All who saw the Italians dancing were struck with the beauty of their womenfolk.'

Oddly, there was barely a mention of the visitors' status as ambassadors for fascism. Mussolini saw sport as a tool for propaganda, and he had ordered his team to London despite the misgivings of Pozzo. Mussolini's message to Italian athletes was: 'When you take part in contests beyond our borders there is then entrusted to your muscles, and above all to your spirit, the honour and the prestige of national sport. You must hence make use of all your energy and all your willpower in order to obtain primacy in all struggles on the earth, on the sea and in the sky.'

At Highbury the game, played in seething mud under drear November skies, boiled immediately into violence, with both sides seeing themselves as victims. In the second minute Italy's Argentinian-born defender Luisito Monti clashed with England's centre-forward, Ted Drake. The collision broke Monti's foot. In pain, he struggled on briefly but soon left the field. 'It seemed at once that the Devil had planted his hoof on us,' said

Pozzo later. Drake always said the injury was an accident, but Monti's team-mates flew into raging retaliation. 'For the first quarter of an hour there might just as well not have been a ball on the pitch as far as the Italians were concerned,' recalled England young winger, Stanley Matthews. 'They were like men possessed, kicking anything and everything that moved bar the referee. The game degenerated into nothing short of a brawl and it disgusted me.' One photograph shows Italian defender Monzeglio apparently trying to strangle Drake in the penalty area after the Englishman had charged the Italian goalkeeper. England's captain, Eddie Hapgood, had his nose broken: 'The right-half, without making any effort whatever to get the ball, jumped up in front of me and carefully smashed his elbow into my face.' Hapgood went to the dressing room to be bandaged, then returned to the field. 'The Italians had gone berserk, and were kicking everybody and everything in sight,' he recalled. 'My injury had, apparently, started the fracas, and, although our lads were trying to keep their tempers, it's a bit hard to play like a gentleman when somebody closely resembling an enthusiastic member of the Mafia is wiping his studs down your legs, or kicking you up in the air from behind.' While the Italians were distracted, England played with swift precision and scored three goals in the first twenty minutes, two from Brook of Manchester City, one by Drake.

In his book *Football Ambassador*, Hapgood noted with satisfaction that the violence was not all from one direction: 'Wilf Copping [the fearsome Arsenal hard man] enjoyed himself that afternoon. For the first time in their lives the Italians were given a sample of real honest shoulder charging and Wilf's famous double-footed tackle was causing them furiously to think.' Hapgood went to the official banquet that night with his nose in plaster and 'a nasty taste in my mouth over the whole affair . . . As I wended my way through the crowd, I passed the table of my assailant of the afternoon. He looked me straight in the eye . . . And laughed. I'm glad I am a pretty even-tempered fellow, or I would have gone across the table at him. But he wasn't worth it.'

The second half was different. In the dressing room, Pozzo ordered his players to stop brawling, reminded them that they were world champions and sent them back on to the pitch with a firm handshake. The skilful Italians then staged a stirring fight-back which, in Italian legend, constituted a moral victory and means they are still remembered as 'the Lions of Highbury'. Meazza (ardour undampened) scored twice, and by the end the English were hanging on. The emotionality of the 12,000 Italian fans in the 50,000 crowd was considered unusual. The *Daily Mail* reported: 'Gay in berets of glorious blue, they screamed, and danced and cried when England scored.' In the second half:

> When the Italians attacked there was danger. Once more the cry 'Italia' went ringing round the ground. Dark-eyed beautiful women danced; they could not sit still. Men threw their hats high in the air, never, I am afraid, to be recovered. Slowly the time went on, it was fast growing dark and then the last whistle came. England had won, but England had had a fright, and ten weary Italians stumbled to the centre of the field while thousands of frenzied Italians chanted that haunting 'Italia'. Ten weary Italians stood and saluted the crowd. Eleven weary and, I am afraid to say, sadly hurt Englishmen, with a broken-nosed captain stood there and bowed.

Mostly, though, the English press was appalled. One paper published a report on the match 'by our war correspondent'. Others fulminated against Italian viciousness. The *Daily Express* said England should 'have no more to do with football on the continent' until the real rules of soccer were observed. 'The big crowd had paid to witness a Soccer match between England and Italy, but what they got was a display of ankle-tapping, tripping, obstruction, free-punching, bawling, brawling, shoulder-shrugging, and a variety of other objectionable things that have never had a place in football.' Complaining that the Italian 'congregation in the stands' was 'in a state of semi-hysteria' the paper said the Italian team was 'no better than a third-rate combination'. *The Times* summed it up: 'The score was 3–2; Italy played with 10 men, but the true verdict of the match, in spite of appearances, is that England is still supreme in a game essentially her own.'

After the war, there was, initially, no serious British animosity towards Italians, despite the recent hostilities; rather, the idea persisted that Italians were over-emotional and not to be taken seriously. In his autobiography, Brian Glanville quotes the derisive attitude of a British diplomat based in Rome in the early 1950s: 'The Italian male is spoilt. He's spoilt by his mother; he's spoilt by his sister; he's spoilt by his wife; he's spoilt by his mistresses; and if there's something he wants and he can't get it, he sits down and cries, whether he's six or sixty.' In Turin in 1948, Geoffrey Green of *The Times* braved the exotic, 'erupting passions' of a shirtsleeved Italian crowd in the Stadio Comunale to see England beat an Italy team containing many of the Torino players who would die at Superga a year later. Green's description of the key moment – Stanley Mortensen scoring with a screaming near-post banana shot from an impossibly narrow angle in the fourth minute – reads a little like George Orwell's famous anti-Empire essay about shooting an elephant in Burma:

It was so astonishing, so unlikely, that it fairly knocked all the breath and arrogance out of an Italian side which, at the time,

was generally regarded as the most talented in all of Europe . . .
The Italians could barely believe their eyes. It was some mirage
surely. That huge crowd, packed tight in shirtsleeves like a
white cloud in the shimmering light, grunted, caught its breath
– and fell silent.

By the mid-fifties, Italy had become a byword for pleasure.
Italians, as they appeared in Hollywood movies such as *Roman
Holiday*, were warm-hearted, wildly gesticulating, harmless
eccentrics. Dean Martin sang of Italy's endless possibilities
for *amore*. Rosemary Clooney (aunt of George) caught the
spirit with one of the era's most popular songs, 'Mambo
Italiano': 'A girl went back to Napoli/Because she missed
the scenery/The native dances and the charming songs.'
The climax of the song is much more daring than fifties Britain
realised: while Clooney moans 'at's nice!', her male backing
group finish with an unmistakably sexual grunt. *Ats* is a
shortened version of *cazzo* – pronounced 'catso' – Neapolitan
slang for penis.

Meanwhile, from Ferragamo shoes to Olivetti typewriters,
Italian design and fashion was beginning to exert a subtle but
pervasive influence on the English way of life. Ferraris and
Lamborghinis were the most desirable of cars and Italian
restaurants supplanted French ones as the chicest eateries. In
1965 Peter Boizot opened his first Pizza Express restaurant in
London. British teenagers too young to be allowed into pubs
met in Italian-style coffee bars to drink Italian-style coffee from
Italian machines. At West Ham, England's tactical football
revolution which helped win the 1966 World Cup was begun
by players meeting at Cassettari's Café near Upton Park. Few of
the working-class English Mods who wore sharp suits cut short
and rode Vespas and Lambrettas realised they were copying
Italian fashion, but they were. It came to them via the shops of

John Stephen, later the 'King of Carnaby Street', who dressed the sixties' pop stars and was hugely influenced by Italian colour and design. English tourists began to visit places such as Rimini in huge numbers in the hope of finding Clooneyesque experiences. In 'Summer Holiday' Cliff Richard revealed that there were just two kinds of Italians – *mafiosi* and happy peasants. (On *Desert Island Discs* Sir Geoffrey Howe chose the song because it reminded him of the sense of liberating sensuality of Mediterranean travel.)

The real Italy was changing fast. Just after the war, 'neo-realist' film-makers made heartbreaking movies about the resilience of the human spirit in desperate Italian circumstances (hunger, poverty, stolen bicycles, etc.). Then came Italy's Marshall Plan-assisted 'economic miracle' and Cinecittà helped define Italy as a place of inimitable glamour. Federico Fellini made *La Dolce Vita* in order to provide generations of British headline-writers with a handy cliché, and stars such as Claudia Cardinale and Gina Lollobrigida became world icons of gorgeousness. 'The basic idea was that Italian women have the biggest tits, the darkest eyes and the loosest morals on the planet,' recalls Barry Fantoni. 'You only had to take one look at Silvana Mangano looking sultry in the rice field, or Sophia Loren gratuitously wearing stockings and suspenders in that film with Peter Sellers to know that no other country had a chance.' Away from the film studios, rapid industrialisation and a fairly benign but corrupt centrist democracy ushered in not merely wealth but a new, Italian style of football: highly disciplined, ruthless and based on defence to a degree never seen before – *catenaccio*.

One of Italy's most philosophical and respected football writers is Mario Sconcerti, author of books such as *Baggio vorrei che tu Cartesio e io . . . Il calcio spiegato a mia figlia* ('Baggio, I would like you, Descartes and me . . . football explained to my daughter'), former editor of *Corriere dello Sport* and briefly general manager of Fiorentina. He argues that Italians developed their tactical system to make up for their perceptions of their own powerlessness. 'The English were always more powerful than us. You always won. After the war, you were still so strong you had no interest in experimenting. But we experimented, and we invented another way of playing: *calcio Italiano* which gives the correct ingredients for a "good minestrone". It specified the roles of each number on the field. We learned to play in a different way. Why? Because we lost the war, because we betrayed.' Who did you betray? 'The Germans. We felt we were a nation of betrayers. So when we started to play football in the 1950s, we played the football of betrayers. The English continued to play the football of winners. We were poor. You beat us until the 1970s. That's why in our football in general, we need to defend ourselves.'

Before fascism, Italian football was underdeveloped, but Mussolini built new stadiums, helped create institutions such as AS Roma and gave Pozzo resources to win the World Cup. English football spent the interwar years in isolation, turning its back on tactical and coaching developments in what was rapidly becoming the world game. Pozzo adapted classic English tactics to create his 'Method', a system which relied on sweeping movements to the wings. But there was a world of difference between Pozzo and the revolutionary home-grown Italian style invented in 1949–50 by two coaches at minor clubs. At Salernitana, Gipo Viani switched his centre-forward to defence, providing an extra defender. Journalist Gianni Brera christened the new defensive position '*libero*', and the idea rapidly spread throughout Italy. Meanwhile, first at Triestina and later with AC Milan, Nereo Rocco – 'the father of holy *catenaccio*' as Andrea Malaguti called him – perfected the new system by adapting it to earlier Swiss defensive tactics. *Catenaccio*

delivered amazing results. From the brink of relegation, Rocco
guided Triestina to second place in the league. A decade later,
with Cesare Maldini (father of Paolo) as his *libero*, Rocco made
AC Milan champions of Europe. Over the next two years, an
even more refined version of the system brought Inter the
European Cup under Helenio Herrera.

There is still argument over precisely who created *catenaccio*.
Other candidates include Carl Rappan, Austrian coach of the
Swiss national team, and Ottavio Barbieri of Genoa, who
coached the Firemen of La Spezia to the wartime championship of 1944. Whoever it was, *catenaccio*'s impact was huge.
After the war, Italy had been like Scotland – a team that never
got beyond the group stages of the World Cup. By the mid-
sixties, thanks to the new tactics and the money poured into the
game by often corrupt businessmen, Italy became the hottest
country in world football.

Sconcerti explains the cultural underpinnings for this revolution: 'In Italy football is invented by the small teams. Why?
Because the big teams win. They don't need to experiment. It's
the same in international football. After defeats, nations try to
reconstruct their image through football. The great Hungarian
team came after the Soviets occupied the country after the war.
Germany won its first World Cup after the war. The great
Austria was created in the 1920s after the country's defeat in the
First World War.' We are speaking in Sconcerti's fabulous
apartment in the centre of Rome, high walls lined with books
and pictures. He mimes the ancient Roman story of Orazi and
Curiazi, about the single soldier who runs away when his
comrades are killed. Three pursuers run after him to finish him
off. When the first gets close, he suddenly turns, stabs him, then
runs away again. When the next one catches up, he repeats the
trick. When the last one arrives, he kills him too. This, says
Sconcerti, is the basic principle of Italian football. 'From a

situation of one against three, he ends up as the winner. The counterattack is the principal idea of Italian football. In England you are the rich and powerful. We are weak and defeated. So we have to try to do the best, by whatever means we can find.'

Weak? Poor? Defeated? From a modern English perspective, this view of the Italians takes some getting used to. Over the last decade or so, Italy has seemed luxuriantly prosperous, elegant, happy and relaxed; a rich, sunny nation thoroughly at ease with itself, spreading soft warmth all around. A country where, as the comedian Eddie Izzard observed, the police are too busy seducing beautiful women to bother with crime, and the rest of the population consists entirely of cool guys cruising around on Vespas, wearing sunglasses, waving to each other and drawling: '*Ciao.*'

This is not how the Italians see themselves at all. They see themselves as survivors of centuries of poverty and misrule, as victims, permanently weak, always under threat, worrying that any momentary good fortune will be snatched away from them at any minute. Henry Kissinger, in his famous football essay entitled *World Cup According to Character*, was right when he said:

> The Italian style reflects the national conviction, forged by the vicissitudes of an ancient history, that the grim struggle for survival must be based on a careful husbanding of energy for the main task . . . The initial objective of Italian teams is to force the opponent out of his game plan, to wreck his concentration and to induce him to abandon his preferred style. In the early stages of a match, the Italian team tends to look destructive and purely defensive – a style achievable only by extreme toughness and discipline. But once the Italian team has imposed its pattern, it can play some of the most effective, even beautiful soccer in the world – though it will never waste energy simply on looking good.

The hard, cautious Italy was the one encountered by Denis Law, Joe Baker and Jimmy Greaves when they signed for northern Italian clubs in the early sixties. Under Rocco at AC Milan Greaves felt 'like a little boy lost'. He thought the Italian game 'spiteful and vicious', detested every second of his four-teen-game, nine-goal career and blamed the experience for turning him into an alcoholic. Years later he described Rocco as being like Mario Puzo's Godfather and claimed: 'The Italian press murdered me. They could not have done a better assassination job had they been given a contract by the Mafia.' Greaves was paid a fortune, but lost most of his money to fines as Rocco vainly attempted to get him to observe the strict Italian codes of sporting behaviour: no booze, no sex before matches, spartan training camps and obedience to the coach at all times. Greaves refused to be, as he saw it, 'just another sheep in his flock of highly paid but unhappy footballers'. Rocco despaired of Greaves's late-night carousing, one night even nailing his hotel door shut with planks of wood. It didn't work: Greaves climbed out of his window three storeys up and crept along a narrow ledge while his manager waited downstairs watching the main exit. His Italian team-mates found Greaves's behaviour incomprehensible.

It was a similar tale at Torino where Joe Baker and Denis Law played. Baker hated training camp so much that he staged a hunger strike. He pushed a paparazzo into a canal in Venice, and was lucky to survive a late-night car crash. Law was appalled by the cynicism and violence on the field: 'Some players were extremely skilful, much more so than we had been used to back home. Those that weren't – usually defensive players – were very, very hard. They really did their job . . . Kicking, punching and elbowing was all part of the game, and something not particularly physical, but which annoys British players: shirt-tugging. Just when you were going up to head a ball, your shirt would be held so that you couldn't move off the deck.' Just before Christmas 1961, Law had to fly south for a game in Palermo: 'Like a good many people, I always associated Sicily with the Mafia – and when we arrived there a couple of days before the game, it turned out to be every bit as forbidding as I had imagined. Of an evening the streets were full of men. The atmosphere was sinister. There were no women to be seen anywhere, just men dressed in dark clothing standing around in groups of three or four.' The match was even worse. At one point, he collected a ball for a throw-in: 'It was just a few feet away from the high wire fence and as I looked up I gazed into a sea of evil faces which all seemed to be spitting at me. They looked just like caged animals and I am sure that if the fence hadn't been there they would have come to get me. I remember thinking to myself, "What the hell am I doing here?"'

The English mixture of abhorrence and fascination towards what they see as Italian charm and danger is captured in E. M. Forster's *Where Angels Fear to Tread*, in which the narrow, hidebound life of an English middle-class clan is convulsed when a woman in the family falls for an Italian man, Gino, who 'carried his iniquities like a feather'.

At Rome's foreign press club, just a few yards from the headquarters of Forza Italia, Silvio Berlusconi's party, I consulted *Irish Times* correspondent Paddy Agnew who has reported on Italian football, politics and culture for twenty years. 'Italian football mixes artistry and thuggery, which seem to us to be contradictory concepts. But the ability to be deeply cynical yet immensely elegant is Italian nature. Italians are the most elegant people in the world. Just look at the streets. Who dresses better than the Italians? Who's got the better sense of style? How come Armani, Versace, Prada are all Italian? But this is also a very cynical country. Only a deeply cynical population could have voted in Berlusconi. In Britain or the United States of America he couldn't possibly have run for the office of Prime Minister or President of the United States. The first time Berlusconi got elected, people could say they didn't know about him. The country was in a state of crisis. A whole ruling class had been swept away by *tangentopoli* [corruption scandal]. Berlusconi seemed a very successful businessman who was going to bring new ideas and energy. Second time round, we knew about his conflicts of interest and his judicial problems. And people still voted for him! In Ireland we used to call it "the cute whore factor". People thought: "Berlusconi might not be clean, but if he's successful he'll make Italy successful and if he bends the law, it's OK with me as long as we all get richer." I think Berlusconi will lose the next election because Italians have not got richer, and they're not going to get richer because he doesn't know how to govern in the interests of Italians. Silvio Berlusconi only knows how to govern in the interests of Silvio Berlusconi. But people won't vote against him for moral reasons. It'll be the economy.' As a political phenomenon Berlusconi would have been inconceivable without football: a successful businessman, he found acclaim through the success he brought as owner of AC Milan in the late 1980s.

Agnew warns against falling into *Italian Job* clichés. 'It's an odd little film, isn't it? And it's strange that the English still talk about it after all this time. Very few people here have seen it, but I always thought the title was a splendidly effective way of summing up the way *Italian* teams have played over the years. They go out to do a job and they do it. Like Maldini's team at Wembley in 1997: one chance in the game, and they took it, and it was the only goal of the night. Classic!' Does he find something slightly racist in the English view of the Italians? 'At the end of the day there's always an element of it. It's a British colonial thing, isn't it? And they were a lot worse about the Irish. One English cliché about the Italians is that they have "hysteria". Actually Italians are never hysterical. They're cold and calculating: you think your way through things. If you want to understand *catenaccio* read *The Prince*. Why did Claudio Gentile mark Maradona so violently in the 1982 World Cup? It's just basic Italian cynical realism. They thought: "If we're going to win the game, we have to stop Maradona" so Gentile kicked the shins off him.'

It's true. In Chapter 18 of *The Prince*, Niccolò Machiavelli explained this aspect of winning the World Cup: 'You must know there are two ways of contesting, the one by the law, the other by force; the first method is proper to men, the second to beasts; but because the first is frequently not sufficient, it is necessary to have recourse to the second. Therefore it is necessary for a prince to understand how to avail himself of the beast and the man.' To the English imagination, Machiavelli was an antichrist who justified evil. The image of 'the Machiavell' (ruthless amoral schemer) became a stock figure of blood-drenched Jacobean dramas in the seventeenth century. Despite all scholarly attempts to reclaim Machiavelli as a rational humanist philosopher, something of the old taint still clings to the name. And the English – along with other northern Europeans – are still apt to interpret Italian methods as being as deep and mysterious as witchcraft.

The Dutch still haven't quite recovered from defeat at Italian hands in the bizarre semi-final of Euro 2000. The Dutch, playing their usual attacking game laid siege to Italy's goal throughout the two hours of normal and extra time. Holland had twenty-four shots on goal, hit the post, and missed two penalties; the Italians spent the entire game in their own penalty area. The longer it went, the more Holland's confidence drained away. Eventually Italy won on penalties with ease.

Dutch writer and film–maker Jos de Putter concluded that
Holland had been destroyed by the metaphysics of a football
civilisation far in advance of his own: 'In Holland we think we
control the game by having the ball. The Italians win by *not*
having the ball. We think defending is ugly but to the Italians,
defence is an art. Their idea that not having the ball is better
than having it implies that they can take it whenever they want
it. It means their best players are the ones who only take the ball
when they need it for the sudden counterattack. It is a kind of
virtuality: by not having the ball, you have it! It is far beyond
anything we can do. Virtuality is an unknown principle to us. It
is part of Italian metaphysical control. If the Italians beat us by
normal means, they would be human. We could understand it.
But they beat us with something else – with Destiny. It's part of
an order you can't understand. And it's hyper-romantic: the art
which is almost invisible, which becomes visible only at the last
possible moment, when it's too late. It's fantastic. It's like
death.'

    Mario Sconcerti is keen not to dispel such romantic percep-
tions. 'Metaphysics? Yes, your Dutch friend is right! You talk of
Machiavelli and assassins, and plots and Gothic novels . . . well
it's all the truth. But the real difference of Italy comes down to
only one thing: the Church. We are the Church. Only we have
the Church.' Hang on a minute! What about the Archbishop of
Canterbury? 'No. The Pope is here!' He points vaguely in the
direction of the Vatican a couple of miles away. 'Just over there!
England had the most important philosophers in the world:
Adam Smith, Locke. And who did we have? Gioberti! At the
time of the Risorgimento, his progressive idea was that Italy
should be led by a Pope-like King. The Pope is the biggest
reason we had such a big communist movement in Italy after
the war. No other country in western Europe had as many
communists as we did in Italy. In England and the United States

you have progressives and conservatives. In Italy this is not possible. You have only the middle. It's terrible.'

By the seventies and eighties Italy seemed to be overtaking Britain on and off the pitch. The economic *sorpasso* was preceded by a footballing one, which was in turn anticipated by another Michael Caine movie. In *Sleuth*, the film of Anthony Shaffer's famous stage play, Caine plays completely against his *Italian Job* character as Milo Tindle, a half-Italian confronting vicious old-style Englishness, in a clever thriller about nationality, class, sexual humiliation and games-playing. Milo's father, Tindolini, was a watchmaker from Genoa who came in the 1930s to a Britain where Italians were expected to 'make-a da-ice cream' and keep their heads down. English racism might have ruined his father's life but Milo has been doing rather well. He's also having an affair with the wife of an aristocratic crime writer called Andrew Wyke (Laurence Olivier). When he arrives at the older man's country estate for what he imagines will be an amicable man-to-man chat, he finds himself ensnared in a vicious game for his life.

The script is loaded with morbid post-imperial English anxiety. The snobbish, ageing Wyke claims to be an 'Olympic sexual athlete' who can 'copulate for England over any distance'. In fact he is impotent. 'I belong to that rare breed of men who genuinely don't mind losing gracefully to a gentleman who plays the game by the same rules,' he claims. 'But to be worsted by a flash crypto-Italian lover-boy who mistakes my indifference for inadequacy is altogether too much.' He is also a ferocious racist who thinks Milo 'a snivelling dago clown' and hates his 'smarmy good looks' and 'easy manner'. 'Above all I hate you because you're a cunning blue-eyed wop, and not one of me.' Because his opponent is Italian, Wyke underestimates him, but by the end the ageing Englishman has been outwitted by the young Italian who turns out to be not only more virile but better at the games the Englishman invented.

On the football field as well as in the bedroom, Englishmen were being outplayed by flash-looking Italians. In 1973, a month after England's World Cup failure against Poland, Italy won at Wembley for the first time, the late winning goal scored by Fabio Capello, the future AC Milan and Roma coach. In the *Daily Telegraph* David Miller noted:

> English soccer, charging courageously forward, head down, took another bloody blow on the nose at Wembley last night. It's time that we retired to our corner for a tactical re-think – or looked for some new contenders. As against Poland in the World Cup, England aimed a barrage of blows that never connected while Italy, deftly defending, took the bout on a counter-punch three minutes from the end – leaving England frustrated and further discredited . . . For eight years the English, encouraged by success at club level and the World Cup triumph of 1966, have preached the virtues of how to play without the ball: work rate, running off the ball, and so on . . . now the Italians quietly but sharply reminded us that football is played with the ball . . . The exquisite Gianni Rivera in midfield, the ungainly but dextrous Giorgio Chinaglia at centre-forward and others such as Franco Causio repeated the lesson that Italy gave us in Turin – that there is no substitute for skill on the ground, for the ability to give and take a pass first time at any height or angle, above all for the ability to beat one's man when face to face.

Three years later it got worse. On the eve of the decisive World Cup qualifier in Rome, Don Revie dropped half his team and the *Sun* offered bombast along the lines that Italians 'don't like it up 'em'. Frank Clough wrote: 'Look out Italy!

England are geared to teach you the hard facts of life in Rome
tomorrow afternoon. Don Revie has picked some of the
toughest nuts in the League for the World Cup qualifying
battle.' And Desmond Hackett took 'a horror trip down
memory lane' recalling the Battle of Highbury, when the
brave and forbearing English and their sporting crowd had
seen off the 'calculated villainy and savagery of the fanatic
Italians'. In the event, even though the Italians played with
caution, England were easily beaten. The *coup de grâce* was
administered by Roberto Bettega, who seemed to float high
over the ground for an unearthly distance before guiding
Romeo Benetti's cross past Ray Clemence with his head. It
may not have been the most beautiful goal ever scored, but
Gianni Brera gave it the most beautiful name: *il volo dell'angelo*,
the angel's flight. Frank McGhee in the *Daily Mirror* offered a
declinist interpretation of the result: 'Losing by two goals to
Italy in Rome is not too bad to bear – until you look deeper.
Then a bleaker truth emerges. It wasn't manager Don Revie's
fault that England lost . . . It was the failure of English football
as a whole. We have men who can run and chase, battle and
work – something they all did manfully, sweatily in this
match. But the Italians have men who can PLAY.'

Meanwhile, Italian standards of living were overtaking
those in Britain. In 1960 this would have seemed inconceivable. The future writer and doctor Theodore Dalrymple
first visited Italy as a boy and fell violently ill when he drank
the notoriously dangerous tap water. Italy was then a 're-
cognisably poor country' with a standard of living comparable to that of Batista's Cuba. Dalrymple: 'In one Sicilian
town, 3,404 humans shared 700 rooms with 5,085 animals
including pigs, goats and donkeys. Animal dung, still used as
fertilizer, was piled up in the Sicilian streets awaiting use.' In
2001 *La Repubblica* carried an article wondering why the

British food supply was so unclean and unsafe. Dalrymple observed:

> This is an astonishing reversal: for two and a half centuries at least, Britain was much richer than Italy in almost everything except its past. Britons pitied and condescended to their Italian contemporaries. Italy was a country of inexhaustible charm, sybaritic pleasure, and cultural wealth, of course, but it was not to be taken quite seriously in an economic or political sense . . . Merely to have caught up with Britain would represent its greater success, but il sorpasso . . . is evident almost everywhere you look. For example, you do not see in Italy the miles of urban desolation and squalor that characterize so much of Britain. Squalor, upon which British visitors to Italy used to remark with effortless and eloquent superiority, is now far more prevalent at home. The Italian population does not look nearly so grey or crushed by circumstance as the British. The shops in every small provincial town in Italy, even in Sicily, offer luxury goods of a range and quality not to be found even in the largest British cities outside London. Bari is incomparably richer and less dilapidated than Dover.

In her apartment in Rome's Via Machiavelli, close to the once-bloody Coliseum, forerunner of all modern stadiums, I meet Lina Unali, professor of English and American literature at the city's University of Tor Vergata. She divides her time between Rome and London and suggests that the main difference between the Italians and English – in football and everything else – is the family: 'In England, they have no information. In Italy the family means you are informed about everything. Teamwork is so natural to Italians, you feel they belong to their clubs as in the Bible it was written for husband and wife: "there is only one flesh". But the English are incapable of being one flesh. They seem almost blind with each other. They play very energetic football which is very entertaining. But it is a bit stupid.' She suggests a test to prove her information theory: 'Go down the road and stand near the Coliseum – but not looking at it – and ask anyone "Where is the Coliseum? And why was it built?" A hundred per cent of the people will give you the correct answers. Then make the same experiment in London. Stand 100 metres from the British Museum, but not looking at it, and ask: "Where is the British Museum?" Only the students will know. If you ask what it is, why it was built, probably even the students won't know. You may also ask: "Where is Heathrow?" They don't know. "Where is the railway station?" They don't know. It is the same on the football ground. There is no information. The English players are disconnected.'

Italy, however, has its own problems. Running a modern corporation as if it were a family business contributed to Fiat's decline and seemed to lie behind the 14 billion Euro collapse of Parmalat. Italian caution also has a price. 'We are all goal-keepers,' says Lina. 'All of us. In Italy we play mainly on the defensive, and there is little energy. My countrymen have other virtues, but they are very conservative.' What are the deep roots of *catenaccio*? 'There is a Spanish word: "*terraño*". It means the earth, being strongly connected to the earth and to the elements. It is about the wisdom of not taking a risk. We are a "*terraño*" society. We are grounded, highly grounded. I see it in my students. They are not full of adventure. Very seldom will a student of mine start a personal adventure. I don't speak of a love affair. British students are different. Their minds are completely empty because their schools teach them nothing. But they have courage. "Where are you going?" "I'm going to Africa." They may be unwise. They do things without the protection of their families. But at the same time I admire their manly courage. In Italy very few people try to build their

destiny by themselves. The Italians are "*terreno*". Our footballers are "*terreno*". What is their purpose? Not to be defeated. So
what do they do? They defend. Just defend. I don't appreciate
this element in Italy, and I don't appreciate it in life in general.
With an excess of defence in life you do precisely nothing.'

The European Championship of 1980 was staged in Italy,
and England qualified for its first tournament in ten years. Denis
Law, working for the BBC, enjoyed one sweet moment of
revenge, walking through the Italian streets late one night
singing the advertising ditty 'Just One Cornetto' to the tune of
'O Sole Mio'. Apart from that, the tournament was a British
cultural and footballing disaster. The fragrance of England's first
match against Belgium in Turin was tear gas as hooligans fought
running battles with the Italian police. The mayor of Turin,
Diego Novelli, decided to risk no more *Italian Job*-style antics
from the northern invaders: when England played the hosts a
few days later, he flooded the stadium and streets with police.
To the relief of the British government, Marco Tardelli scored
the goal that stopped England reaching the semi-final.

By the early eighties Italians were laughing at the English. Or
at least they were laughing at one particular English footballer,
the centre-forward of the national team, Luther Blissett. In the
summer of 1983, a year after Italy won the World Cup,
Graham Taylor's Watford ace ('one of the most feared forwards
in English football') signed for AC Milan for £1 million. 'In the
next three years, Blissett can expect to live the life of a
superstar,' predicted the *Watford Observer*. 'The Italians are
fanatical about their football stars and if the pacy striker
continues scoring goals at such a phenomenal rate he will
quickly become a favourite.'

'Yes, in Milan, we still love Luther Blissett. He is still very
popular,' confirms football writer Tommaso Pellizzarri, Inter
supporter and author of *No Milan*, a witty diatribe against AC

Milan which seeks to prove the wickedness of Silvio Berlusconi's club. 'Blissett played only for one season twenty years
ago, but you still say his name and everybody laughs. "Blissett
Miss It" he was called. He just looked physically ridiculous, this
big man running in his strange way with his long legs, and he
failed to score goals in the most incredible way. The worst
player we have ever seen! Joe Jordan also came to Milan and
played quite badly, but he wasn't considered ridiculous. Maybe
it was Blissett's size. At that time our players were still small. But
his name became synonymous with "Really Terrible Player".
You laughed because . . . how can I say it? You were overwhelmed by his incapacity . . .'

In 1994 a secretive group of Italian anarchists adopted the
name 'Luther Blissett' as a collective identity for a series of
playful assaults on the 'nihilistic tyranny of the spectacle'. One
early 'Luther Blissett' stunt involved sabotaging an event
devoted to the national poet of Finland by handing out tickets
advertising 'FREE BOOZE AND STRIPPERS' to local
youths: hundreds turned up with dud tickets and stormed
the barriers when they were refused entry. Later, like a sort
of non-comedy Italian version of Chris Morris, 'Luther Blissett'
spread false media stories about paedophilia and satanic cults in
high places.

There were also novels. *Enemies of the State* by Luther Blissett
concerned the state of emergency in Italy amid the terrorism of
the late 1970s. *Q*, written by four Genoans under the name
Luther Blissett, was an anti-clerical thriller set during the
bloody repression of the sixteenth century, and was nominated
for a literary prize by the *Guardian*. The real Luther Blissett, by
then a coach at Third Division York City, appeared baffled by
the phenomenon. 'It's got nothing to do with me,' he said.
'When I played in Italy I was one of the few black players over
there so they picked on my name for that sort of reason . . .

When you've played professional football or anything in the public eye you tend to get tarnished with whatever nickname, and that's what happened. But I'm happy to have gone through my career with a name like that scoring the number of goals I have scored.' But as one of the surreal Blissett websites explained:

> Luther Blissett is not a 'teamwork identity' as reported by the journalists; rather, it is a MULTIPLE SINGLE: the 'Luther Blissetts' don't exist, only Luther Blissett exists . . . Sabotages, hoaxes, urban legends, performances, magazines, bulletin boards and TV or radio broadcasts are spreading the name all over the world. Especially in Italy, this merry prank is reaching new heights of subversion and mythopoesis. Anyone can be Luther Blissett simply by adopting the name. Become Luther Blissett.

There wasn't much merriment – or 'mythopoesis' – when Ian Rush moved from Liverpool to Juventus for a single year in 1986. He told the story in his autobiography in a chapter (inevitably) entitled 'The Sour Taste of la Dolce Vita'. 'See Naples and die, that's a famous Italian proverb. Well, I have a different one: spend a year with Juventus and die a thousand times!' Everything about Italy unnerved Rush, from man-marking to intrusive *tifosi*. In his diary he recalled being besieged by 'frenzied' fans early in the season: 'I wasn't ready for the antics of one supporter, who grabbed me round the neck and planted a huge kiss on my mouth. What made it really embarrassing was the fact that it was a man! For a split second I felt my blood boil and I was ready to belt him one. But then, luckily, I saw the funny side of it all and all I did was laugh. People sure are different over here . . .' Rush and his wife, Tracy, were so homesick in Turin that they spent £1,000 a month on phone calls home to Flint in north Wales. Tracy later wrote: 'I'm glad we went. We would have spent the rest of our lives wondering otherwise. It's changed our whole attitude to life and I think we are both far more appreciative of living in Britain. We all moan and groan about it, but a year away helps you to realise what a fine country it really is.'

Yet through the 1980s – even after Heysel – Italians retained a fondness for England and its footballers. As a child, writer Tommaso Pellizzari adored Liverpool when they won the European Cup four times between 1977 and 1984: 'I played Subbuteo and Liverpool were my favourite team. They were not on TV all the time; football was not globalised yet. You just had the impression: this is the best team in the world. I remember Kevin Keegan was a great right-wing, Kennedy, the defender, Hughes, Thompson . . .' The hooligans of 1985 seemed to be from another world. 'I don't think it changed the perception of English football,' he continues. 'For us it was something to do with politics or sociology, not with football. At first, people here thought it was something to do with poor people who through football made some kind of vengeance on society, but when Bill Buford's book *Among the Thugs* came out it showed it was people who like fighting. When there was the fire at Bradford, and the stadium where the Liverpool supporters died . . . we thought that English football is suffering something very big. But we are talking about something which is not strictly football.'

Pellizzari says Italians still see England as the land of fair play. 'In English football, you play tough, make hard fouls, use kicks, and hands and elbows and everything . . . But at the end of the game everybody shakes hands and everything is over. And all the people say in Italy: "This happens in England and it never happened here in Italy" because in Italy we are not fair at all.' He admires the fact that in Britain there are no Italian-style TV discussions about football: endless chatshows in over-lit studios with hatchet-faced journalists, politicians and former players, sets decorated with perpetually smiling, scantily clad babes. 'In England you don't think about football so much as we do. In Italy, we think seven days a week about football. We talk six days a week about the match: waiting for the new one talking about the old one. Always discussing about the referee, about the penalty, about the fouls, about everything. We are the country with the biggest number of sport-only newspapers. We have three national sport newspapers. We have horrible TV shows where you watch horrible people horribly shouting for hours and hours about penalties and geography. The so-called journalist from Rome shouts against the one from Turin, saying: "Because you have Fiat, and you have Agnelli, you buy the referees." Maybe they are right, but you cannot go shouting on TV. For twenty years we have seen these things on TV. People in Italy think: in England nothing like this happens.'

Italians still look up to Britain in other areas too. 'Even if we don't like to say it, we have a great inferiority complex with countries like England or France,' Pellizzari admits. 'Especially now with our political situation. We always say: in great democracies like France or England [Berlusconi] could never happen.' Equally intriguing from an English perspective is the Italians' struggle with their own shortcomings. 'When we win in football, it's not the natural order of things. It is the opposite. We are a small country trying to show that it is not so small. When Ferrari win the F1 championship, everyone here says: "Look how brilliant is Italian industry." We were the greatest country – but 2,000 years ago, and also 500 years. But we lost that memory. I think in England you still have the memory of your great past. We don't look to the past, and we are not patriotic or nationalistic at all. For the cynical Italian, his sense of his small town is much stronger than the sense of the nation. Yes, we know about our victories in '34 and '38 and also in '82, but we are always more involved in the present. Football in Italy is hysterical. We are always shouting and crying about the last loss. Everybody says the trainer is an idiot, but when he wins the next match he is a "genius".'

On the other hand, the Italians do take pride in their sense of themselves as being smarter and tactically superior. One popular TV programme called *Mai dire goal* – never say goal – shows the worst defending and stupidest goals from around the world. Most clips come from England, whose defenders are ridiculed for being tall, slow and incompetent. When a handful of top Italian players such as Zola and Ravanelli came to the Premiership they enjoyed English sportsmanship, the relaxed atmosphere, and the huge amount of space they got to play in. No British player has made himself a legend in Italy since John Charles in the fifties, although Liam Brady was appreciated at Juventus, Sampdoria and Inter in the 1980s. Pellizzari says: 'The Italian championship is too difficult for English players. We are too tactical and our defenders are too nasty. I think Beckham would have great problems here. But we look at the English national team as a great unfulfilled potential. As we say: a man who misses a cent to have one million. You are always nearly there. You reach the semi-finals. But, in the end, you never arrive. We can never exactly explain this. When we look at your players, we always think of England as a favourite, but then we write: "Once again England didn't succeed." '

In England, footballing attitudes towards Italy have changed since the early nineties. Mike Ticher, former editor of the fanzine *When Saturday Comes*, recalls: 'After the 1990 World Cup, Italy seemed to have everything we didn't: brilliant new stadiums, the world's best players. Now I think we've got a much more balanced picture of Italian football.' After a brief infatuation, Channel Four's Serie A audiences decided Italian football was actually rather cagey and dull and viewing numbers dwindled. Back in Turin, the once-admired Stadio delle Alpi is derided for being cavernous and lacking in atmosphere. Juventus look with envy at the colourful, passionate, tighter stadiums of the Premiership and hope to build something in the English style for themselves. There are some in England still inclined to cede cultural superiority to Italy. Most English observers found the cautious 2003 Champions League final in Manchester between AC Milan and Juventus tedious. Simon Barnes of *The Times* saw it as a masterclass: 'Football is an Italian game that just happens to have been invented in England. That was the only conclusion to draw from . . . a match played with the rhythm of a rapier duel and the passion of a chess world championship.'

But the Italian public largely shunned their team during their awful Euro 2004, and the self-inflicted humiliation of losing to South Korea in 2002 (a defeat caused by Italian lack of adventure) still haunts the *azzurri*. Meanwhile, increasing athleticism and globalisation are changing Italian football.

Says Pellizzari: 'We complain now a lot about our players' technique. It is not as good as twenty years ago. They don't teach children any more how to stop the ball . . . well, they teach but they don't insist. They talk about tactics. If you compare the small 1982 team physically with the big players of today, they seem to belong to different sports. In 1998 we played a very old football, still with man-to-man marking. Now everybody in Italy plays with the zone. We think of that now as the Italian way. But when Eriksson brought it to Italy in the eighties, it was as if he came from Mars.'

Italians now admire England's top three teams. 'But they are very different. The Manchester United way is to play somehow as if they were robots: a perfect machine in a system which is the same year after year. We don't see Arsenal really as an English team. They don't play in the classical English way, as we imagine it, with big centre-forwards always jumping for crosses. And we thought the Chelsea of Ranieri were good because they had an Italian trainer.' The Bosman Law changed Italian football almost as much as it did the English game. 'At Inter you now have very few Italians playing. Sometimes it is eleven foreigners. So national differences are being eroded. Within ten years national teams are all going to play in more or less the same way.'

England and Italy are probably closer to football parity than they ever have been. But in the longer term, says Mario Sconcerti, the advantage is with the English: 'When the English era in football comes, I will study it with great interest.'

By C. MALCOLM
HINCKS.

# Such a Sportsman

## ENGLISH GRACE

My dear, gentle, wise American friend Suzan Harvey often talked about the 'grace of the English'. She could have been talking about herself. She was proud of the deep English roots of her family in Massachusetts, and although she was no expert on football, she knew a mountain about integrity, spirit, strength and courage. In one phone conversation just before she fell ill for the last time we talked a bit about the distinctively English-flavoured virtues of men such as Bobby Moore and Nat Lofthouse. Among her many gifts Suzan was a remarkable psychic. In her intuitive way, she sensed what was special about them, why they still matter. It wasn't just the obvious stuff such as their modesty and decency on the field, she detected something spiritual too: that they represented a deep culture of generosity and mutual respect.

Suzan wasn't the first great American to embody or talk about this kind of Englishness. During the Second World War, the journalist Ed Murrow detected something similar, and in his radio broadcasts during the Battle of Britain and the Blitz conveyed the courage and dignity – the grace – of Londoners under attack. These days the 'spirit of the Blitz' has become something of a distant cliché, but in the summer of 1940 it was real. Britain – the single light shielding the world from absolute darkness – seemed on the verge of being snuffed out. Murrow's electrifying reporting of the Nazi air assault helped to shock neutral Americans into support for entering the war. On 18 August, for example, Murrow visited a London suburb after an attack. 'There were two women who gossiped across the narrow strip of tired brown grass that separated their two houses. They didn't have to open their windows in order to converse. The glass had been blown out. There was a little man with a pipe in his mouth who walked up and looked at a bombed house and said, "One fell there and that's all" . . . About an hour after the "all-clear" had sounded people were sitting in deck-chairs on their lawns, reading the Sunday papers. The girls in light, cheap dresses were strolling along the streets. There was no bravado, no loud voices, only a quiet acceptance of the situation. To me those people were incredibly brave and calm. They are the unknown heroes of this war.'

A week later, on the heaviest night of bombing yet, Murrow visited eleven air-raid shelters around the West End. 'No words of mine can describe the spectacle over London tonight, so I'll talk about the people underground . . . Each time I entered a new shelter people wanted to know if I'd seen any bombs and if it was safe to go home. At one shelter there was a fine row going on. A man wanted to smoke his pipe in the shelter; the warden wouldn't allow it. The pipe smoker said he'd go out and he'd go out in the street, where he'd undoubtedly be hit by a bomb and then the warden would be sorry . . . I have seen a few pale faces, but very few. How long these people will stand up to this sort of thing I don't know, but tonight they're magnificent. I've seen them, talked with them and I know.'

Sometimes the quiet private defiance he witnessed verged on the crazy. German bombs that were fused to explode at any time after falling were one of the nastiest problems for emergency crews on the ground. On one occasion Murrow found an area roped off around one such device. Nervously, he peered round the corner of a building and saw a big policeman standing over the bomb rhythmically, slowly tossing his whistle into the air and catching it. 'I've seen cops in New York perform something of the same operation with a truncheon on a warm spring day. If that bomb had gone off, the bobby would have been a dead man and the whistle would have fallen to the pavement. After watching him for perhaps two minutes I withdrew, convinced that it would have been impossible for me to catch that whistle in a washtub. What the policeman was doing there, I don't know. He may be there still.'

Unlike war, football isn't an arena of life and death, yet some of its greatest practitioners have exhibited those same qualities of quiet courage, grace under pressure, forbearance and decency. This sporting grace is occasionally reflected in acts of selfless compassion. For example, playing for Juventus in the fifties, John Charles accidentally flattened a defender and was left with only the goalkeeper to beat. Instead of attempting to score, Charles kicked the ball into touch and went to aid his fallen opponent. As Michael Parkinson notes: 'Even in those days it was a remarkable act of sportsmanship. Nowadays he would be bollocked by his manager, derided by the fans and lampooned in the media for doing such a silly thing. Who says the game is better now than then?'

Integrity also comes into it. The ludicrous attempt to charge Bobby Moore with shoplifting in Bogotá in 1970 failed because picturing the England captain as a thief was as plausible as imagining the Dalai Lama as a Millwall fan chanting: 'You're going home in a fucking ambulance.' Perhaps English sporting grace has above all been about forbearance and generosity in adversity. When Basile Boli of France cynically head-butted Stuart Pearce in the face during a Euro '92 game, Pearce made no fuss. At the post-match press conference, he refused to criticise Boli. 'It was just an accident,' he insisted, saving the Frenchman from an automatic two-match ban. Boli was so astonished and grateful that he sent Pearce a bunch of flowers to thank him.

Such behaviour is the benign part of the legacy of the Victorian ideals of manliness inscribed into English football's genome at the moment of its creation. As we saw in the second chapter, public-school headmasters sought to turn boys into chivalrous sporting warriors who would be modest and indomitable, and as patriotic as they were honourable. Later, this upper-class sporting code was quite successfully proselytised to the working classes where it meshed with older strands of English manliness. But this moral code was also shaped and reflected to some degree by the physical conditions in which the game was played: heavy, toe-capped leather boots and hefty, mud-caked leather footballs. Even such a rebellious, ball-playing artist as Billy Meredith subscribed to the Victorian moral code of football. For him, football was 'my only love, for it is a noble and manly game'. In a television commentary, the big-hearted Kevin Keegan memorably once described a player's qualities: 'He's using his strength. And that *is* his strength: his strength. You could say that it's his strong point.' For as long as anyone can remember, much the same has been true of English football as a whole.

One of the finest exemplars of the tradition of graceful strength is Nat Lofthouse, the 'Lion of Vienna'. When we think of footballing grace now, we tend to think of a Thierry Henry rather than an oak-hearted English number 9, but when Lofthouse played he seems to have embodied rather spiritual qualities. 'There is English football; there are English footballers: and Lofthouse is, perhaps, in our time the most English of them all,' wrote the historian Percy Young. 'In Lofthouse all the native traditions were incarnate. Not the most skilful of players (although his tactical ability and appreciation of placing and timing had probably been underestimated), he proved himself to be at least the most resolute of his generation.'

In his 1954 autobiography, *Goals Galore*, 'Lofty', as he is still known, thanked all the bruising defenders he had faced. 'Believe me, it is meant from the heart when I say that footballers such as these have given me a lot of fun. I must stress once again that football followers who think a hard tussle between footballers means bad blood are wrong. The harder the struggle the better friends we are after the match. That is as it should be and is how I hope it always will be.' The sentiment was completely genuine. His friend and Bolton colleague, full-back Roy Hartle, recalls: 'It was a considerable honour to play with Lofty because he *was* graceful, and he was tough, and he could play against the best centre-halves. But he sort of made friends with them all, and they stayed friends over the years. I think there was more friendship in the game in those days. You played against someone and it was tough, but at the end of the game everything was forgotten, and the next time you met, you'd shake hands and go out and play. Lofty was probably the best of all in this respect. He's not a big guy, except in his heart. He's only 5 ft 9. But he was so powerful. In training sessions we'd play first-team defence against first-team forward line, and Lofty was terrible to play against because he always played flat out. You'd be waiting on the far post and he'd come clattering in behind you with his knees, elbows and everything. Terrible!

He couldn't play it any other way. He'd say: "I can play 100%, but I can't play 90%."'

Lofthouse's modesty is reflected in the book:

I'm no pin-up boy, and when youngsters hang about outside the dressing-room I feel almost as embarrassed as they do when they jump forward for my autograph. As a boy I used to do the same, and I know they think of me as something out of the ordinary. But I am not. Like other footballers, I'm just an ordinary chap who enjoys the simple things in life. There's no glamour about me, a fellow who often washes the baby's nappies, and gets a kick out of taking his young son out for an ice cream. You've only got to sit down and talk with me to realise that I'm just the kind of fellow you'd meet in a railway carriage, in a restaurant, or come to that in the local YMCA. The fact that my job of scoring goals sometimes put my name into the headlines is embarrassing.

He revealed that his favourite food was Lancashire hot-pot. He enjoyed a glass of beer once a week, and smoked five cigarettes a day. His favourite film star was Greer Garson. He liked rock gardening. He and his wife Alma's favourite hobby was making rugs: 'We completed a rug for the living room. Now we are engaged making one for the sitting room. Why rug-making? I find it most relaxing!'

He was also strikingly open-hearted and eager to learn. When Brazil visited Burnden Park, Lofthouse was the first person at the training ground to watch them, and when a Rest of Europe team drew 4–4 with England in October 1953 he enthused: 'People who had never regarded soccer as something possessing a creative beauty of its own were made conscious of the fact by the accurate passing and skilful movements of the continentals. Their acrobatic ability lent to the game a colour

which seems to have departed from our own football.' In
Florence in 1952, when a broken bottle thrown from the
crowd missed his right eye by inches, instead of being furious,
Lofthouse preferred to praise the reactions of the Italian players:

> The scene that followed has gone down in my memory as one
> of the most remarkable I have encountered in any walk of
> SPORT. Pincinninni, that grand Italian left-half and sports-
> man, followed by four other players, black with anger, rushed
> over to the bottle-throwing section of the crowd and began
> remonstrating with them . . . It was quite clear the Italian
> players were giving the hotheads quite a roasting . . . I shall
> always appreciate the way those Italian footballers dealt with the
> hotheads in the moment of crisis.

When the Hungarians destroyed England in 1953: 'When the
goals began to rip past Gilbert Merrick a lump came to my
throat. I found myself wishing I could have been playing in that
match, not because I thought I could improve upon the men
preferred to me, but because it would have been a wonderful
education to play against such accomplished soccermen!'

He also understood that his own talents were very different:
full-bodied aggression, a tremendous shot and remarkable
power in the air, honed by countless hours as a boy heading
a ball against a stable door. Early in his Bolton career, coach
George Taylor had told Lofthouse: 'You can do three things.
You can run, shoot and head. You couldn't trap a bag of
washing. So don't get fancy.'

Lofthouse served – no other verb will do – Bolton for more
than sixty years as player, manager and official; although at the
time of writing he's been ill, he remains the club's honorary
president. Other great players have been loyal to their clubs,
and have won more honours, but the affection for Lofthouse

reflects something deeper, something almost spiritual. Hartle says: 'I took him last season to a supporters' meeting and I have never seen anything like it. It was absolutely incredible, the way they looked up to him and honoured him. Young people in their twenties who never saw him play. I couldn't believe it. There were 300 people and he must have had 100 photographs taken. They just could not get enough of him. It's pride. He is them. He is the best of them. He is the club as far as they're concerned. He's bigger than the club, but not in a way that he detaches himself from the rest of the people. He is still one of them.'

Close to the centre of Bolton, on Chorley New Road, there's a pub called the Lion of Vienna. The great man (routinely referred to in Bolton as 'Sir Nat' even though the Prime Minister ignored a local campaign to have him knighted) opened the place himself in 1984. The walls are decorated with pictures of his exploits, including his second goal in the 1958 Cup Final, when he shoulder-charged Manchester United goalkeeper Harry Gregg into the net. (Perfectly legal at the time. English goalkeepers weren't protected and foreign keepers – who were – were sissies.) The pub's name celebrates Lofthouse and his most famous game, the one that defined him, against a 'crack' Austrian team in Vienna in 1952. In his fearless, blazing style, Lofthouse led the England forward line with almost insane heroism and got himself knocked out in scoring the late winning goal. When he regained consciousness, he simply shook himself and carried on.

At the end of the match, British soldiers in the crowd carried him on their shoulders. As Geoffrey Green wrote later:

For anybody who has ever seen football or read football [Lofthouse] will always be known as the lion of Vienna . . .
It was the heart of Lofthouse that won the match. The two

goals, including the winner which turned the game, are only a part of the story. It was his example all through the match that brought the scores of British soldiers pouring through the crowd at the end of the game to cheer him, lion-hearted, from the field.

Lofthouse's description of the decisive moment in *Goals Galore* evokes the spirit of a thousand boys' stories. In front of a passionate crowd in what was billed as the 'championship of Europe', the Austrians had 'tried to dazzle us with their grace, artistry and power play', he wrote. But England were holding on. With the score 2–2 and only minutes to go, Austria pushed their defenders into attack. England's goalkeeper, Gil Merrick, caught a corner and quickly threw the ball out to Tom Finney, whose flick sent Lofthouse clear. Three team-mates shouted: 'You're on your own Nat!' and Lofthouse raced towards the Austrian goal:

> In the distance I could see Musil, the Austrian 'keeper, bobbing up and down between the goalposts. While I sensed the situation and quite clearly remember the scene in front of me, it was only by some sixth sense that I whipped the ball under control and as if my life depended on breaking the 100 metres record closed in on Musil at the fastest pace I could muster. It did not take the Austrians long to realise what a tactical error they had made in putting all their attacking eggs in one basket. But they did not stop to ponder long. Like a pack of hounds after a fox they began to chase – me! The whole of Vienna seemed to have gone mad. I found myself the centre of 60,000 pairs of eyes, few of them friendly ones, and as the ball bobbed at my feet I could hear the thud of Austrian boots behind me as their nimble defenders began to overhaul me . . . 'Shall I have a crack and chance to luck?' I asked myself. The

speed with which I was travelling gave me my answer, for just when I had decided to shoot, Musil, like a frightened stag, suddenly darted from his goal. At that precise moment I hit the ball hard to the right at the Austrian goal and then felt a searing pain in my right leg as the goalkeeper missed the ball and gave me a tremendous – but for all that accidental – kick on my shin-bone. As I went sprawling on the dark turf I heard the crowd begin to roar. Then darkness came. Only when Tom Finney, Eddie Bailey and Billy Elliott rushed up, hauled me to my feet and shouted 'It's in Nat!' did I realise England were in front. My one regret is that I never saw the ball into the Austrian net for the best goal of my life.

Best goal it may have been, but it also sounds like the triumph of spirit over technical shortcomings. 'Exactly,' says Hartle. 'His first touch wasn't so good, and it's given the goalkeeper a chance. The goalkeeper thought: "That's mine." Lofty really shouldn't have chased the ball. He was 40–60 down, and the keeper was obviously going to get there first. But Lofty never pulled out of anything. He chased lost balls and lost causes and he would just keep running and running. It meant so much to him. He always said: "I would walk to London to play for my country." That's the kind of guy he was. It was his ball and he was going to make it his. What happened is history. But he scored the goal, didn't he?'

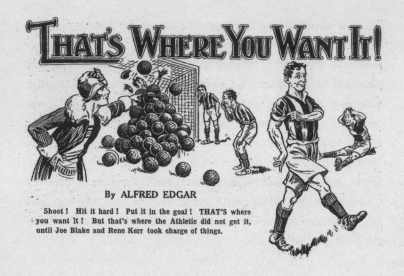

# THAT'S WHERE YOU WANT IT!

## By ALFRED EDGAR

Shoot ! Hit it hard ! Put it in the goal ! THAT'S where you want it ! But that's where the Athletic did not get it, until Joe Blake and Rene Kerr took charge of things.

## BOOTS AND BALLS

Nat Lofthouse played, as English footballers had always played, in traditional, high-ankled, devoutly dubbined heavy leather boots. Bolton's players were allowed one pair each year, trooping down to Albert Ward's on Bridgegate each summer before the season to be shod. 'They were awful things,' recalls Roy Hartle. 'You used to end up with blisters and everything trying to break them in. I used to sit for hours on the side of the bath at home with my socks and boots in warm water, trying to mould the damn things so I wouldn't get as many blisters.' Players of the fifties would rarely admit to pain, even when seriously hurt. 'It was just the way we played the game. For instance, Denis Law was quite tough to play against and one day at Burnden he whacked me. It wasn't deliberate, just very painful, but I would never give him the satisfaction of letting him know he'd hurt me. You just got up and got on with it. I got an even worse kick from Frankie Blunstone at Chelsea one

day. He hit me on the knee and it was *so* painful it was killing
me, but I got up immediately and jogged away. Then you'd
sort of wait your turn, and whack him back. You would never
go out intentionally to hurt anyone. But that's just the way the
game was played. It was tough and everybody accepted it.
These days . . . "Cheat" is a horrible word to use, but I feel
sorry for the boys in black: the referees have no chance at all,
have they? Players throw themselves down at every little touch.
And the shirt-pulling! That was never *ever* used in our day. It
just wasn't the way a man behaved. The moral code changed.'

Strength and the ability to withstand punishment were still
more essential when football was even tougher, in the 1920s
and 1930s. Dixie Dean of Everton, statistically the greatest
goalscorer in the history of the English game, lost a testicle at
the age of seventeen when playing for Tranmere in a reserve
match. Dean had angered the opposing centre-half, one Davy
Parkes, by scoring twice. As Dean passed him going down the
field, the two bantered. Parkes: 'Tha'll get no more bloody
goals today, you've finished.' Dean: 'By the looks of you,
you've finished, you've had it.' Next time Dean got too near
Parkes the defender kicked him with full force in the groin. In
hospital Dean was strapped to a table while his balls swelled,
and then was given gas while surgeons removed the damaged
organ. After five weeks he was back on the field, and the injury
didn't affect either his football or his ability to go on to father
four children. Seventeen years later Dean was in a pub in
Chester when a stranger sent him a pint across the bar. He
stared at the man's face for a while before it dawned on him that
the man was Davy Parkes. Dean strode over and greeted his
former assailant . . . with a savage beating. 'I done his face up
and they took him to the hospital, so we're evens,' Dean
recalled in a radio interview in 1978. 'It was the only time that I
ever retaliated.' During his later career, he played with a metal

plate in his head, the result of a life-threatening motorcycle accident which left him with a broken skull and a fractured jaw.

Doctors told him he'd never play again. But Dean was a phenomenon, both physically and as a footballer. As a small boy, he could kick the ball as hard as an adult; when he was twelve, the power of his shot broke the arm of a school goalkeeper. Dean's principal gift was his astonishing heading talent, enhanced by the ability to leap like an Olympic high jumper. Even with defenders holding on to him, he could out-jump anyone. One of his tricks was to lob a goal by heading the ball into the ground with such force that it bounced up and over the goalkeeper's head. Dean was also one of the few players ever to head a goal from a penalty: when the goalkeeper punched away the spot kick in a match at West Brom in 1936 Dean headed it straight back into the net. He could also be subtle. His range of flicks and touches was extensive and he occasionally scored with back headers, using the sun and the goalkeeper's shadow to judge the angle. Dean was contemptuous of modern equipment. In his 1977 biography, *Dixie Dean; the Life Story of a Goal Scoring Legend*, Nick Walsh quotes Dean saying of the new lightweight football: 'It's more like Lewis's balloons;' Of the new footwear: 'Today they play in bloody carpet slippers instead of boots.' He was convinced that modern players' lack of technique was to blame for head injuries. Yet the old balls were sometimes dangerous even to Dixie Dean. In a match against Wales in 1928 (in the season during which he'd scored a staggering eighty-two goals, sixty of them in the league), he rose for a header and came down half blinded. The lace in the ball had come loose and whiplashed into his right eye. Despite being in pain and barely able to see, Dean, naturally, insisted on finishing the match.

This ethos goes back to the Old Etonians and beyond. Playing at the dawn of sport in the 1870s, Arthur Kinnaird caught Charles Alcock, creator of the FA Cup, with a ferocious late foul. 'Is it to be hacking then?' asked Alcock. 'Oh, by all means let us have hacking,' answered Kinnaird cheerily. And they did. The pleasure taken in rough play has always cut right across class lines in England. As Barry Fantoni puts it: 'The Anglo-Saxons are great warriors. They are murderous. Those fucking lads in white vans: I don't pick fights with them. Some pansy out of fucking Eton I might have a go at, but even then I'd be careful because they are the same people. They'll all give you a good fight.' This view is confirmed by the Edwardian classic *Association Football and the Men Who Made It*, in which William Pickford reflected:

> When you can eliminate the spirit of the Anglo-Saxon from the national elements and substitute the mildness and patience of the Hindoo for it, we may perhaps arrive at playing football in a purely scientific manner, with no more physical danger than is incurred in a game of lawn tennis or golf. When that day arrives may I have laid down my pen and rested my bones in their last pilgrimage, for I don't want to be present.

The respected journalist and former player Ken Jones reflects that such spirit informed every aspect of the game. Jones's first manager when he turned pro at Southend was the iconic hard man Wilf Copping, England's terrifying two-footed tackling hero at the Battle of Highbury in 1934. 'It always used to make us chuckle to hear Wilf described as "hard but fair", when in fact he was violent,' says Jones. 'Copping taught us that you rattled people as early as you could in the game, because that might give you a bit of an advantage. If the guy came back for more then you'd think: "Well, I've got a game on here." But if the guy buckled a little bit, you'd say: "Right, he's looking for when I'm coming . . ."' Copping was merely an extreme example of the prevailing culture of the game: 'Training was not nearly as concentrated as it is now, but a lot of it was based on actually hurting each other. If you played a game of head tennis, for example, boots would be flying about over the top of the net. And in a practice match, there would be a lot of nastiness: "Get him out the way and I might get his place in the team." When I was growing up I never really thought of it as a "manly" thing. You just wanted to play, didn't you? And at that time, of course, ball skills were basically just moving it along the ground. Flicks and tricks were frowned upon. You tried to develop your dribbling skills and your touch, but you wouldn't see players in those days, right up into the fifties, out on the field before the game, flicking the ball up. They just went out there and practised shooting.'

Jones was born into a formidable football family. His uncle Bryn, who played for Wolves and Arsenal, was one of the stars of the 1930s. His cousin Cliff was a key member of the Tottenham Double-winning team of 1961. 'When I was at Swansea I lived with my cousin Bryn, who was also playing at Swansea at that time. We used to walk to the ground together every morning, and we'd chat away amiably. And we'd get to the ground, and we would invariably be on opposite sides in a practice match. And then he'd kick shit out of me. I'd say: "What is it with you?" "Ahh, get on with it." I think there was a certain pleasure taken in all that hardness. There was something manly about being able to stand up for yourself on the field. But the emphasis was never on just being hard. The emphasis was on being able to play. And in those days, athleticism was a bonus. Nowadays it's the other way around.'

Historian Richard Holt has shown how, in the north of England, this ethos may have dovetailed with a longer tradition of admiration for tough local sporting heroes who reflected the way the region liked to see itself. This was as true of nine-

teenth-century prize-fighters, runners and rowers as it was of
the 'gritty, unadorned, indomitable masculine style' of Yorkshire cricketers such as Wilfred Rhodes, Herbert Sutcliffe and
Freddie Trueman. In football, Holt singles out Newcastle's
1950s hero 'Wor' Jackie Milburn, uncle of the Charlton
brothers, and predecessor of seventies star Malcolm Macdonald
as the perfect example of the deeply loved 'big, open-hearted
ordinary man'. While he sees Nat Lofthouse as 'the acceptable
face of northern football hardness', there was an unacceptable
face as well: 'Not all northern heroes were nice; some were
famous for their willingness to be sent off for injuring the
opposition. Clubs like Barnsley, fed by miners from the nearby
coalfield, abounded in stories, polished in the telling, of men
working double shifts and walking twenty miles to play a
match. These men did not like to lose, especially if there was a
hefty side bet illegally placed on the outcome. There was a self-
conscious cult of northern aggression, which applauded the
violent antics of some players . . . Plenty of teams had a hard
man but some clubs, it was widely believed, made a fetish of
aggression. When Barnsley played Swindon in the cup semi-
final in 1912 Barnsley deliberately kicked Harold Fleming, the
star Swindon player, until he had got seriously injured, and the
local press jeered at the southerners for making an official
complaint. These hard men were never heroes in the sense of
commanding wide admiration as athletes, but there was a side
of northern masculinity that admired anyone who could "do
the business". Being able to give and take punishment was
universal, part of the male ethos of football.'

It was certainly the main claim to fame of Frank Barson,
arguably the most brutal of all English players, who played for
Aston Villa, Manchester United and England in the 1920s. A
former Sheffield blacksmith who suffered four broken noses
and two serious back injuries, Barson was a 'character', 'a truly

great footballer and personality and a card', according to Billy Walker, who played with him at Aston Villa. He was also violent enough to be cautioned *before* a match. Just before the 1920 FA Cup Final, referee Jack Howcroft went to the players' dressing room to tell him: 'The first wrong move you make, Barson, off you go.' Barson's on-field repertoire included late and over-the-ball tackles which put victims out of action for weeks. Off the pitch, he was even scarier. Towards the end of his career, when he was offered a smaller pay rise than he thought he deserved, Barson is said to have gone in to contract negotiations with his manager carrying a gun. Barson's pals included Lawrence and William Fowler, Sheffield gangsters in the style of the Kray twins. The Fowler brothers terrorised the city in the 1920s and earned it the nickname of 'Little Chicago'. Awaiting execution for stabbing and kicking to death a local boxer who stood up to them, the brothers sent Barson a pre-match good luck message from the condemned cell.

The nineteenth-century codes of manliness which governed English football – and its style and equipment – went virtually unchallenged until the 1950s. In the first decades of football, boots had been, in essence, adapted workmen's boots. In a game of power and manly endurance and violence, footwear was designed for strength. Adverts of the time reflected this: 'permanent indestructible block toe' . . . 'protects the ankle wonderfully well' . . . 'solid leather'. By the 1920s earlier designs had evolved to produce the classic English football boot: the super-sturdy, ankle-high 'Manfield Hotspur', man-ufactured and sold in great numbers by a company in North-ampton. As an ad for the boot makes clear, robustness and dependability were the principal selling points:

1. Solid butt toe, non-kinking
2. Rounded sole to edge prevents mud clogging and smartens action
3. Waist arch of strength and spring
4. Bevel-edged stiffener fits snugly and protects heel
5. Lock-rivetted studs, placed for most grip and support

Balls, reflecting the same ethos, were advertised in similar style. In the 1900s sports goods manufacturers Frank Sugg Ltd of Liverpool promoted a ball called 'Football King' ('Best in all the world. Round, sound, waterproof, durable, lasting') by showing it being run over by a two-ton agricultural roller 'which did not burst it!'.

In his autobiography *The Way It Was*, Stanley Matthews describes the leaden qualities of the balls of his era. Before the Second World War, there were basically just two makes – the Tugite and the Thomlinson 'T': 'The Tugite was more expensive because it was considered a superior ball – it didn't gather mud on heavy grounds – whereas the "T", which did collect mud on a sludgy pitch, was favoured only when pitch conditions were firm.' Specially treated, super-heavy 'T' balls tended to be used from March until the end of the season. Matthews recalls:

In a matter of weeks the conditions of pitches changed from being quagmires to being rock hard. As anyone who has played football at any level will know, playing on a bone hard pitch in windy weather, the ball seems to be overly light and always bouncing up around your knees. To counteract this, trainers would soak the 'T' ball for 24 hours in a bucket of water, then insert another bladder, additional to the one already inside the leather outer case. From being light and balloon-like, the ball took on all the attributes of one of those large concrete balls

used on the gateposts of stately homes. You knew when you
had headed this ball, I can tell you. What's more, if rain fell
during a game, as the match progressed the leather expanded so
that the ball grew to almost beachball size . . . It says much for
the general standard of skill that for all the cumbersome weight
of such balls, the players still managed to produce football of
high-quality.

Although the ball was supposed to weigh 16 ounces, soaking and
an extra bladder could double this. If it rained, 'the "T" ball with
its penchant for gathering clinging mud became heavier still'.

After the war, balls were better made and more likely to keep
their shape but they still had to be dubbined to make them
water resistant and remained a world away from the resilient,
lightweight balls of today. In his 1955 book *Soccer Revolution*,
the Austrian Jewish exile Willy Meisl was baffled by English
attitudes. Why, he wondered, did the English always insist on
using the heaviest and biggest balls?

Everybody knows that wet weather and muddy ground conditions prevail in Britain throughout the soccer season to a
much greater extent than in most other soccer loving countries.
A ball frequently immersed in water gets soaked; that is,
heavier, and very often tends to extend a bit. The logical
conclusion would be – for a person with imagination anyhow –
that in Great Britain the lightest ball, and above all, one near to
the minimum circumference, should be used to guarantee the
best sporting conditions. The very opposite is the case. We
happen to be the only soccer nation to use the ball of maximum
weight and circumference exclusively.

Meisl saw this as an example of lack of imagination: 'One of the
prime virtues and main deficiencies in the British national

character. It sometimes has the same effect as the lack of vitamins or hormones has on the diet of mind and soul.' It wasn't lack of imagination; the English preferred it this way. But as English footballing hegemony became increasingly under threat, contact with the outside world and new ideas began to challenge the old codes and eventually brought profound change.

Stanley Matthews was one of the first major players to glimpse an alternative universe when he travelled to Brazil for the 1950 World Cup. Before England played Chile, he went to the Maracaña to see Brazil beat Mexico. The experience was a revelation. The atmosphere was 'provocative, animated, impassioned and intoxicating' and the Brazilian players excited him:

> Breathtaking skill was coupled with precise passing and explosive shooting . . . Brazil played a game that was fast and accurate with an inordinate amount of skill. Although attacking play was the order of the day in England, the fluidity with which Brazil took the game to opponents had a controlled grace and style about it I had not seen before. In England, teams loved to attack, but in comparison to the Brazilians, our style came across predominantly as hell-for-leather running and chasing.

He left the stadium with his mind 'buzzing with new ideas and possibilities', he wrote in his autobiography.

He had also noticed something interesting about the Brazilians' feet. 'Their boots . . . were shaped to hug the foot, light and far less cumbersome than the traditional English boot.' The day after the game, he bought a pair of Brazilian boots – size seven – in a Rio de Janeiro sports shop and marvelled at their construction:

The boots were made of thin leather. They had no bulbous toe.
And no steel plate in the sole, which was also made of a thin
strip of leather. The boots were streamlined in design and barely
reached the ankle, unlike British boots which, in affording
complete protection for not only the ankle but the couple of
inches above, were weighty and not conducive to speed off the
mark, especially on heavy grounds . . . I realised that with a pair
of these lightweight, streamlined boots I could be even quicker,
if only by inches over a yard or so.

When he got home, he went to the Co-Op boot factory in
Yorkshire and asked them if they could make new boots
specially for him, along the lines of the shoes from Brazil:

It took a few goes before they came up with the boots I wanted,
but once they were right it took only one game for me to fall in
love with them. The leather was thin as card, the boots were
hand-stitched. There was no bulbous toe, no steel plate in the
sole. In fact, the leather sole was so thin they had to produce
special nails small enough to tag it to the upper and for the studs.
The boots afforded little protection to the ankle in much the
same way as boots do not today, but my theory was if a
defender caught me, it was my fault for not being skilful or
quick enough to evade his tackle. The boots weighed just a few
ounces and were so supple and flexible I could fold them up
and put them in my jacket pocket without them being
cumbersome. From 1950 until my retirement from league
football in 1965, I wore that style of boot in every game I
played. Heaven knows how many pairs I got through; they
were so light and delicate they would last for two or three
games at the most, sometimes not even a game. I always had
four or five pairs in the dugout as a precaution. One pair has
survived the years, and looking at them now they are not far

removed in design from the boots current players wear, but they were certainly revolutionary in the fifties.

Matthews recalled an advert in the official 1951–52 *FA Year Book* for the 'Official Association Boot', the Hotshot. 'This boot hadn't changed in decades, and indeed among the advantages listed were "reinforced hard toes", "non-stretch instep supports" and a back that came some two inches above the ankle. Made of "best materials" they may have been, but they were not conducive to the game that was rapidly changing on the continent and in South America.' By coincidence, on the opposite page was an advert for the tracksuits worn by Blackpool, featuring a photo of the team, including Matthews, wearing his handmade, lightweight boots – 'the old and new world of football facing each other across the page'. Matthews persuaded the Co-Op to design and market a brand of lightweight boot bearing his name for the general public. The Stanley Matthews Boot sold nearly half a million pairs. But the game as a whole remained indifferent. 'Stan was light-years ahead of everyone, wasn't he?' recalls Roy Hartle. 'Training on his own, taking all the orange juice and pills. But nobody copied him. Everyone thought he was strange.'

Much-loved as he was, Matthews couldn't change the culture of the British game on his own. In boot design, the transformation had to wait almost a decade. When it came, it was fuelled by external influences and was part of a wider challenge to the old Victorian codes.

In Switzerland in 1954 an innovative football boot designed by an obscure German craftsman called Adi Dassler helped the amateur players of West Germany to beat the apparently invincible Hungarians in the World Cup Final. Few games have had such long-term consequences. Hungarian football never recovered from the defeat, but winning made the

Germans feel good about being German for the first time since the war. All future German football successes can be traced to that afternoon, which is still celebrated as *das Wunder von Bern* (the miracle of Berne). And Dassler's little known company, Adidas, went on to dominate the world football boot market (alongside his estranged brother Rudi's company, Puma, which used similar designs). The Berne game was played on a pitch that heavy rain had turned to quagmire. While Ferenc Puskas and his team-mates wore more traditional Hungarian leather boots, the Germans had Dassler's lightweight boots fitted with adjustable studs, which he had invented three months before. Hungary took an early two-goal lead, but the Germans' footwear helped them master the conditions much more effectively and they fought back to win 3–2. Reports of the game created a bit of a stir in England. Under the headline 'What a Dazzler!', a British tabloid described the new wonder boot, less than a third the weight of the Hotspur, and urged the England team to switch to it immediately.

Eventually, they did. When Geoff Hurst scored his hat-trick in the 1966 Final, he and the rest of the England team were wearing Adidas. The company had struggled for years to break into the ultra-conservative English professional market. One desperate tactic was to leave boots in players' dressing rooms together with cash-stuffed envelopes. Another marketing method was to send boots unsolicited to clubs. Future Everton star Jimmy Gabriel had grown up in hand-me-down Hotspurs given to him by his father just after the war. In 1957 he was a youngster with Dundee United when the club coach picked him to try out 'the strangest pair of boots I had ever seen':

The boots were black in colour with three white stripes down the outside and inside of the instep. They also had some lettering on the side which spelled out the word Adidas. They looked much lighter than normal new boots, the toe caps were softer, the uppers which protected the ankle lower, and there were no bars on the bottom to hammer the studs into. They were as far removed from my pair of Manfield Hotspurs as you could possibly get.

The boots were ridiculed by supporters and players. But, according to Ian McArthur and Dave Kemp in their book *Elegance Borne of Brutality*, Gabriel was entranced and said: 'Once I'd played in them, I wasn't going to swop them for any. They were as comfortable on my feet as made-to-measure boots, and my touch and timing, passing and control improved every time I wore them. Soon enough the spectators' catcalls turned to cheers and my team-mates' guffaws to questions like "Where can you buy them?"'

In the sixties the cultural shift saw the arrival of slipper-style boot design – and a new language of advertising. 'Play in Comfort', urged ads for imported 'chaussures françaises fantastiques' in the late sixties. 'George Best endorsed the Stylo Matchmaker – specially designed' in 'luxurious softie leather' to give 'lightness, flexibility and maximum comfort in wear'.

Cameron Kippen, historian of footwear and eroticism and lecturer at Curtin University of Technology in Perth, Australia, sees a sexual dimension behind the shift from big old boots to the new slippers. The first football boots were modified engineers' boots – 'very macho and manly' – and for more than a century there were only minor modifications to the basic design:

'The main purpose of football boots was always protection. In the late 1950s and the 1960s, they found they could drop the height of the boot. Instead of the hard-working traditional British player, you started to see the continental nancy-boy who was smart and exciting, who could move and dart. Through the sixties you had a greater awareness of the feminine side of males. For the spectators they became sensual beings.'

Kippen insists that footwear and sport are always sexualised:

The whole attraction of human movement is that you're replicating the sex act. When you go to a dance club and are attracted to someone, what you see is their brain in total control of their movement. Someone who can't coordinate her movements is unattractive. In football, when you see fantastic control, you are instantly fascinated because the primal part of your brain recognises: here is someone to emulate or copulate with.

Football boots are now part of an image-driven global sports equipment market. The most important buyers of football boots today are the middle-class Soccer Moms of the USA who care nothing for old English manliness and simply don't want their kids hurt. Image is all. As Kippen says, in the professional game, marketing tends to cut little ice and most players stick to boots they find reliable. But among the general public, new models of sports shoes go out of fashion in three months. 'In professional football it has been very difficult for Nike to break into a culture which has been dominated for so long by Adidas and Puma. But Nike can appeal to children – or to kids of all ages. So you see the fat wheezy boys who want to be like Ronaldo, so they wear his boots. People don't buy the football boots to compete, they buy boots to look like somebody else.'

When it comes to sex, Kippen sees surprisingly little difference between 120 years ago and today:

In Victorian times, on the outside, you had a very suppressed sexual conservatism, but there was a very volatile sexualisation inside. Muscular Christianity was highly sexualised. You wanted to make as much of your body as possible for theological reasons. But there were also lots of folk turned on by fit young bodies. The public schools tried to make men uninterested in touching and loving. But these feelings came out in another way: by beating up on other men. Being tough with each other was a way of cuddling. The violence came from a suppressed sexuality. It's two sides of the same coin. One is repressed, the other open. Men are always the same, but at different times they express it in different ways. The machismo of today contests the old hard image; but in some ways it's the same thing. It is continuously moving and evolving.

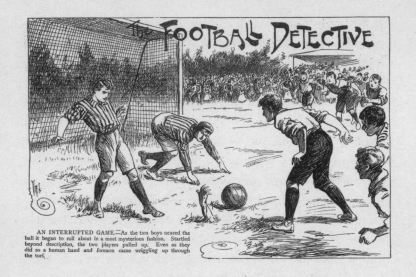

AN INTERRUPTED GAME.—As the two boys neared the ball it began to roll about in a most mysterious fashion. Startled beyond description, the two players pulled up. Even as they did so a human hand and forearm came wriggling up through the turf.

## MEET THE ANCESTORS

When the Duke of Wellington said the Battle of Waterloo was won on the playing fields of Eton, he really did mean *fields*: cold, thick, loamy slabs of former agricultural land. It's late March and I've come to the most important of all English schools searching for sporting dinosaurs. Eton College is where James Bond, Bertie Wooster, Arthur Kinnaird and nineteen British prime ministers were educated. It's also a place which guards its sporting heritage with pride. Modern football was, in large part, created here, adapted from older games which continue to be played at the school. I suspect that the ancient Wall Game and Field Game still contain part of football's original DNA code.

Eton looks fantastic. Oxbridge-style architecture. Coach-loads of tourists. Spotty teenagers in tail coats who will one day run the country. The place glows with a sense of its own excellence and power. For the Wall Game, security will be tight, I have been told mysteriously. First up, though, is the peculiar and punishing Field Game, played nowhere else on earth, which seems to incarnate the spirit of English football yet plays havoc with its rules. This, of course, is to see the thing from the wrong historical perspective: the game may look a weird cross between soccer and rugby, but it predates both by at least 150 years. (It was also the basis of field hockey.) The game is played at a frenetic pace on a football-sized field and there are two ways to get points: scoring a goal (but there's no net or goalkeeper) or getting a 'rouge', which is a sort of cross between a soccer corner and a rugby try. As in soccer, the ball is round and players kick and head it. They tackle each other and dribble as much as possible, and there's also a rugbyesque scrum called a 'bully'. Players attack and defend in packs and wedges. When someone kicks forward, his team-mates move smartly away from the ball. Complex codes of honour are also involved: switching play to the open space of the wings is 'sneaking'.

Confused? Me too. Dr Angus Graham-Campbell, who, as well as being Eton's head of games is also a playwright, editor of the *Keats–Shelley Review* and head of drama and creative writing, kindly tries to explain some of the many rules: 'You see, these red guys can't just sweep up without passing a blue guy on the way. So these guys are offside. The guy running up is offside because he didn't run past a blue person. Those blue players are now offside, which is why they hang back. Now they can run up. Now the reds are all offside. That boy who's running up there is offside and the referee hasn't spotted it.' I confess I haven't a clue what's going on. 'It seems complicated but you can actually learn it in about half an hour. The basic idea is: get the ball and run with it. But it's also a game of free-kicks. All the fouls are the same as soccer: no kicking, pushing, holding, tripping, handling. It's all the same.' How about spitting or calling the referee a wanker? 'Ungentlemanly conduct!'

It's a Saturday, and from all corners of the sleek, 350 acres of playing-fields, boys saunter by wearing ancient-looking football kit – each house has different colours with halved shirts and narrow stripes predominating. Parents, girlfriends and dogs look on with pride. The milky sun arcs low across the Berkshire sky, over the spires and old walls of the college. Field Game players spend most of the time charging up and down the field chasing long balls or weaving across their lines to comply with the complex offside rule. The game looks bruisingly manly; not so different from watching Wimbledon in the days of the Crazy Gang. Games master Mike Grenier, who's referee for this one and will take part in a Wall Game later in the afternoon, suggests the game's rugged aesthetic is connected to conditions under foot. 'A good bully player should be strong, but he also has to be skilful in controlling the ball. In the old days the grass at the Field Game was much longer than now. The idea of a bald surface over which you can dribble a light artificial ball is recent. It's like English rugby. For many years it was crash bang wallop, straight down the middle. The idea of releasing wingers and using the full-back as a front runner was a French and Welsh invention, a bit of Celtic flair. But I think we played in our way for pragmatic reasons too. Playing in England in winter, using a big old leather ball, by the constraints of the conditions, what else can you do?'

Today's big Field Game pits the school team against an old boys' side and turns out to be a bit of a classic. The more skilled old boys take an early lead, but are gradually pushed back by the fitter, younger team who equalise with the last kick of the match. The scorer celebrates by pulling his shirt over his head and racing away with arms outstretched like a plane. Post-match formalities – handshakes, speeches, team photos and champagne with parents, wives and girlfriends – are conducted amid an odd mixture of high decorum and weapons-grade testosterone.

In its style and tactics, Graham-Campbell suggests, the game I've just witnessed was remarkably similar to how the Old Etonians must have played when they won the FA Cup twice in six finals between 1875 and 1883. Indeed, the school newspaper at the time disparaged 'unsporting' working-class opponents such as Blackburn Olympic who passed the ball between themselves rather than doing the decent thing, which was dribbling. 'If the other side were passing the ball about, you couldn't get hold of it, so you couldn't "play football",' he explains. 'The sort of selfishness you saw going on in today's game is regarded as "good play" and "good sportsmanship" because you're putting yourself on the line: can you take responsibility and dribble and try to beat a man rather than give it to a team-mate which in those days was seen as cowardice, not being "man enough" to play the game.' The school has come a long way from the late nineteenth century, when, under headmasters like Edmond Warre, compulsory and highly organised games were used to instil the values of sexual purity, militarism and imperialism. Graham-Campbell has undone Warre's legacy a little further by restoring to boys their ancient right to organise games themselves. But the game is still a forging ground for English manliness. 'I think you saw that today. There were no cups or trophies, but there was a hell of a lot of pride at stake.'

It's time to wander over to witness the much stranger ritual of the Wall Game, regarded as an oddity even by most Etonians. In old photographs, the big annual St Andrew's Day match between 'Collegers' (scholarship boys) and

'Oppidans' (the rest of the school) seems to resemble the *Monty Python* sketch about Batley Townswomen's Guild's theatrical productions which always involve mud-wrestling and battering each other senseless with handbags. Up close the Wall Game is much less frivolous. George Orwell called the game 'an afternoon of mud, and blood, and rain'. The school's own website says it's 'exceptionally exhausting' though more skilful than it appears. The skill lies in the 'remorseless application of pressure and leverage as one advances inch by painful inch through a seemingly impenetrable mass of opponents'. Another Old Etonian, Princess Diana's brother Earl Spencer, observed:

> Two sides flounder in the mud for half an afternoon, hoping that today is going to be the one which will produce a score, idly grinding their opponents' skulls against the wall, or treading it into the oozing quagmire that is the playing field. Play is rarely interrupted by the referee's whistle; although calling for air does result in a brief cessation in hostilities, while lungs are emptied of mortar and mud, and refilled with the air wafting over from neighbouring Slough.

Mud is usually a vital ingredient, and the field – once known as the Furrow – is ploughed to make the ground softer. Today's practice match, however, is on relatively dry ground which soon turns to choking dust.

Goals are staggeringly rare. It's almost certainly easier to carry the Ring of Power to the River of Fire deep in the heart of Mordor than to score a goal in the Eton Wall Game. At one end of the long thin pitch (5 metres wide, 110 metres long), the 'goal' is a dark green door in a wall. At the other end, the target is the whitewashed upper portion of a tree trunk. With such small targets, so much pain, and so many obstacles in the way, no goal has been scored in the St Andrew's Day match since 1909. Even John Barnes, a part-time teacher at Eton in the early eighties, in his days at Watford, tried to hit the tree from 80 yards and failed. But then goals aren't what the game is about. Even more than the rituals of football, the Wall Game celebrates and reinforces the primal essence of ancient English manliness. It's a highly disciplined contest of raw endeavour and pain as two teams of huge lads – organised in a scrum-like phalanx – try to grind each other back in the shadow of a lowering roadside brick wall. As an *Economist* journalist who used to play the game wrote recently: 'It's fun. Buried in that sweating, unmoving bully are skills and achievement that few watchers . . . will see, let alone understand. Boys like rough games. They like to have skills, even arcane ones. They like to compete, however eccentric the game.'

Another veteran, the former Foreign Secretary Douglas Hurd, recalled sweat and steam rising from the players' bodies. 'I played wall, which is the three people inside, nearest the wall, and you need to be fairly resistant to pain and tough and physically strong, and I was those things. In those days it was much tougher – you had to put on helmets and uniform. Now they don't. It has become rather a soft game now.' *Soft?!* 'The Wall Game is the most vicious game I've ever played,' says Mike Grenier. 'In rugby, when the front row of Gloucester and Newport come up bloody, you don't know what's gone on in the scrum. Whatever it was, it was over in twenty seconds. In the Wall Game it can go on for ten minutes.' But why would anyone want to play such a type of football? 'You have to go back to the idea of the primal struggle. The thing is to impose your will and your physical strength over somebody else.'

In Rome, the footballers Giannini and Totti are both known as 'the Prince'. Here, however, under the cold and lowering wall of the Slough Road, they have the real thing. Amid the amiable, relaxed pre-match rituals I wonder why I'm sensing such a buzz among the small crowd, and why there are so many police present. Then I notice that one of the tall lads in blue tracksuit trousers and cream and blue halved shirt looks vaguely familiar. Suddenly I realise why. It's the most eligible young man in the world: Prince William, who left the school a couple of years ago but has made a special trip to play for the old boys' team. When the game starts, he strains and groans along with the rest and, appealingly, none of the players or the umpire accords him any special status. The game itself is an unexpectedly electrifying spectacle. The heaving contest produces a series of bizarre static tableaux of contorted bodies. Serious injuries are rare, but when someone falls beneath the grinding feet and cannot breathe, he has to be dragged to safety by his arms. In one incident the game is stopped to rescue a player crying out in distress. A man beside me explains: 'They're entitled to shout for air if they can't breathe. How you shout for air when you can't breathe, I'm not sure.' The referee is armed with a walking stick, which he uses to poke into the mass of bodies, barking commands that outsiders cannot understand.

The onlookers are no more than a few yards from the action. Foolishly, I edge a little closer still to get a better view. Suddenly, the ball breaks loose and one of the school team hammers it straight at my head from about two yards. He's not aiming at me, he probably doesn't even register me. He's kicking for distance, because the game will restart at a point level with where the ball comes to rest. As I spin to get out of the way, I lose my balance and fall awkwardly on my camera. Luckily, thanks to the soft ground, the camera survives, but my ribs, bruised, ache for a week. A second surprising flurry of movement leads to a spell of frantic pressure on the green door.

For a moment I think I'm about to witness a goal. The school team has somehow driven the ball to within range and someone hoists it powerfully and precisely towards the green door. As if in slow motion, the ball sails perfectly towards its target. At the last moment, a tall ginger-haired boy who looks a bit like Prince Harry leaps like a top-class goalkeeper, stretching brilliantly to claw the ball to safety. I look again. *Dash my buttons!* It *is* Prince Harry!

In spirit, these games at Eton are reminiscent of the School-house match described in *Tom Brown's Schooldays*, another ferocious example of an ancient public-school game in which the 'great science of football' was in essence a war game without weapons. 'It's no joke playing-up in a match, I can tell you,' East tells Tom. 'Why, there's been two collar-bones broken this half, and a dozen fellows lamed. And last year a fellow had his leg broken.' Thomas Hughes's description, published in 1857, was based on the game played at Rugby School in the 1820s. In the novel, plucky little Tom becomes a hero in his very first match because he allows himself to be battered and crushed for the sake of the team.

Like the Wall Game, the pre-modern sport Hughes describes resembles modern soccer much as dinosaurs resemble humans: they share basic design features, but the heavy older models are redder in tooth and claw. Tom's heavily outnumbered house team has about twenty goalkeepers spread five yards apart. In midfield the 'captain of quarters' commands 'the light brigade'. Ahead of them the 'heavy brigade' is made up of smaller units. The 'fighting brigade' or 'die-hards' are known as the 'bull-dogs'. One wing is led by 'a true football king. His face is earnest and careful as he glances a last time over his array, but full of pluck and hope – the sort of look I hope to see in my general when I go out to fight.' At kick off, as the narrator explains, the game involves 'a struggling mass of boys, and a leather ball which seems to excite them all to great fury . . . A battle would look much the same to you, except that the boys would be men, and the balls iron.' After forty-five minutes, weight and numbers begin to tell. Yard by yard the house are driven back and 'the bull-dogs are the colour of mother earth from shoulder to ankle'. Having taken the lead against the odds, Tom's team face an onslaught. The narrator urges: 'Meet them like Englishmen, you Schoolhouse boys, and charge them home. Now is the time to show what mettle is in you; and there shall be a warm seat by the hall fire, and honour, and lots of bottled beer to-night for him who does his duty in the next half-hour.' As the battle rages in front of goal: 'This is worth living for – the whole sum of school-boy existence gathered up into one straining, struggling half-hour, a half-hour worth a year of common life.'

Such warlike public-school games are descended from much older, more chaotic and brutal forms of folk football, some of which still survive. A fortnight before my afternoon at Eton, Prince Charles travelled to Derbyshire to support the Ashbourne Shrovetide match, ceremonially hurling the first ball into the mob. While the Wall Game is a highly disciplined, codified contest with ten combatants on each side, Ashbourne's game is fought out by hundreds of beefy working men from the village on a 'pitch' three miles long, through muddy fields, village streets and a river. Despite the different scale and the different class origins of the players, the basic principles and values don't seem so far apart. One of Ashbourne's few rules states that a player is not permitted to commit manslaughter during a match.

Historians have made much of folk football's past potential as an unruly vehicle for radicalism and protest, but it's just as good for barrel-chested patriotism. Locals proudly refer to it as the

*Royal* Shrovetide Game because the Prince of Wales – the future Edward VIII – started the 1928 match. Now the current Prince of Wales was serenaded with a lusty rendition of 'Land of Hope and Glory'. Accompanied by sixty players, he carried the match ball down a street decked with Union Jacks and was hoisted on to the shoulders of three strapping locals. Later he told the crowd: 'I do adore coming up here whenever I can. It is still a part of old England at its best.' Prince Charles sees the sport in terms of heritage: 'What I love is that you have managed to retain your tradition in an age when tradition seems to be viewed in some quarters as some communicable disease to be eradicated. Plenty have tried over the years. Even during the two world wars men on active service wrote asking for [the game] to be carried on. Why? Because they said it was one of the things they were fighting for. Part of the old traditional England which has survived innovation and invention at a time when a lot of familiar things are swept away.' The Royal Shrovetide Game's official song celebrates its 'friendly strife':

> *And they play the game right manfully,*
> *In snow, sunshine or rain*
> *'Tis a glorious game, deny it who can*
> *That tries the pluck of an Englishman.*

All-weather pluck (preferably demonstrated while blind drunk) has been an ingredient of all folk football games, but such games also had deeper spiritual significance as rituals of pagan nature worship. 'If you really want to understand these games, think sex and sacrifice. Think *Wicker Man*,' says the writer Derek Hammond, who has studied them around Britain. 'Football is a magical rite designed to raise energy and direct it toward "the fructification of crops, cattle, people and the land." Most of the games basically re-enact primeval fertility rites. That's why, in Durham, at the annual Sedgefield Ball Game, a thousand drunken men chant: "When the pancakes are sated/Come to the ring and you'll be mated." ' In the Warwickshire village of Atherstone, Street Football is played with balls symbolising eggs: a straightforward fertility rite which marks the vernal equinox. Lunar worship is the essence of Silver Ball Hurling in the Cornish village of St Columb Major, where a silver ball is dipped into jugs of ale and players drink large amounts of the resulting 'silver beer'. At the dawn of the game, pitches would be chosen for their magical properties. The Shrovetide Football match at Alnwick in Northumberland takes place along the sacred energy network formed by the route of the high street, aligned with an abbey and a church.

One of the darkest games of all is the Haxey Hood, which takes place on Twelfth Night deep in the old bog country of Lincolnshire. Derek says: 'It's a really weird one: there's a "Lord" in charge, a painted "Fool" who can kiss any girl he fancies, and twelve flower-decorated "Boggins" acting as referees. The ball is a leather tube "swayed" by a large scrum between pubs. Sadly, they stopped swinging the Fool across a bonfire 100 years ago, but the "ball" probably represents the leather hood archaeologists have found on lots of bog mummies. The players probably don't realise it, but they're re-enacting a midwinter human sacrifice.'

The game with the best name is unquestionably the Hallaton Bottle Kicking and Hare Pie Scramble, contested every Easter between the Leicestershire villages of Hallaton and Medbourne. 'Once you've seen it you wouldn't want to miss it,' enthuses Derek. 'You go to the top of this hill. They throw a lot of hare pie up in the air. You all have to grab a bit and eat it. And then they start.' The 'bottle' is a small cask of ale which the two sides fight to drag back over the parish boundary to their territory. Hallaton always win because they only need to go half a mile down a 45-degree slope to their village whereas Medbourne is miles away over fields, hedges and an escarpment. With the result a foregone conclusion, the essence of the fun is to get battered and caked with mud.

Medbourne haven't scored since about 1740, but, again, that's hardly the point. 'Imagine a scrum of about sixty big bastards bent on extreme violence, pissed out of their heads and surrounded by about a thousand people. If somebody throws the bottle over a hedge, the players smash straight through the hedge. They demolish people, too. If you're at the bottom of the scrum, you go to hospital. Every year they have ambulances waiting to take away the injured. Just broken legs and concussion mainly. I don't think anyone's been killed, but broken necks, or paralysed? I wouldn't be surprised.' It's almost as dangerous to watch. 'These guys don't stop if someone throws the bottle into the crowd: they just plough straight through 200 women, children, pushchairs, ice-cream vans. It is absolute anarchy. Primal! Fantastic! Just don't get too close.'

Some historians have speculated that the hooliganism surrounding modern football may be a continuation of such ancient rites, but they are also clearly connected to what happens on the field of play. Says Hammond: 'Modern football and bottle kicking are both at some level rituals of war. That's the dark side of football. You're symbolically killing the other tribe. These are pre-Christian, pagan rituals which only survived because they were in places everyone forgot about. They're probably part of the original heathen, naturalistic British religions which were about the earth and the sun and killing and fucking and getting what you want. Football as a game is just a very small reflection of that.' We are talking in a London pub while the cagey all-Italian 2003 Champions

League semi-final comes in live from the San Siro. Inter are playing AC Milan and there's not an Englishman or drunken riot in sight. Derek waves dismissively towards the big screen: 'Look at those boys. Put any one of them in the Hallaton Bottle Kicking and they wouldn't last ten minutes!'

# INDEX

# NOTE ON THE AUTHOR

David Winner is a freelance journalist.
He lives in London and Rome.

## NOTE ON THE TYPE

The text of this book is set in Bembo. This type was first used in 1495 by the Venetian printer Aldus Manutius for Cardinal Bembo's *De Aetna*, and was cut for Manutius by Francesco Griffo. It was one of the types used by Claude Garamond (1480–1561) as a model for his Romain de L'Université, and so it was the forerunner of what became standard European type for the following two centuries. Its modern form follows the original types and was designed for Monotype in 1929.